Experience, Caste, and the Everyday Social

Experience, Caste, and the Everyday Social

GOPAL GURU

SUNDAR SARUKKAI

OXFORD

UNIVERSITY PRESS

OXFORD
UNIVERSITY PRESS

Oxford University Press is a department of the University of Oxford.
It furthers the University's objective of excellence in research, scholarship,
and education by publishing worldwide. Oxford is a registered trademark of
Oxford University Press in the UK and in certain other countries.

Published in India by
Oxford University Press
2/11 Ground Floor, Ansari Road, Daryaganj, New Delhi 110 002, India

First Edition published in 2019

ISBN-13 (print edition): 978-0-19-949605-1
ISBN-10 (print edition): 0-19-949605-6

ISBN-13 (eBook): 978-0-19-909789-0
ISBN-10 (eBook): 0-19-909789-5

Typeset in ITC Giovanni Std 9.5/13
by Tranistics Data Technologies, New Delhi 110 044
Printed in India by Replika Press Pvt. Ltd

Contents

Preface

The origin of this book can be traced back to our earlier volume *The Cracked Mirror: An Indian Debate on Experience and Theory* (2012). This was a book that was in the form of a 'debate' and we contributed four chapters each. We were quite happy at the reception and the critical appreciation which the book received, among academics and students in India and abroad. While we were extremely glad to acknowledge the growing scholarly interest in the *Cracked Mirror* (CM) shown by the students from different educational institutions, we felt deeply heartened by both the cognitive generosity and constructive criticism of reviewers and academics who belonged to different research backgrounds in the humanities and the social sciences. Although we were not in a hurry to write a follow-up to the CM, our public engagement with students across the country, and the feedback we got from the larger community, encouraged us to think of the possibility of writing this book. We were aware that the CM had perhaps raised more issues than resolving them and the process of thinking about the social came quite naturally to us in this reflection. As was clear from the tone and tenor of the CM, that book was the result of dissatisfaction with the scholarship in the practice of social sciences in India that followed a sociologically skewed route often leading to the exclusion of certain groups from the epistemic domain. This book also began with a different kind of dissatisfaction with the description of the nature of the socials that are endemic to the many varied experiences of living here, of 'being-here'.

We believed that social theory had to find a different voice to speak about the everydayness of the multitude of the socials surrounding us. And, like in the CM, we went back to the question of experience—this time the experience of the social. We were well aware that this was a step that was intellectually discomforting if not dangerous given the reaction to the category of experience within the social sciences in general. But perhaps that was also the incentive to work through this difficult task of integrating different disciplinary approaches, including philosophy, sociology, political science, and literature, to the idea of the social. We also wanted to write in a way that was accessible but also intellectually rigorous and unlike the CM, we wrote this book jointly. We do not know if our readers will be as generous to this book as they were to the CM; however, we hope that they will at least be provoked to find new ways of thinking about the complex social experiences that are particularly special to the non-West.

As always, we are indebted to many people in various ways. To those who have contributed in one way or the other to our journey in this book: The faculty and students who engaged with us in Hyderabad Central University, Tata Institute of Social Sciences, Jawaharlal Nehru University, Manipal Centre for Philosophy and Humanities, National Institute of Advanced Studies, English and Foreign Languages University, and other institutions. We are also thankful for the support of these people who have been in conversation with us, wrote about, or organized discussions around the CM and themes in this book: Raghurama Raju, K. Satyanarayana, Probal Dasgupta, Rustom Bharucha, Rita Kothari, Srinivasan Ramanujam, Samir Banerjee, K.V. Akshara, S. Parasuraman, Arjun Appadurai, Sheldon Pollock, Sudipta Kaviraj, Mary John, Rajeshwari Sundar Rajan, Anupama Rao, Udaya Kumar, Arvind, Rajan Gurukkal, Sanil, Milind Wakankar, Satish Deshpande, Lakshmi Srinivas, Tulasi Srinivas, and Akeel Bilgrami. A special word of thanks to our colleagues and students who have engaged with us on these topics for long and with patience and friendship: Gurpreet Mahajan, Babu Thaliath, Meera Baindur, N.S. Gundur, George Verghese, Nikhil Govind, Kaveri Haritas, Apaar Kumar, Anindita Majumdar, Gayathri Prabhu, B.K. Anitha, Carol Upadhya, Shivali Tukdeo, Hamsa Kalyani, Saurabh, N.Y. Manoj, Asim Siddiqui, Madhava Chippali, Pooja Nayak, Kaushik Ramu, Aivin Aivinor, Jobin Mathew, Renny Thomas, Nitesh Choudhary, Leya Mathew, Varun Bhatta, Srajana Kaikini, Nitesh Anchan,

Savita Suresh, M. Rashmi, Shireen Azam, and Subroto Dey. We are grateful for the generous friendship of Carolyn Rouse, John Bornemann, Parvis Ghassem-Fachandi, and Carol Greenhouse, and also for having us as a part of their 'engaged anthropology'. A special thanks to Gordon McOuat and words of gratitude to Bruce Kapferer for critical and illuminating conversations on these topics.

As always, we are indebted to Hema and Dhanu for continuing to make the everyday special and also our thanks to Dhanu for editing the manuscript.

1 Introduction

We are experientially pervaded by the social in many ways. There is no one universal 'social' but a multitude of socials that character- ize societal experiences. These multiple experiences of the social influ- ence the ideas we form of the social, as well as give cognitive access to the different socials. In true empirical spirit, we begin with the fact of an experience which is recognized most commonly, and across members of a society, as being an experience of the social. This experience catalyses the way we see the social world and also influences how we act within this world. Within these set of experiences constituting the social, can we say something more meaningful about this term, how we use it, and how it matters to understanding societies? Can it offer us a new way of understanding the social processes of societies in Asia, Africa, and the Middle East, all of which exemplify complex experiences of the social? To emphasize this aspect of experience, we focus on the everyday social, the world of experiences of the social which is part of everyday life. While what we say may have implications for other forms of the social, such as social institutions, we restrict ourselves to the everyday experiences of the social that become part of the everyday talk of the world. The aim of this book is to explore the nature of the everyday social, based on the multiple ways of experiencing and articulating these experiences, with particular focus on the experiences of caste in the everyday social.

Sociologists and philosophers have long pointed out a simple fact that the idea of the social has always been ambiguously defined. Latour (2005) famously begins his work on reassembling the social by claiming that both the terms 'social' and 'science' are poorly understood. Halewood (2014) shows how this concept was defined in quite contradictory ways by Weber, Durkheim, and others. The problem of correctly understanding the nature of the social is important for the social sciences since clarity on the object of discourse will help clarify fundamental questions about the nature of knowledge in the social sciences as well as the methodologies involved in their study.

For some, the problem of the social is really nothing more than the problem of wholes and their relation with their parts. The notion of the social is really a matter of understanding the nature of collections in general and the core question about collections is whether a collection is 'more' than its parts. Equivalently, this is the question of whether the social is nothing more than the individuals who constitute it. Thus, to understand the social along this trajectory, it is only necessary to consider the individuals and there is nothing else that stands for the collective over and beyond its members. This view is also enshrined methodologically as 'methodological individualism' and this also leads to well-known debates that often places the category of the social in opposition to that of the individual.

However, this way of understanding the social is problematic unless it manages to include the special nature of the individuals who constitute the group. What can differentiate a collection of things and a collection of humans? At the level of a collection, there is really no difference although one may discover the difference when the relations between the members of the collection are specified. Debates on social ontology—the nature of the thing called 'social'—are also deeply influenced by ontological approaches to the notion of the whole. There is a strong analogy to this approach in philosophy of set theory where the question of the independent existence of a set over and beyond its members has been much discussed; this approach has certain obvious connections with the philosophical discussions on the ontology of the social.

However, there is another model to understand the social, one that is relatively independent of the conceptual problems related to parts and whole, to individuals and the collective. This approach understands the social in terms of social action and the actions corresponding to an embodied individual. Some of the earliest models of society often drew their conceptual sustenance from the notion of the body. Society was ordered like the body and even today the use of terms like the

'Head of the State' carry with it bodily connotations. The mapping of caste groups modelled on the hierarchy of the body is also well known. The privilege of the mind over the body and the emphasis on the so-called rational tradition leads to similar constructs of society. Higher order social processes are often associated with the rationality of the social. In the Indian context, the body acquires seminal importance, both in terms of creating social boundaries as well as producing corporeal distance. It also produces a language of sensations used to talk about the social. For example, the sensory faculty emanating from the physical body performs not just the cognitive function of classifying the foul from the perfumed, but also constructs the 'natural' substance such as the air that carries with it not just the smell of foul but the very idea of foul. Thus, these sensory phenomena appear along with their distinct cognitive function.

The Everyday Social

What really can be the object of study of the social sciences? Social structures are an important component of what constitutes the social and society, but these larger structures of the social are built not just from individuals but also from a conglomeration of everyday socials. Often, the tendency to not take the everyday social seriously is a reflection of the intrinsic problem of the social sciences, as well as of the location of the individual within the social. However, we argue that the everyday social fills an intermediate gap—it is a site where the individual is not yet the social as embodied as an agent within social structures but has already lost the naivety of being 'just' an individual. The everyday social is the domain where the first experiences of the social are formed and these experiences influence to a great extent other engagements with the structural social. Equivalently, this shift to the everyday social is also a shift to the domain of the experience of the social as a fundamental category to understand the formation of the social.

What do we mean by the everyday social?[1] The everyday social is life as lived every day, by individuals who function within relationships

---

[1] The everyday social has been of interest to phenomenological sociology. See, for instance, Overgaard and Zahavi (2009). Their approach, and in general that of phenomenological sociology, differs in many respects from ours.

with other individuals. This social consists of the socialities of house-wives, maids, children, women in the market, city sanitation workers, interaction around small shops and bakeries, little eating joints, auto drivers, public transport, and other such countless everyday things and processes around us. It is a collage of experiences which occur in rural and urban areas, inside and outside houses, within and without insti-tutions. It captures the way by which the first experiences of the social are experienced and articulated. Many of these modes of understand-ing the social begin to influence the ideas of the social in the larger structural sense. Thus, these experiences of the social influence how the sense of the social gets formed in categories such as nation, religion, caste, and gender. These experiences which go to form an awareness of the experience of the social influence the way individuals interact with the impersonal or the institutional social.

Individuals make meaning of the social not only from being taught about socialization, for example, but also from experiencing it. It is possible to claim that they experience it as realistically as they experi-ence the physical world. Much has been made of the abstract nature of the social and the claim that there is nothing more to the social than individuals who go to make up the social, as mentioned earlier. But this claim, which has found some criticism in discussions on social ontology, does not take into account the possibility of describing the experiences of the social which are not reducible to the experiences of the individual components of the social.

What really is the fundamental issue in making a realist commitment to something called the social? One could be the difficulty in accept-ing the existence of something which does not seem to be available to the five senses. Many would argue that unlike an individual entity, the social is an abstract category and cannot be meaningfully experienced in any manner. This conclusion would be too hasty. There are many entities which we invoke as if they have some notion of reality and experience. The concepts of 'people' and 'individual' are simple exam-ples. Other such examples include money, society, tradition, market, space, time, and numbers. Space and time are, of course, paradigmatic examples of seemingly un-sensed entities that are nevertheless taken to be 'real' in some sense. Independent of the theories of space and time one might hold, what is important is to recognize the 'ontological pressure' of these entities, the pressure to acknowledge their existence in our everyday talk. So even if the social is seen as an abstract entity, one can meaningfully talk about it in many different ways.

However, we can begin with something more concrete: the experiences of the social. This is not because we postulate the social as an experiential entity to begin with but only because we believe that it best describes the nature of our everyday social experiences, particularly in a place like India. Before somebody jumps to the conclusion that we subscribe to one homogenous experience called the Indian experience or even a homogenous entity called the Indian social, we would like to emphasize that this is not what we are aiming to do nor is it an assumption that underlies our analysis. In fact, by the end of the book it will be clear that there are many socials and it is the interactions of the many socials that are really important to understand the nature of a diverse society. Reducing this diversity to individuals misses a crucial aspect of the relation between the socials.

We need to further clarify here that we rely on the experience of the everyday social only to gain a deeper understanding of different social actions happening at the empirical level on an everyday basis. We also argue that such a perspective would approach the notion of the social in terms of its diverse manifestations. In the fragmentary lifeworld, such a social tends to operate with different conceptions of rationality. For example, the caste and gender socials will act along different rationalities. Thus, some women find the practice of imposing 'untouchability' for menstruating women for three or four days to be rational since in their estimation this is a great opportunity to enjoy freedom from crushing domestic work. The nature of time in such cases is contingent upon the individual experience. Since the same individual (an upper caste woman) practices untouchability against another Dalit woman, the former will operate in a social time which is defined through the collective practice of untouchability. Hence, the social life of untouchability corresponds to the conception of social time, a point we will discuss in detail later in Chapter 7. This could be understood as the rationality of the weak or the subaltern while the touchable might find it quite rational to practice untouchability, particularly as it would help the former avoid inter-caste marriage. Similarly, different people would have different senses of the rational in terms of accessing sound, smell, and touch. But in this work, we argue that this is not an adequate view of the social. For gaining an adequate understanding, we would have to use the ethical and the moral in order to creatively dissolve the lifeworld into a social world. Thus, at the end of the book, we argue that the new language of *maitri* would help us to conceptualize this social world.

The process that interests us is how the idea of the social comes to the cognitive awareness of those members who constitute that social. Individualism would force us towards starting with the building blocks of individuals who then go on to form a society but this does not capture the lived reality of the social. The lived experiences of the social are made up of sensations which are perceived to stand for the social. How does this come about? Why does this come about? The position we are searching for is one that is between the belief that individuals are autonomous entities and that the individuals are always, and perhaps completely, socially determined. By shifting the focus back to experiences, we are then able to relook at the question of the social as an experiential term and then look at how these unique experiences actually go on to define our established notions of the social.

For gaining a clearer understanding of the notion of the social, let us cite a simple example from the Indian situation. In relatively more recent times, India has been experiencing a significant growth of religious and quasi-religious communities headed by various gurus. The social formation of these groups does not originate entirely from the guru or even from the collection of individuals who decide to collectively come under the guru to be part of that community. Rather, the guru herself or himself becomes the condition, as manifested in such a collection, which gets crystallized. How do we characterize this crystallization? In what sense do people realize that they are members of the group? Are people's perceptions and beliefs the sole basis for the formation of quasi-religious communities?

Perception alone does not show the presence of an object. Some might argue that different perceptual modalities create a sense of an object. Objecthood itself is an inference built from certain perceptions we have. The idea of the object might lie in nothing more than the unity of these perceptions. The reality of an entity might be nothing more than an inference; like the famous Nyāya dictum (Chakrabarti 1992) that multiple modalities—'I touch what I saw'—make us infer that there must be an object which can both be touched and seen. Thus, instead of asking what kind of an entity the social is, we could begin with asking how the social is perceived. This might seem like a circular or even an absurd question, but it is not circular because the way people talk about the social is often in terms of its perceptual awareness as we will discuss in detail in this book. We smell, touch, and taste the social and from this can try and understand something of the nature of the social. This argument is one of the central claims of this book.

In taking this approach, we are focussing on the act of sensing in contrast to believing or conceptualizing as a central mode of constructing the social. The everyday social exemplifies this all the time. There are states of experience that are more than mere claims of belief that one is part of a group. Just as perception is the first step in forming beliefs about what we see, there is a first modality of perceiving the social which leads to forming beliefs about our belongingness to the social. Our focus on 'sensing the social' is an empirical account of the social, which we believe captures the unique nature of many societies in Asia and Africa.

There is a problem in the way we commonly use the term 'social' in that it seems to be diffused and omnipresent. Almost everything becomes social these days and there is a need to delimit the meaning of what we exactly mean by the social. In many accounts of the social and sociality, the idea of the social seems to be all pervasive. Individuals are seen to be infused with the social and so are linguistic and discursive activities. One of the major justifications of the qualitative method also rests on this pervasiveness of the social because of the belief that engaging deeply with few people is enough to generate data that is actually about their social world and not only about these few individuals. However, this pervasive notion of the social is too strong and hence too weak. Instead of this universal homogenous social, it is more reasonable to hold the position that there are many socials and these socials get materialized and particularized as specific communities. Thus, it is important to delimit the meaning and extent of the social in different contexts.

First of all, a universal social is not all-pervasive; it is also quite vague. Saying that 'nothing is outside the social' is like saying 'nothing is outside the text' or that there is nothing outside language. It is possible to argue that they are many forms of the social and yet they exist with their complete and coherent 'normative vision'. Thus, entities like markets and nations are themselves composed of different socials. The limits of each social, in terms of their claims of being complete or coherent, give the boundaries of meaningful social action and ethics. Experience as the realm of ethical action has a definite bearing on the question of the meaningfulness of the social.

Bringing the question of experience of the social into the forefront might seem like yet another way of invoking the body metaphor to describe the social. Although the body image as related to societies has long been used, what we are doing here is as much using the complexity of the body as of the social. The body does not signify only an individual; it already includes the social. Perhaps the right way of describing the body is as a unity and not as an 'individual'. The multiplicity that characterizes the social is already implicated within any body. Yet the body functions as a unified whole, but the whole is not a collection or sum of all its parts. There are always elements of the body which continuously destabilize any stable notion of the body. The elements that do this include the soul, mind, self, consciousness, life-force, and so on. The influence of the images of the body in describing society and nation is well known. Images of disease and health are often used to describe 'undesirables' in a society. Bodily functions are often used as a frame of reference to refer to such undesirable groups.

While a particular scientific and philosophical turn shifted away from using bodily metaphors for the social, it has nevertheless failed to capture the processes of many societies. This turn, away from the body image of the social, may have served one purpose of focussing the conceptual domain of the social away from its constituents such as human individuals and focus instead on social structures, those that are centrally constitutive of modern societies. The sociological theories of the social, dominantly influenced by European and Anglo-American scholars, may perhaps map well the so-called advanced modern societies in those regions. However, they seem to miss some essential aspects of the social that characterize societies in Asia, Africa, Middle East, and perhaps some of the European countries as well. Without wanting to club all these diverse social experiences of these societies into one monolithic one, we would like to nevertheless point to the importance of relooking at the conceptual presuppositions surrounding the idea of the social derived from dominant Western scholarship. Thus, instead of beginning with a theoretical attempt to define the social, we want to merely invoke ways to understand and categorize experiences that are experiences of the social.

We will argue in what follows that the most powerful experience of the social is in terms of the categories of human sensation and through it the metaphors of the human body. An important task of social theory and social philosophy is then to expand the ways by which we understand processes such as bodily perception and bodily action. In other words, we experience the social as if we experience the world through our bodily senses. Thus, it is possible to talk of a social sight, social touch, social smell, social taste, and social hearing. In the same way, it is possible to talk of a social self for the social and a 'life' of the social. Through this approach we begin with the social as a primal, given experience and do not construct it as assemblages or collections of other individual elements. Following from this premise, it is easy to see that the individual is already social and is immersed in the experiences of the social.

The reason why we need to make a move like this is also related to a methodological problem, which is arguably a deep problem in studying the social. The difficulty is not really in dealing with numbers in a group or the messiness of dealing with relations between members of a group. The fundamental problem lies in the difficulty of studying something of which we are already a part of. This is not the usual problem of the whole and parts, although it is related to it. The simple question is this: How do we study something to which we belong? The problem in knowing something which we are a part of is based on the way we understand knowledge and objectivity. When we study an object, we first propose to study it as if it is an object 'outside' us. This allows us, among other things, to consider the various perspectives of the object under study; it also allows one to conduct experiments on the object in order to discover new qualities of the object. The most influential models of knowledge-making today, influenced by a long and domineering tradition of Western science and Western philosophy, are based on this metaphysical possibility of distinguishing the subject who knows and the object which is known. The problem is that the social has to be defined while already in a state of being social. It is not possible to stand outside the 'social' and define it since the standpoint of the observer is not possible for the social. A similar problem arises in attempts to describe 'nature' as if we were not part of the nature that is being described.

All experiences are social experiences although located within the individual. A society built on individualism and solitary individuals becomes more radically social through the belongingness of these solitary individuals to a much larger social formed through social media, social forums, and the networked world. All it does is to replace a simplistic notion of the social as aggregations into something more complex, more disembodied. This is a classic instance of the 'mind' of the social, the ways by which the social is completely displaced into a 'mindspace'.

The object corresponding to the social is quite different. The difficulties in conceptualizing the social point to the difficulty in isolating a stable transcendent object called the social which is amenable for critical study by the subject. The object called the social is an integral part of the subject; hence, attempts to study the nature of the social as if the social was obviously outside the subject are problematical. The definition of the social as aggregates, collections, and assemblages, or viewing the social in opposition to the individual, are symptoms of this larger problem of epistemology. Instead, the only access we have to the notion of the social is in the kinds of experiences that demand the invocation of the social. Thus, the very origin and creation of the idea of the social is a deeply phenomenological process and has to arise from such accounts of the social as well as methodological attempts to recover the social from those experiences that we seem to recognize as social. The social reaches us not as an abstract collection of individuals but through our perceptual capacities of sight, touch, sound, smell, and taste. Our experiences of being social are often captured through the sociality of these perceptions. The society around us is filled with such examples. The examples we give below are from the daily experiences of cities, towns, and villages in India.

We can start with music and the idea that it is the quintessential essence of the social. Music is a social event. It is impossible to imagine a musical gathering which is only about some sterilized notion of an individual. Music captures the sociality of the social. Music is always with others and also for others. Music as a profession can become individualized, can become a pursuit of the lonely soul, but this stage reached by a musician is a stage that is reached through a conscious removal of the social from music. Why is music most powerfully played, almost always, by a group? Why is music the only common activity that needs other musicians to play with you? What would jazz be if played only by one instrument or even classical Hindustani music with only the singer without accompaniments? (In contrast, in academic lectures it is only the speaker who holds forth without any 'accompaniment'!) This creation of sound through a collective process is the experience of the social which is essential to music.

Consider the practice of music in communities—where many sing together, dance together, make sounds together. The togetherness is not in all of them doing the same thing since it is an activity where different skills in different instruments come together to create a unified sense of music. Why is it so important to have other instruments, other players to create music? Music is social in two ways—not only is music essentially played with others, it is also something that is always for others. The presence of an audience—of whatever kind—is a social event. It is a first marker of sociality when an act by a few is meant for others. This performance is not defined through aesthetic alone; it is first catalysed by the sense of the social created through music. In particular, the social is very deeply connected to the political through music since many musical performances have a transformative purpose. Music is much more than cultural consumption or a form of entertainment. At the subjective level, it adds to the formation of political consciousness. The many powerful protest movements in India often draw upon music in an essential manner. These should not be looked at instrumentally as either an exercise in group bonding or as a way to attract 'common' people. There is something intrinsically social about music, something that helps the musician transcend herself into a social being. Music as a very important form of accessing and creating a social is not only seen in Dalit and tribal music but also in various bhakti movements that occurred in India at different intervals in historical time.

Music, therefore, is an exemplar of the social and allows us a different way to access the idea of social—as something which always has two components, being-with and being-for. The social is a mix of the 'with' and 'for' to varying degrees. The social as created by a collection of individuals is focussed on 'with' alone and even this 'with-ness' is quite often just a 'togetherness'. The other component is always 'for-ness', doing something always for somebody or the other. The social created merely out of individuals as a conceptual category can weakly accommodate the with-ness but not the for-ness. How do we conceptualize the social which takes into account both these elements? This is important since this is the mode of access of the social for the everyday world.

Music thus captures the sense of an activity that is primarily social in character. There are also other such activities which generate a sense and experience of the social among those who are part of those experiences. Music is primarily about the sense of sound through which an experience of the social is formed and it is different from ordinary speech. There is no collective speaking like there is the collectivity in music. However, there is a deep sense of the social when an individual speaks and this is manifested through the sociality of language. The languages in which we speak are already social in that they are socially formed and have meaning only in this sense of the social.

All the other senses also contribute to the experience of the social. The sense of touch is an extremely important sense of the human body. It is also a sense by which the idea of the social comes to us. Touch is potentially social in that it always needs the presence of something other than the toucher to be experienced as touch. The very idea of multiplicity is given to us through touch in a far more primal sense than sight. Often we tend to think that we see multiplicity when we see many objects in front of our eyes. But this multiplicity is always given simultaneously and they have to be conceptualized as multiple. In other words, the appearance of many different things appears as a unity, as 'one' appearance. There is nothing in principle to indicate that they are all different and that their appearance together, as one, does not make them one. However, touch engages with multiplicity in a different way. When touch encounters the social, it does so with the two characteristics mentioned above—being-with and being-for. Experiences and meanings of the social arise through our experience of 'social touch'. So also for sight, taste, and smell. Each of these senses is our first gateway into the experience and conceptualization of the social. They also catalyse other social categories such as caste and class. We will discuss each of these senses in Chapter 4.

The phenomenon of consuming food is an important social experience in many of our communities. Whether it is in a casual restaurant, or in a marriage hall or in a public function, we can see how consuming food together leads to a profound experience of the social. This phenomenon occurs across all spaces, whether rural or urban, private or public. Eating has a quintessential Indian element and there is much about the sociality of our communities within that act. It is, therefore, not an accident or mere contingency that caste is intrinsically connected with food prohibitions. There are at least two types of prohibitions that are important to caste practices—the type of food one eats and the group with which one can eat. Through these proscriptions and permissions, one aspect of the sociality of caste comes to be experienced. Food is also a wonderful example of how all the senses function to create a 'social sense'. The act of eating is often accompanied by loud talk and laughter; it is surrounded by smells and colour, and there is an extended notion of touch through the licking of the fingers. Food is paradigmatic of the way all the senses function together in order to convert the act of eating into a social experience. Eating food in public spaces in India without this unity of senses would be to miss out on the sociality of eating together. Both the kinds of street food and the modes of eating them (along with the mess around these places!) are illustrative of a complex sociality catalysed by the sensorial experience of eating food. More importantly, this experience gives us an entry point into the experience of the social—that is, one of the ways we experience the social and know what it is to be social is through the many different ways of consuming food.

We can use this analysis to understand caste, for example. What really is the sociality of caste? How does caste manifest its sociality, its social nature, and its social experience? The argument here is that it manifests its sociality and becomes an experience for us through these five perceptual modes. In the experience of the everyday social, caste manifests its sociality and becomes an experience through these perceptual modes. So, caste cannot be only in the mind since it appears through the ways we see, touch, smell, taste, and hear. Each of these modes becomes representative of caste; they become the markers and signifiers of caste. The implication of this argument is the following: One, there are experiences of the social which are experienced as perceptual modes of the five senses; two, they form the basis for our conceptualization of the social; and three, they become integral parts of social practices. Thus, to understand the idea of the social we have to first understand the sociality of our perceptions in their social modes. We will illustrate these points in greater detail in each of the chapters that follow.

Social structures are an important component of what constitutes the social and society, but these larger structures of the social are built not just from individuals but also from a conglomeration of everyday socials. The moment of creating the social is also the moment of removing the individual as the discursive point of analysis. The everyday social fills this intermediate gap—it is a site where the individual is not yet the social (as embodied as an agent within social structures) but has already lost the naivety of being an individual. The everyday social is the domain where the first experiences of the social are formed and these experiences influence to a great extent other engagements with the structural social. Equivalently, this shift to the everyday social is also a shift to the domain of the experience of the social as a fundamental category to understand the formation of the social.

The chapters that follow explore each of these points in some detail. The next chapter discusses the various conceptualizations of the social within the social sciences. After discussing the contentious debate on the nature of the social, we discuss one specific relation between the social and the natural, and show how the processes by which the idea of the natural is constituted within the natural sciences leads to important insights about the nature of the social. We then discuss some contemporary accounts that attempt to make sense of the idea of a non-reducible social. The domain of social ontology has been quite active, more so in recent times, and we look at a few examples of how the social has been conceptualized in them.

With these preliminary observations on the conceptualizations of the social, we come to the core of our arguments from Chapter 3. The third chapter describes what it means to experience the everyday social through the senses of smell, touch, sound, and taste. The lived experience of the social is made up of sensations which we perceive to stand for the social. Thus, instead of asking what kind of an entity the social is, we begin by asking how the social is perceived. The social reaches us not just as a collection of individuals but through our perceptual capacities of sight, touch, sound, taste, and sound. Our experiences of being social are often captured through the sociality of these perceptions. The society around us is filled with such examples. The examples we draw upon in this book are from daily experiences in cities, towns, and villages in India. They range from the experiences of music (and sound in general) and its relationship with the social, to the domains of taste and touch as manifested in sharing food or in the practice of untouchability.

Consider the sense of smell. We associate, detect, and define objects through their smell. Smell is not merely perceptive in the sense that it shows the presence of a thing; it is also a source of knowledge about that thing. The pollution that arises from touch is also relevant for smell. Thus, it was that smelling corpses, for example, would cause 'ritual pollution' for Brahmins as much as touch did. The social not only can be perceived by sound but it is also the case that the basic experiences of the social is also formed by sound. It is only by hearing many things that one thinks of the social and this is related to questions of language and music. Sound is, perhaps, the most important element in the creation of the social. Sound creates the social in a way which cannot be created by vision. Touch is another way to perceive the social and is an important way by which the social is experienced. Sociality of caste is primarily created through the sensation/repulsion of social touch. When the people of the same caste touch each other, there is a different sense of touch which may be love and care. But when the upper caste touches the lower caste, what is the quality of this touch? There are many illustrations of touch/untouch that go to form the experience and narrative of the social.

Along with these sensory experiences related to the everyday social, there is an extremely important notion of belongingness that characterizes this experience. In the fourth chapter, we discuss some empirical examples of the function of the social in the Indian context. We first start by discussing the idea of the sense of belongingness. Every social collection is defined by its own unique sense of belongingness and the experience of 'being-with'. We belong to a family, to a community, to a religion, to a caste, to an organization, to a nation, and, perhaps, even 'belong' to the universe. But in each of these cases, the nature of belonging is different. The experience of belongingness to a family is extremely important as it has a great influence on the way we socialize with others. It also illustrates a long-standing tension between the idea of the social and the natural: Do we have a 'natural' affiliation to our family? If so, what distinguishes our belonging to a family in contrast to belongingness to society, religion, tradition, and so on? Is the family more 'natural' than other group formations?

Beginning from this description of the experience of the social, we describe four important characteristics that help us to understand everyday social processes. In the fifth chapter, we discuss the idea of identity and self. How is it that individuals invoke concepts like 'We' to describe certain kinds of processes and experiences? We suggest that if there are good reasons to acknowledge the existence of the individual self then there are similar reasons which should make us take the notion of social self a little more seriously. We will argue that the philosophical themes around the idea of self are very useful to motivate an understanding of the idea of the social through the notion of the social self. Most importantly, the argument that we propose is that the social self is phenomenologically real and has implications for understanding the sociality of caste.

The sixth chapter engages with the idea of the authority of the social. One of the intriguing aspects of the discourse of the everyday social is the invocation of the 'authority of society' such as in expressions like 'social pressure'. The invisible hand of the social is quite pervasive and powerful in many social actions, and is also explicitly acknowledged as such. But what can a disembodied form of authority really mean? How can it act to so profoundly influence individual action? What are the contours of authority that are special to the social? How does the social get its authority? Or is authority an intrinsic and necessary part of the idea of the social? We discuss the notion of authority and show how the authority of the social is similar to the way the 'natural' gets authority in the natural sciences.

The seventh chapter begins with the ethics that is 'naturally' associated with the everyday socials. In this chapter, we begin by analysing how Narayana Guru understands inequality and through it try and understand the uniqueness of the inequality in caste experiences and its interesting relationship to time. We motivate this discussion by showing how time has always been instrumental in changing social norms and practices. Ideas of labour and production are as much creations of new notions of social time. By looking at everyday narratives of caste, primarily its relation to heredity and rebirth, we show how the question of equality in such systems is related to what we call 'intergenerational equality'. Through this idea, we suggest that caste is characterized as much by its sense of 'social time' as by its outward practices.

The last chapter introduces the concept of maitri to understand the ethical relation between the different socials. What we call a society is composed of many socials. According to our argument, it is the relationship between these many socials that really define larger experiences of socialities. We argue that the most important ethical relation is one between the various socials which is not reducible to the relation between individuals. The relation which best characterizes the relation between socials is that of maitri, a concept which we borrow and extend from Ambedkar. Using this idea, we attempt to understand the ethical in social processes. Maitri as an ideal relation between socials really defines the nature of the social.

Any analysis of social processes and social change, as well as mechanisms for social policy, must first take into account the nature of the social. Very often the ambiguous nature of the social is an impediment to a meaningful understanding of complex social processes. We believe that the complex social processes in the Indian context need a diversity of conceptual terms as well as diverse approaches. Our exploration of the social is driven primarily by this sense of dissatisfaction that social theories today are not able to effectively speak to these experiences that characterize the everyday socials of societies like the Indian and many similar non-Western societies. Our attempt is a small step in this process of activating new forms of thinking about the diverse socials that are active around us today.

2 Conceptualizing the Social

There have been many attempts to understand the nature of the social which range from reducing the social to individuals to postulating the existence of the social as an independent entity. For some, the notion of the social is the subject matter of the social sciences in that any analysis of society or aggregations must engage with something called the social. There are many examples of aggregates in the natural world that also function as a model for the possibility of the social as being independent of, or more than, the individual. Molecules are a simple example of aggregation of parts, but the properties of the molecule are 'more' than the properties of the individual atoms that make up the molecule. Views similar to this made Durkheim look to chemistry to draw a parallel with the social as an ensemble of human interactions. At the other extreme, the social could be seen as a unity, a given whole which cannot really be broken into parts made up of individuals. Or it could be seen as a field which is spread out, located in space and time, and having properties that are 'experienceable'. Such entities are also endemic to the natural world and to the natural sciences. Or the social could be an entity like space and time—and depending on which theories of space and time we hold, we could have different ideas of the social. For example, space and time could be seen as extensions of some kind or as non-material substrates or as conditions of empirical experience, and one could model the ontology of the social analogously.

At another level, the phenomenon of the social could be studied as an object of discourse of philosophy or of science. What this means is that we can understand this object in the way philosophy understands objects through metaphysical categories such as universals, qualities, inherence, relation, and so forth. For instance, the social could be seen as a universal that either exists in itself or as instantiated in its members—those who belong to the social—just as we would understand colour. The colour red could be seen as if it existed by itself (which is problematic for colour as a category) or as being instantiated or located in every red object. This does not reduce the red colour to the object; rather, they are two distinct entities which are related in some manner. So too, the social could be instantiated or located in every individual but that does not mean that it is not possible to have a special entity called the social which is different and independent of the individuals in which it is located. For philosophy, objects do not have to be restricted to physical ones and there are, in addition, mental as well as abstract objects, and hence even if the social is not a physical entity, it could still be seen as a mental or an abstract entity.

Similar questions arise when we consider the social within the discursive structure of a science. Although science is often reduced to methodology or to knowledge, it is necessary to recognize that the scientific discourse is as much about the objects of discourse that it creates. We would perhaps take the view that it is far more dominantly about its discursive objects than anything else. Science sees the natural world as being populated by all kinds of entities and does not use naive empirical constraints to inhibit this ontological surplus. Arguably, the ontology of science prioritizes fields (and abstract entities like laws and mathematics) more than concrete individual objects (Einstein, in the foreword to Jammer (1954), emphasizes that for physics, the infinitely extended fields are the ultimate constituents of reality). The idea of objects that is present in science range from physical things to abstract entities. Entities that are at the core of its disciplines are 'real' although their manifestations are often not obviously concrete or physical: for example, the reality of chemical bonds or the laws of nature or the reality of non-spatiotemporal mathematical entities. In fact, one could persuasively show how the power of science arises from its capacity to possess a complex ontology and allow for entities which are not commonsensical. Given the complexity of the objects of science, to consider the social as an abstract, non-spatiotemporal entity is quite a conservative claim!

There is yet another way of understanding the ontology of the social and this is through relations. There is a lot about the social that parallels the way we talk about space. Both are diffused, spread out, and have individual elements within them. Space has been understood either as an independent entity on its own or as reducible to relations between objects.[1] The relational view of space, notably associated with Leibniz, suggests that space has no independent existence of its own and can always be reduced to objects since what we call as space is perhaps nothing more the relation between objects. The analogy with the social then is that there are only individuals and it is the relation between individuals that form what we call the social. However, even if this is the case, it is possible to have an ontology of relations which argues for the reality of relations. Force is one such powerful example. Although it occurs most powerfully in the natural sciences, the notion of force predates that use and is often used in a more general sense. For example, force has been understood in terms of the power to change the behaviour of the other according to one's dominant design. In the case of science, force can be seen as a relation between objects, but we often talk of gravitational force or the electromagnetic force as being real constituents of the world. So even if social is a relation between individuals, there is nothing that stops it from being 'real', either as an abstract entity (since abstract things could be 'real') or as a real (physical) relational term.

Thus, there are many reasons that motivate the arguments that amplify the adequate sense of the reality of the social. The reality of the social could also be manifested either as progression or regression in the process of social change. Talk about social change and social transformation is based on beliefs about the nature of the social: for example, as a substratum on which changes can be detected. Analogous to the model of change in objects, say, the changing colour in a leaf, social change too is often spoken about as changes in qualities that inhere in a substratum of the social. These beliefs about the social have a serious implication for understanding social processes. When scholars observe

[1] See Nerlich (1994) for a good introduction to the philosophical ideas of space.

that caste in India is almost impossible to eradicate, they are assuming certain qualities of the social. To make sense of how caste constantly morphs into other forms, gets reproduced in new ways, or finds new sources of authority to sustain it, it is not only necessary to look at the nature of caste but also at the nature of the social since it is the particular sociality of caste that is often the culprit. So, before we are able to meaningfully talk of social change, it is necessary to understand the nature of the social and the hidden presuppositions about it.

Nature and Scope of the Social

What is the precise sense in which the idea of the social could be rendered more intelligible? Firstly, this word is used across a broad range of processes such as the following: social factors, social circumstances, social conditions, social media, social life, social rules, social practices, social position, social movements, social action, social power, social domination, social influence, and social upbringing. Why are all these social processes? What is social in these processes? Is there a diffused nature of the social which is different in each of these references? Is the social of a religious group different from the social of a caste group or the social of a group of friends? There are different ways of answering these questions. For example, one could say that a particular group becomes social to the extent it exercises power on its members. In such cases, power becomes a common element which is universally present in all these groups. Power is incomplete without the social in the Indian case—family, caste, and language are required to complete power and thus any invocation of power has to explicitly acknowledge the qualification of the social. Similarly, the terms mentioned above such as media, life, rules, and upbringing are incomplete without the addition of the social. One may thus argue that these uses of 'social' point to how the second term is incomplete without the former.

There is an analogy with human cognition that may be useful to understand this point. Consciousness is seen as an essential element of human beings and is an integral aspect of sensation and cognition. The difficulty in understanding consciousness arises from a unique problem which is that individual objects are cognized only through (and mediated by) consciousness and at the same time, consciousness itself is only known through its awareness of objects. Consciousness and the object are intertwined in an experience (which we often think of as the experience of the object) and it is not immediately possible to know what is contributing what to a particular experience. This conundrum can be best exemplified by the example of sugar. Sugar is experienced to be sweet but how can we know whether the sweetness of sugar actually arises from the nature of our saliva and the gustatory contribution of our body? Our experiences say as much about the objects that we experience as about the nature of our consciousness. One might argue that the social functions in a similar way—we might think that we are perceiving individual properties or action, but that perception is already and intimately part of the experience of the social. Every perception related to human individuals (in a world already suffused with the social) is an experience of the social as well as of the individual. Like consciousness and objects, we need both the social and the individual to illuminate the other. In this sense, the social is the consciousness of society and functions in a similar manner. Many of the examples given above of the use of the word social illustrate this intricate embeddedness of the social and the individual in every perception of ours.

Now it is possible to understand what the different meanings of social are in the context of their adjectival use. The word 'social' in the terms mentioned above are not really referring to the primary social or a primary group or even an aggregate. The terms they qualify are already social and hence the social in those terms are actually doubly qualifying. This can be understood either as an explicit reminder of the social that is forgotten in the use of the first term or it actually hides another meaning for the adjectival social. For example, consider the term 'social movements'. First of all, movements are themselves social, but this character is not explicit in the use of the term 'movements'. Thus, the use of the social to qualify 'movements' might serve as a reminder of this implicit presence of the social. But there is a second function which is that the 'social' in 'social movements' is not the same as the 'social' which is implicit in 'movements'. The qualifier social is a universal social, a social that is presumed to be common to all or most 'movements'. We would argue that the primary purpose of the qualifier social is not to draw attention to the social nature of the second term but more to function as a universal, to present a universal social that is common to all the socials of movements. Consider three movements—caste eradication, girl education, and anti-corruption movements. All these three as movements are already social but there is an implicit assumption that the 'social' in all of them are the same 'type' of social. But this is what we dispute—there is no one idea of the social but only multiple socials or only multiple socialities. And it is important to give an account of what these specific socialities are, what distinguishes them from each other, and why all of them can be put under the larger family of the social. The use of the social in 'social movements' betrays this anxiety that the socialities of all these movements are not quite the same and thus one word 'social' can serve to unify these different socialities. In the chapters to follow, we will explore ways to make sense of this multiplicity as well as the tendency to work within a universal social.

Social in Social Science

Why are we raising the question of social in the social sciences? Is it not a redundant question? It could be seen as redundant, as there is already the word social in 'social sciences'. We could do the same exercise for 'social sciences' that we did above for 'social movements'. But we can also note other aspects of the use of the word social in 'social sciences'. The mere inclusion of the word 'social' in this phrase does not make sciences social. They become social in a double sense. First, they are social because they deal with the social relationship which binds groups into sociality. This ranges from caste and religious groups to the social clubs of the elite. Second, social sciences are social because they are not physical sciences in that the social sciences deal with human beings. Physical sciences can also deal with human beings but more as a substance or a thing to be examined and observed through experiments.

In the common usage of the term, social is often understood as the framework of relationship within which people relate to each other based on certain commonly accepted norms. One of the norms, for example, is to be civilized or associative rather than atomistic. Social is other-regarding rather than self-regarding. Social norms are therefore about the imagination of a 'decent' life. Being hospitable is social and being hostile is anti-social. Being alienated is the loss of the social. However, the social sciences are not about human beings in a broad sense but about the social organizations and institutions which order societies.

Social is the bedrock of sociology and in a different way of the social sciences. For Durkheim, the concepts of the social and society are the foundational concepts for sociology and can be distinguished from each other. Durkheim argues that the objectivity of sociology is based on 'social facts' which are real and empirical. In his *Suicide: A Study in Sociology* (2005: xxxvi) he writes: 'For sociology to be possible, it must above all have an object all of its own ... a reality which is not in the domain of the other sciences.' However, it is not obvious that the social must be seen in the sense of an object. As Giddens (1986: 163) points out, 'the term "society" has two main senses (among others, such as "society" in the sense of "high society"). One is the generalized connotation of "social association" or interaction; the other is the sense in which "a society" is a unity, having boundaries which mark it off from other, surrounding societies.'

Now, either the object for sociology is directly available to the discourse or it has to be specially constructed and crafted which makes it amenable for use in sociology. It is not only the social as a concept that has this character. All disciplines first create their own objects of discourse. The natural sciences create an object of interest to each of their disciplines, namely nature. It is important to realize that while 'nature' is the bedrock concept of physics, chemistry, biology, geography, or the environmental sciences, it nevertheless has a different meaning in each of these disciplines. Although the word is common to all the natural sciences, the meaning of 'nature' differs in each one of them since each of the disciplines mark out their uniqueness by specially defining the object of nature for their own use. For physics, the essential mark of nature lies in the 'laws of nature', for chemistry in the combination of elements, for modern biology as embodied in the evolutionary principle, and so forth. Geographers have pointed out that in their discipline, nature is inherently social and is constructed such as in Castree and Braun (2001).

Similarly, the social is uniquely created as a discursive concept and in a manner similar to the natural sciences, the concept of the 'social' in each of the social sciences is different. However, the problem is that the concept of the social is itself very contentious. Latour (2005) begins by showing how the term 'social' is hopelessly confused. He suggests that as long as the word social is used to refer to an assemblage it is reasonable, but the problem arises when we use it to refer to the nature of that assemblage. In doing so, the process of assembling gets confused with the assembled product. Thus, he claims that it is 'no longer clear whether there exists relations that are specific enough to be called "social" and that could be grouped together in making up a special domain that could function as "a society". The social seems to be diluted everywhere and yet nowhere in particular' (Latour 2005: 2). He argues that the social, if it has to function as a special term, as an object that is of interest to sociology, is often defined negatively: as not-politics, not-economics, and the like. Thus, he suggests redefining 'sociology not as the "science of the social", but as the tracing of associations'. In this adjectival meaning of the social, it is not an entity but a 'type of connection between things that are not themselves social' (2005: 4). He points out that the social as in the 'social contract is Rousseau's invention. "Social" as in social problems, the social question, is a nineteenth-century innovation' (2005: 6) thus leading him to claim that the word social is the residue left after all other terms like politics, biology, economics, and so forth have taken their share.

Latour's suspicion towards the social as an entity, as a noun term, depends on the ontology of his own discourse and on the way he understands the ontological status of a term. As we discussed above, the multiple examples of scientific objects which are not physical/concrete objects, illustrate alternate possibilities within which one can understand the social as a noun. Nevertheless, Latour has an important insight into the way the social is formed and used. It is true, as he notes, that the social is often spoken about as a pre-given; even if not directly as the social, often as a pre-given social term like society, community, group, and so forth. When these terms are used, there is often a matter-of-factness about them, as if they are transparently cognizable. Latour notes that

> they begin with society or other social aggregates, whereas one should end with them ... They believed the social to be always already there at their disposal, whereas the social is not a type of thing either visible or to be postulated. It is visible only by the traces it leaves (under trials) when a new association is being produced between elements which themselves are in no way 'social' (2005: 8).

This goes to the heart of Latour's project in that the pre-given of the social is biased and looks for connections between members of an already defined social/society/group. If we do not begin with this and instead ask how something can become a social, we will have a different social since associations can be formed between humans and things, for example. If groups are not given, then they are always forming and being formed through relations and associations. Thus, 'the central intuition of sociology should be that at any given moment actors are made to fit in a group—often in more than one' (2005: 28).

If the social is not an entity of any kind but only a 'very peculiar movement of re-association and reassembling' (2005: 7), then it presumably does more work in describing social processes and other related socialities associated with the social. Rather than enter into the limitations of this view here, we want to merely highlight the gap in the way we talk and experience the social, along with this view of the social as decentred reassemblings. What really is the source of suspicion about the social as an entity? Is it merely evidential? Then is this suspicion merely a reflection of positivist prejudices about ontologies? Instead of focussing on a pre-given social, we could, as Latour suggests, look at the constant formations but why do these groups form in the first instance? Why is the notion of experience so central to these formations and what does this tell us about the nature of the social? As we saw earlier, the ontology of natural science can give us a different framework to enquire into the ontology of the social. This, coupled with the experiences of the everyday social which we will discuss in the next chapter, should allow for a robust ontology of the social which would include that of Latour but also other entity-type ontologies of the social.

Halewood (2014), in his study of the social among the pioneers of sociology, suggests that Latour is not correct in saying that sociologists always were unclear about what they meant by the social. None of the founding fathers of sociology could be accused of this and each of them had a formulation of social and society that was relevant to their ideas. But it is also true that the way sociologists like Weber, Durkheim, or even Marx understood the social is quite at odds with some of the later discussions on this concept. Nevertheless, it is useful to consider a few points from these thinkers in order to highlight certain common thematics in ideas of the social that are relevant today.

The two themes that we will focus some attention on are that of the moral and the natural, and their relation to the social. Durkheim is a good example of a thinker who includes all three together. Although he did not make explicit references to the concept 'social', his work is nevertheless concerned deeply about its ontological status. Halewood (2014: 23) points out that, for Durkheim, 'not only is the social natural but the social is moral and, in an important sense, the moral is natural'. Ultimately Durkheim locates the social in morality in his book *The Division of Labour*. To create the association between social and morality, Durkheim needs to invoke a specific conception of the natural since his axiomatic beginning is that the moral is natural. How then can one move from the naturality of morality to sociality? For Durkheim, the moral could be considered as a force like gravity and thus it 'gains its authority, and hence its ability to constrain, from collectivity' (2014: 126). Since 'collective thought expresses something in nature' it is natural. Thus, the very idea of the social, and all other cognate terms around it, arises from the authority present in collectivity—which is a 'collectivity of morality' (2014: 126–7). This approach is perhaps to be expected given that Durkheim, as Halewood emphasizes, generates his sociology from criminology.

Durkheim seems to be making the mistake that Latour cautions against—starting with a pre-given collective. But what is different is that the pre-given collective is one that is naturalized and also one which is related to morality. In fact, the two concepts that support the idea of the social, if we follow the argument above, are that of the natural and the moral. The association of some notion of morality with naturality problematizes this formulation. It is instructive to remember this as we will argue later in the book how notions of the natural, in association with that of the moral, influence social processes deeply in the Indian context (and presumably in other contexts too). Below, in this chapter, we will explore the link between the natural and the social in greater detail.

As Halewood points out, Weber uses the term 'social' rarely and not as it arises in the debate on social ontology. However, his invocation of the social as in 'social action' has been influential and hides various metaphysical presuppositions about the social. For Weber, the social occurs in a specific form of awareness of the others in a group, so that our actions are dependent on this awareness. In this sense, there is a pre-given group analysis which will illuminate social action. However, this analysis does not explain the formation of a group or what distinguishes one group from another as a group. Meaning-making becomes an important requirement that marks the social. As Weber argues, even if all members of a group speak the same language, it is not enough for it to be a social; it also requires that we are aware that others are speaking it and respond to this awareness. Thus, while society is made up of individuals, it needs rational interaction between the individuals to make it such. The object of study of sociology for Weber is 'meaningful action' and not all individual behaviour. From meaningful action we can move to social action which is action 'directed to other people' (Benton and Craib 2010: 78). As is well known, Weber classifies four types of meaningful social action as follows: traditional, affectual, valuing action, and practical action.

Some of the problems discussed above in the context of Durkheim also hold for Weber's description. What does the emphasis on 'meaningful' and 'social action' do to our understanding of the 'social'? The social is still built from the individual and is still relational in essence. More importantly, does this have the capacity to capture the complexity of the social in Indian contexts? Or in Asian and African contexts? Is it an idealized description of a particular kind of society? How does it capture the essential diversity of socialities and the different types of social such as the regressive social, progressive social, ideal social, embodied social, conflicted social, contaminated social, as well as the anti-social? We will explore some possible responses to this through our formulation of the social in the chapters to follow.

Natural and Social

The second theme drawing from Durkheim is the trope that the social is irreconcilably split from the natural. This view, according to Halewood, 'has infected much sociological thinking of the 20th century' (2014: 124). But this was not so for Durkheim when he held the position that social was natural. One important reason for this position was that only then could it be treated scientifically. What this implies is that although there are and could be special properties of social, they cannot be divorced from the natural. For Durkheim, even 'division of labour'—so important for his analysis of social—was natural in that even animals had it. As he writes, 'association is natural; what is interesting is the manner of association' (2014: 125).

The explicit relation between the natural and the social is fraught with problems especially because of views that understood the social in opposition to the individual, and the autonomy of the individual as a particular form of value. The nature of autonomy and authority becomes too closely linked to resistance against the natural—either as an individual or as a social group. The social begins to be seen as constraints on the individual and notions of freedom come to be situated entirely within the individual. By denying any natural state to the coming-together of individuals, this view at the same time makes the state of individualism the natural one. So, it is not that the idea of natural has been removed in a formulation of the social, but it has only been displaced to the individual and to her propensities including that for 'freedom' and 'choice'. Moreover, the argument that the natural is itself to be seen as social, motivated by geographers and Science and Technology Studies (STS) scholars, reverses the priority given to the individual, which itself was based on an unstated assumption that our views on individualism are natural in some sense. Ranging from biological arguments to philosophical ones, the claims to an individual's autonomy are suffused with ideas of pre-giveness and naturalness. But with the view that the natural is itself social, it puts the onus back on the social.

Our argument is that the notion of the natural often functions as an invisible conceptual substrate in any definition of the social, and the task is to make it explicit. For example, a common problem today is the essentializing that has become part of the discourse of identity politics. Essentializing itself has a deep relation to notions of the natural and thus identity politics is suffused with hidden notions of the natural. The notion of the individual may itself not be 'natural' since the individual is already social. The point is that the idea of the autonomous individual has one type of sociality that characterizes it. The fact that today's individuals far more socially interact with technologies is only an illustration of how technological objects becomes surrogate for other individuals. The experience of the autonomous individual is still a social one and functions according to the forces that generate and sustain that social. So, the very idea of the modern individual today is a consequence of the resistance to certain characteristics of a particular social and should not be mistaken as being against the idea of social itself, as some contemporary debates tend to do.

The collective which is created in a technological society is one that is not the collective associated with the moral but one that aggregates and flows around the functions of those technologies. The radio is a good example to illustrate the formation of a technological social mediated by the contours of that technology. One of the most powerful influences in the formation of a particular type of social—such as that associated with nationalism—is the government radio service, the All India Radio (AIR). Through its many innovative music, entertainment, and news programmes, AIR succeeded in building a sociality that was mediated around the technology of the radio but managed to connect, aggregate, and relate dispersed individuals to each other in many interesting ways. For example, there is a long-running programme called 'Sakhi Saheli' (companion and friend) which is broadcast every weekday afternoon combining music with recipes and titbits about domestic life. This is primarily seen as a programme for women and succeeds in creating a sense of the social which relates the listener to anonymous people in various small villages and towns in India. The experience of being a listener is equivalent to being a part of a larger group of imagined women all clustered around radios in their houses. The social that is experienced through this listening experience remains after the event is over and influences many of the other socials that get formed and dissolved through the course of their daily lives.

Like AIR, India's national TV Doordarshan, with its egalitarian content, has become another effective catalyst of the social. It has brought together aggregates whose relationships are mediated by this technology in various ways. Sports is a good example of how AIR and Doordarshan create socialities associated with sports in India, particularly cricket. We still remember that one defining moment of Indian cricket which was broadcast in Doordarshan in 1983 when India won the World Cup in limited overs cricket for the first time. It was a time when not every house, even in urban areas, had TV. People congregated in small groups to watch the match in houses which had TV sets. The socialities which defined these gatherings were duplicated in countless places and all these smaller socials not only were related by the live broadcast of the match, but it was also reproduced in various ways after the match was over. These socialities get revived, modified, and performed repeatedly after the event in so many different ways. The technology, as much as the sport, creates a sense of the collective, of a group, with its own unique set of relations between these groups and the people in them. The relations are ephemeral, and in today's time, global. Very similar phenomena continue to happen in millions of homes in India today even though TV is now a common sight in most houses. The spurt of sports bars where people come together to watch games—a phenomenon very common for World cup competitions in cricket or football—is nothing but a controlled reproduction of the earlier socialities related to this technology.

Technology today has come far beyond the capabilities and ambitions of the radio and TV. It might seem that there is a counter move towards the social in today's extensive personal technologies. Instead of sharing the listening space of a radio or the viewing space of a TV, we are immersed in personal technologies. Although this might at first glance seem to be counter to the experience of socialities, it is not really so. The sociality that is created by the experience of these technologies can best be described as corresponding to an 'anonymous social' or a 'surrogate social'. This is a social that is formed through the aggregation not of physically related individuals or related through the shared spaces of a TV or radio, but through virtual relationships in a digital space. The important point to note here is that even in the extreme cases of hyper-individual action through these technologies, we are most often only creating other kinds of social spaces or, in other words, creating different experiences of sociality. Or, equivalently, creating experiences of different socialities. The point that we are making here is that what appear to be extremely individual actions located within the practices of personal technologies today are still experiences of the social that can be described as anonymous or surrogate socials. The pervasiveness of the human attempt to be social—although manifested in diverse ways—makes the everyday discourse of the social move towards the belief that there is indeed a 'natural' disposition of humans towards sociality.

Thus, we can notice the interplay of the natural and social in almost every phenomenon, including the different disciplines of the social sciences. The first point to note is that the meaning of the term social in the different disciplines of social sciences is different for each discipline. Moreover, this meaning is based upon particular ideas of the natural in these disciplines, which is sometimes articulated but many times not. Thus, it seems as if the notion of the social in these disciplines draws upon—covertly sometimes—certain conceptions of the natural and, in this sense, the natural mediates between the individual and the social. There are also implications of this in the way certain concepts can be understood. Later, we will illustrate the working of this in the case of caste and argue how the idea of caste as social rests on, and needs, a particular idea of the natural.

We can motivate the discussion of the meaning of social in the different disciplines of the social sciences by considering the differing definitions of nature/natural in the disciplines of the natural sciences. As mentioned earlier, the meaning of nature in physics, chemistry, biology, geology, immunology, and other disciplines, differ although they seem to be talking about the same thing, namely nature. The contours of these disciplines are as much influenced by the theories of nature that are used in them. We will discuss more of this in the next chapter but here we will briefly discuss the origins of the idea of nature in the sciences. The origin of modern science is often located within a methodological move, such as the experimental method (Bacon and Galileo) or the use of mathematics (Galileo). But, the disciplinary formation of modern science is as much indebted to how nature is reconfigured in terms of the idea of the 'laws of nature' from the late eighteenth century onwards (Daston 1992, 2002, 2014). (This is particularly true of physics and, as mentioned earlier, chemistry and biology have different assumptions about nature.) The notion of the 'laws of nature' changes the way nature is perceived and also influences the meaning of doing science. Within this notion is also hidden an often-unasked question about the agency of nature that this notion seems to presuppose. This shift of understanding nature not in terms of natural beauty, not in terms of diversity of individual objects, but as a set of structural laws has important implications for the meaning of nature. An important consequence of this is that the diversity of objects in nature is reduced to a multiplicity of classes of objects which are defined by their appearance in laws of nature. For example, objects of nature can be classified universally in terms of mass which is defined by how it responds to or creates inertial force or gravitational force. Another implication is the origin of naturalistic fallacy and as Daston (2014: 582) notes, 'the sources of the philosophical confusion over the naturalistic fallacy are specific to a historically particular understanding of nature that emerges in the late eighteenth century'. The decoupling of nature from the moral is a social consequence of the way science as an institution accepts particular definitions of nature as essential to the definitions of science. As Daston argues,

> Nature in the Enlightenment had been quite openly saturated with values, but its authority over human affairs was exercised through rational assent rather than physical necessity. Nature during much of the nineteenth and twentieth centuries had been purged of values because it ruled entirely by physical necessity ... Within a will-centered, Kantian ethics, nature does not qualify for moral agency, much less moral authority: nature neither deliberates nor dictates; the natural and the moral belong to different ontological categories. (2014: 585)

This brief description is merely to point out that nature is first conceptualized in particular ways for a science to become possible. This is true as much for the social sciences. Durkheim's view of the natural cannot be the natural of the natural sciences for this view of nature is one that delinks itself from morality and yet has a notion of authorless authority (more on this in a later chapter). But neither does Durkheim go too far away from scientific nature since he reduces morality of nature to causations related to punishment. Moreover, his position is also different from the eighteenth-century view of morality as natural. This confusion exemplifies the problem in any claim that the social is natural and yet there is a link between the two that needs to be explicated, especially in the context of the everyday social.

In the case of the disciplines of the social sciences, what are the specific views of the social that are either implicitly or explicitly invoked? The socials as understood in economics, political science, anthropology, sociology, or history have to be conceptualized separately for each of these disciplines. What this means is that when an economist is using the word social, it is highly likely that she means something quite different from an anthropologist using that word. It is possible to find broad contours of the meaning of the social in each of these disciplines. Here is one simple and suggestive classification: The social in economics is situated within the relations of transaction (for example, transaction of money); in political science in the relations of agential authority/power; for anthropology in human kinship; and in sociology as institutionality. These are just suggestive structures of the social and it is possible to see many variations of the social even within the subdisciplines of these disciplines. We mention this in order to show the importance of recognizing how the ideas of the social are uniquely formed in each discipline and also how these socials are essentially related to particular ideas of the natural, which often remain unarticulated.

One could map the different naturals within the social as described above. For example, the notions of the natural which are specific to these disciplines could be the following: human rationality as the natural for economics; authority/power as the natural for political science; naturalness of family for anthropology; and the naturalness of aggregation ranging from counting, collections to institutionalizing for sociology. These notions function firstly as the defining notion of the natural which supports the idea of the social in these disciplines. For example, human rationality is a given natural disposition which makes the social that is needed for economics as a discipline. The social for economics is not really about kinship or even power as much as it is about certain assumptions of 'natural' human action. Similarly, for anthropology, an important idea of the social is derived through the emphasis on relations such as kinship and is not dependent on whether these relations are mediated by rational, utilitarian action. These intrinsic assumptions end up defining the scope of the social in these disciplines. So, the domains of the social can be seen to function in the following way in these different disciplines: Economics—transactional, Political—power, Anthropology—affectual, Sociology—cognitive/normative.

These are just the basic contours of a much more complex structure of the social and natural in these disciplines. We can similarly map the social that is inherent in the natural as defined in the natural sciences. (The work on social geography is a good instance of how the specific social that defines the natural of geography can be found.) The central point in this discussion is this: The idea of the individual is not really the essential counterpart to the social and this is well exemplified in the case of societies like India. The tension around privileging particular (especially modernist) notions about the individual without a clear understanding of the social contributes to many conflicts of the everyday social. Our claim is simple: Social, particularly the everyday social, is not in opposition to the individual but is in a tripartite relationship with the individual and the natural. Thus, when we invoke the social, we are essentially talking about two other terms, the individual and the natural, as well as relations among all these three terms.

There are two important issues that are essential to the discussion of the social: The question of authority (with or without an agent) and the mechanisms of the function of the social. We will address these issues in the chapters that follow but first we will discuss one example of the influential use of the natural within the social of caste.

Natural and the Social of Caste

What is the natural that is essential for the social of caste to be defined? By the very definition of caste in terms of caste groups, it appears to be a pre-given aggregate, a pre-given collection. It does not seem to form into aggregates as in the Latourian picture since it is quite rigid and does not allow individuals to form arbitrary castes. But how is this pre-giveness possible? What grounds this possibility? There is a strong and persisting notion of the pre-given social in the case of caste through biological association. It is analogous to the pre-giveness of a family in the sense that when a child is born there are at least two people who are part of the 'aggregate' in which the child is present, that is, the family group that a child belongs to is already decided by the parents even at the moment of birth. The relation between caste and family are strong on many counts, and themes such as biological relation, hereditary relation, and the notion of reproduction are routinely manifested in caste actions. The pre-giveness of caste, like that of a new born child, is reinforced by the association between caste and birth. One is born into a caste and does not choose to belong to any caste, just like the case of the 'natural' family. It is reemphasized by the association of hereditary biology with caste. The ideas of reproduction in the case of the family are similar to those that are often articulated in the 'reproduction' of caste within society. These mechanisms convert a social phenomenon like caste into a 'natural' grouping like family. Thus, it is not a surprise that the structures of the family like a patriarchal head are also reproduced within caste practices. The special association of caste with labour is only a pointer to how even the social division of labour gets naturalized.

But there is a complexity inherent in this question that needs more careful analysis. If we accept as a starting hypothesis that notions of the natural are themselves social, then we need to explore more carefully the natural that is inherent in the caste social. There are two worrying puzzles about the question of caste in India: one, the lack of strong and consistent ethical critiques of caste practices, and two, the authority that is needed to be able to sustain these practices in spite of various forms of social challenge. In fact, we observe that in the face of many such challenges, caste practices are getting consolidated in various new ways indicating a kind of a fluid identity of caste but with the essential core being undisturbed. Gail Omvedt (2001) argues that even when racism was compared with caste, racism was morally condemned because it was not compatible with modern life, but this view did not extend to caste. While practices of untouchability and exclusion have been criticized, it has been more difficult to sustain a consistent ethical response to the larger idea and function of caste. Part of this resistance arises from the strong sense of the natural which is associated with the caste social. There are two related arguments that help answer these two puzzles about lack of ethics and the notion of authority that sustains caste. The ethics issue in caste is very similar to that about nature itself and we can see that it is the extension of the naturalistic fallacy from nature into caste. The sustenance of caste functions through the mechanism of an authorless authority, which again is very much a part of how the natural functions. Given the uniqueness of caste in the Indian context, an understanding of this relation between the natural and the social in caste has to engage with the ideas of nature in Indian intellectual and cultural traditions, and also how these practices and beliefs around nature get morphed into ideas and practices about caste.[2] The remaining chapters in this book will deal with some of these issues.

Caste can have elements of the political, the historical, and the economical, but this relation between the natural and the social through which the social gets taken into the domain of the natural is the primary mode by which caste is sustained (caste 'as' a biological process) and remains outside the bounds of morality (naturalistic fallacy). So the many claims that the social is that which is not natural are often based on a particular social definition of nature itself but once we understand that there is little that is natural about nature, we can begin to see how the natural and the social cohabit in many interesting ways.

The natural arises in many explicit and implicit ways in the public discourse on caste and in the everyday talk about caste experiences.

---

[2] On the ideas of nature in Indian traditions, see Baindur (2015).

Images from nature lead to metaphorical descriptions of caste and other social phenomena. The imagery of waste and its relation to nature is deeply influential in the social imagination of caste. So also, another image that is often invoked in the everyday understanding of caste is that of trees on the seashore being forced to change their direction due to the strong winds from the ocean. These trees succumb to the force of the wind and have no control over their 'natural' growth which has often been equated with strong social winds of Brahminism or patriarchy, which attempt to force Dalits and women to change their 'direction' towards Brahminism. This process gets related to the notion of hierarchy since hierarchy is derived from the ideas of natural orders as seen and interpreted in the natural world. The interpretation of hierarchical behaviour among animals and plants (like in the case of the coconut trees) gives a template for articulating natural notions of hierarchy that become part of the sociality of caste. So, it is not uncommon to hear the claim that the domination of the upper caste within a society is 'natural' and thus all the members, including those of the upper castes, have to behave according to these natural expressions of hierarchy. It is most forcefully articulated in the case of the hierarchy of men over women accompanied often by arguments from the natural (or more correctly, the socialized natural). In the unfortunate case of Rohith Vemula, the reaction against him included the argument that it is the father who decides the caste and not the mother, thereby consolidating the naturalization of caste through these forms of the natural. Even the court has played a role in naturalizing caste through patriarchy.

The formation of the naturalized social is exhibited clearly in the way the State responds to the hierarchy of caste. One of the ways by which the natural is exorcized from the social is through making exceptions and locating the autonomous social within the language of exceptions. Caste as a 'natural entity' found its source of defiance and relevance in its exception. Even historically, caste rules were always about exceptions and the definitions of caste practices are so much based on ideas (and the anxieties) of exception as in the *Manu sāstra*. The modern State produces exceptions by treating Dalits as exception cases. Justice requires that some people need to be treated as exceptional (for example, the second principle of Rawls) but this rule cannot sustain itself without the difference principle. The Indian state or any welfare state has to create its own exception through the provision of reservation. Being exceptional, therefore, is being reasonable and thus the idea of the reasonable comes to be counterposed to the natural. It also rules out market rationalism based on Darwin's principle (the survival of the fittest argument). Moreover, only those who have the capacity to participate in the market can survive. The survival of the fittest is an unreasonable natural rule and it is exception that confirms or defines the rule of the natural. The natural cannot exist without concomitant notions of the unnatural or exceptional (and this is itself the mark of the socialization of the natural). In the case of caste, the domination of the upper caste is articulated in terms of it being natural. Thus, the natural behaviour of social groups is to behave according to the rules of hierarchy such as graded inequality.

Appointing Dalits to some decorative, if not decisive, positions is an exception that proves the dominance of the social. For example, a President of India as a Dalit is an exception and is referred to as such as it happened when K.R. Narayan went to Paris and some of the French journalists were reported to have referred to him by saying a 'Dalit President has come'. However, such journalists would not use a caste prefix to refer to a president who has an upper caste association such as a Brahmin President or one belonging to other castes. Dalit becomes a curious exception to the rule that is the high caste Hindus. Exception, thus, has the function to legitimize the reign of the social. Along with exception, it is necessary to democratize the social and humanize it as well, for democratizing the social offers only a partial condition for destroying the rigid hierarchical society.

The natural protects the dynamics of caste in various other ways. A common example of how caste is transmitted indicates not just the complex social imageries associated with caste but also indicates a powerful tool associated with the natural. One way to express this is by saying that a Dalit, as a part of dynamic social reality, has both legs and wings. In the case of a transfer of a Dalit officer, it is often the case that her caste travels faster than her transfer papers and before the people in the new post know about the new transfer, they know her as a Dalit. Thus, a Dalit in her exceptional state of being flies across time and space. But, to continue the natural imagery, the caste of a Dalit is like an inauspicious or grotesque bird like a flying fox. It flies as if it is a danger to the social. Hence Dalit, in the Indian context, is a walking carcass in its materialist manifestation while Dalit as a repulsive idea, flies. The deep relationship to the structures of the natural gets exhibited in this social dynamic as it manifests the work of an authorless authority (more on this in Chapter 6). Authority expresses itself both as a materiality as well as an idea. In the modern conception of the social, a Dalit begins to lose control on her caste as an embodiment.

Every doctrine remains hypothetical and can only be confirmed by being somehow associated with some notion of nature. Even the caste system is hypothetical and can be confirmed only by basing it on the foundation of nature. In evolution, a relatively undifferentiated, implicit arrangement or potentiality is rendered explicit, or actual, by its own development (Bookchin calls it dialectical naturalism). Does caste in this sense evolve? Has it evolved? Or is it that its own consciousness lacks self-reflectivity? In this sense, caste functions like a 'natural entity' in that it is reflexively not conscious. But caste as a social form has to be aware of itself but it is only mechanically self-aware. Thus, it functions entirely based on ritualized performances of caste, both in the personal and public domains. To understand what it could mean for caste to 'naturally' evolve, we first need to understand these deeply imbricated structures of the natural and social which sustain caste. One of the most important ways by which the social gets naturalized is through its association with the natural senses. In the next chapter on sensing the social we will see how the experience of the everyday social through the senses influences our understanding of various socialities including that of caste.

Social Ontology

There have been scholars who have taken the object of social as non-reducible and as a primitive ontological term, and there are different arguments that are available in support of such views. For example, Searle suggests that 'where the social sciences are concerned, social ontology is prior to methodology and theory' (2009: 9). Similar to the discussion earlier, he argues that we need to first know the object of our investigation before we can choose the right method and right theory. He begins by pointing out that the function of language in the description of social reality has been misunderstood right from the Greeks. (If he had known and been conversant with other philosophical traditions, like that of the Indian Grammarians, he might not have asserted this so strongly!) Searle's basic point is that it is necessary to reject the belief that language is given and can be taken for granted. Instead, he points to language as a primary agent in the formation of the social. One way to understand this is based on the observation that language is already social, as he notes, 'once you have a language you already have a social contract' (2009: 10). He shows how language is a more 'fundamental social institution' that makes it a foundation for other institutions since these institutions need language, or, more precisely, 'linguistic representation'. Although he considers money, government, and property, for example, as deriving meaning through language, they nevertheless acquire powers that go beyond these meanings. Thus, meanings 'are used to create a reality that goes beyond meaning' (2009: 25) whereas language does not exhibit this property. In other words, there is a priority and autonomy to language which makes possible social institutions.

Any discussion of the ontology of the social has to engage with the potential reduction of this entity to its presumed constituents, the individuals. Demeulenaere (2009) makes the important argument that the thesis of methodological individualism has two independent components: one, that only individuals act and two, that the social is built from individuals. He argues that these are two separate elements of this thesis; he takes the first interpretation to be 'obvious' whereas the second is ambiguous because of the ambiguity of the term 'social' (2009: 61). This ambiguity leads to dispersive meanings of the word 'social'. For example, Bratman's use of the social has three characteristics: shared intentionality, social as against individual norms, and individual and social as being at different 'levels'. He is suspicious of the view that the social emerges from individuals since the social is already everywhere and already 'pervading individual activities' (2009: 66). Since individual action is always social, there is really not much achieved in opposing individuals and the social. In this and similar approaches, the central element is individual action and not experience although he concludes by saying that 'social life is first given in our experience' (2009: 66). In line with a general hesitation in the literature to talk more seriously about the experience of the social, he does not discuss what this experience of the social life is or how the social is experienced as such.

One of the difficult problems regarding the social lies in the difficulty of conceptualizing the nature of group agency. Pettit (2009) attempts to describe how group agency is possible and uses the aspect of behaviour to do so. He suggests that in a simple theory of agency, 'a system is an agent just to the extent that it instantiates an agential pattern in its behaviour' (2009: 69). But it is not enough to merely talk of patterns in group behaviour. Taking into account various objections, he builds on this account to argue that agency should show 'purposive-representational pattern' which should satisfy 'systematic perturbability, contextual resilience and variable realization'. It is in this form of agency that 'a group of people might be an agent' in the sense that its members act without necessarily recognizing that they are doing so (2009: 75). This is one type of group agent, what Pettit calls 'transparent group', where all members of the group have 'equal awareness' and 'equal participation' of the desire for agency. He then concludes that the straw-vote assembly does indeed stand as a model of group agency.

Pettit points out that prejudice against group agency has two components. One is the epistemological problem: if groups have agency then there should be a corresponding mental life, but this would not be accessible to the members of the group. In the case of individual action, the agent can access her mental life, and can most times 'know' the intentionality behind an action. In the case of a group action, should all the members of the group be aware of the intentions of each one of them? Or is there something called a group intention which makes the group action possible? The second fear, which is metaphysical and political in origin, is more pervasive and this is the fear that there will be a group that mysteriously operates as an agent and that might adversely affect individual rights (2009: 88). Pettit dismisses both of these objections, at least in the case of the straw-vote assembly. But one can defend this idea even beyond this particular example and particular approach. As a general principle, there is no necessity of assuming a model of mental life for every notion of action. The belief that there should be a mental life that is needed to give an account of agency is itself based on a questionable model of the dualism of body and mind since there are other models of the mind which do not invoke this dualism. Importing this structure to group action without justification is not a good idea. The metaphysical fear about the group as an entity is also quite unfounded, especially for a discipline that sees itself as a science. Embodiment is not the only form of the real. Natural science is filled with causally efficacious entities that are not materially embodied. Not only the fundamental phenomena of nature but also the very structure of nature is fundamentally reducible to fields which are not materialized entities of any kind. Fields are real, have properties, influence individual particles, are spread out, and have other such characteristics. This does not mean the individual-social is exactly analogous to the picture of the particle-field in physics but those who hold these metaphysical fears would do well to enquire into this analogy further.

Similar metaphysical fear of groups is also related to ideas of rational action, a trope that is quite common in talking about actions of the individual in economics. Even the Weberian classification of social action privileges actions that are seen as 'rational'. However, this could be a mistake of wrong application of 'kinds' since the rational in all its manifestations is modelled primarily with respect to the individual. The difficulty is not just in imagining a rationality of the social or a group as much as in rethinking what group thinking would be like. Pettit's elaborate argument is as much a way to talk about group rationality but at the same time locating the locus of rationality within the individual per se. Therefore, he retains individual characteristics of rationality and simplifies the group as a collection with certain behavioural characteristics. What we are suggesting is a different way of understanding the possibility of both group agency—namely change the way we understand the nature of group as well as find a way to talk about agency which is not modelled on individual agency. We do this by beginning with the experience of diverse socials and then discussing the dynamics of the relation between the various socials. In Chapter 5, we indicate how we could understand group agency without reducing it into individual agency.

Abbott in his analysis of social entities accepts a form of 'social localism'. Little, who also supports this position, describes it as follows: 'that all social facts are carried by socially constructed individuals in action' (Little 2009: 159). Little carries this further to what he calls as 'methodological localism which accepts that social action is based on the "local, socially located and social constructed individual person"' (2009: 174). Thus, he holds the view that a person is not only 'socially constructed' but also 'socially situated'. As far as ontology is concerned, the point he wants to make is that the social is not an order or system but is made up of diverse mix of institutions, phenomena, behaviour, and so forth.

In these debates on the ontology of the social, there are at least two points we need to take note of. One is that the social is often spoken about as if it is a universal term. However, we argue that all collections or grouping are not the 'same' social and there is a multiplicity of socials. Two, a serious obstacle to the possibility of group action lies in the difficulty of conceptualizing group agency and this is primarily because of an excessive emphasis on agency as being essentially related to intention. This is a residue from particular models of individual action. One of the dominant ways of understanding individual action has been in terms of the intentions of the agent and then the performance of those intentions. Thus, any invocation of group agency is infected with the metaphysical and conceptual presuppositions of individual agency. There are two ways of dealing with this: one is to articulate alternate conceptions of group agency (a later chapter attempts to do that). The other is to draw upon other theories of individual agency, such as from other philosophical traditions. As one example, we can consider the contributions from theories of embodied action which make it meaningful to consider group agency as pure actions without prior group 'intentions'. For instance, one could act merely as a response to another act. Such actions are not deliberate, meaningful decisions but responsive actions, actions that respond to other actions done in the framework of the social which is the enabling condition for an individual's action. Modern forms of the social arise as more abstracted forms of the loci that generate a large number of such responsive actions. In small communities, responsive actions may arise in the immediacy of the locus of the action. For example, actions in a neighbour's house create social action in the whole street—this could be a social event like a common celebration of a festival. From the immediacy of these loci, we could have more displaced loci. There could be a new shopping centre some distance away which might become the loci of some other related set of actions. More displaced centres such as the government office or the legislative assembly or the high court remove the immediacy of the loci from which action is generated. It would be simplistic to reduce the origin of a set of actions at a particular place to an agent. It is only an origin to the extent that it catalyses various other actions around it and is soon independent of it.

We conclude this discussion with a brief comment about two approaches that may share some overlap with our approach. One is that of 'Phenomenological Sociology' (PS) and the other is some recent approaches to 'social ontology'. We have responded to a few issues in the latter, particularly those points that relate to group agency and the metaphysics of groups. Regarding the former, the approach we take is through the paradigm of 'sensing the social' and although this has some overlap with the centrality of experience in PS, the conceptual terminologies that PS invokes, following the Husserlian tradition, for example, differ from ours. When scholars have invoked these terminologies within the discipline of sociology, they have been a point of contention. Heap and Roth (1973) point to the various problems in the 'casual' use of terms like intention, bracketing, reduction, and phenomenon. Moreover, even within a phenomenological approach, one can make a distinction between the Heideggerian and Husserlian frameworks as Aspers (2010) well illustrates. Even the study of the every-day social through the phenomenological framework, as described by Overgaard and Zahavi (2009), is still concerned with concepts such as intersubjectivity, meaning-making, life-world, and so forth. After all, Alfred Schutz, the pioneer of PS, argued that everyday life should be the 'primary object' for sociology. Although the modes of experiencing the lifeworld are a starting point, they are then understood in typified manners based on prior experiences. As these authors point out, it is also the case that PS in general has had a greater focus on individuals through an undue emphasis on their intentional meaning-making, a problem which we avoid in our account of the social. Furthermore, if Schutz was deeply interested in knowing how a community of 'we' is created, we are interested in discovering how the sense of the 'we' is created and experienced.

The approach of PS and social ontology mentioned above also tends to privilege particular notions of the 'theoretical'/'philosophical' in order to make sense of the 'natural attitude' of the human subjects, and through this creates a hierarchy of method and knowledge in understanding humans. This is only one aspect of being human and it runs counter to the experience of being-social. Our focus is not on discovering social structures through these everyday experiences but to work towards understanding the importance of being-with rather than knowing-that. Our vision of the social, drawing on people like Gandhi and Ambedkar, is one that is based on an essential ethical relation between different socials. Thus, we reject this suspicion towards the subjects of the everyday life since these ideas of the theoretical or the philosophical are already contaminated with a history of bias against the social, which is many times manifested as a bias against cultures, communities, colour, and gender.

Some of these problems with the 'theoretical attitude' of social theory spill over into social ontology. It seems much easier to accept the possibility of a social in terms of collective beliefs, collective desires, and collective intentions, or somehow connect it to linguistic facts that refer or seem to create institutional and social facts (for example, Thomasson (2003)). There have been quite a few approaches trying to describe what the ontology of a social group could be, and readers might have found some similarities in our discussion of the social with some of these approaches. For example, Thomasson (2016) argues that it is obvious that there are social groups but the best way to understand them is as normative structures supplying various norms for the members of the group. But in general, these approaches seem to miss the most primal experiential sense of the social and the ways by which it influences other individuals and other socials. These views on the social may be much more representative of the intellectual or social cultures which these scholars are part of, rather than a 'universal' description of the nature of the social. Or it may be that the social of their societies catalyses such reflections. Whatever be the case, we want to understand how reflecting and thinking about the experience of the social in the Indian context might generate another view of the social, without necessarily creating hierarchies between the academic enterprise and the experience of living in the everyday world. As a first step towards this, in the next chapter we will illustrate how the everyday social is experienced through different sensory modes.

3 Sensing the Social

The fact that we talk about the social as if it is experienced through the different senses might suggest that the social is something that is available to our senses. Alternately, we could also consider the possibility that the social stands for certain kinds of experiences that we have and in this sense, it becomes a category of naming those kinds of experiences. There is a sense of seeing, touching, smelling, tasting, and hearing the social. Does this mean that the social is a 'real entity' which can be experienced with our five senses? We would suggest that this question should be bracketed and kept aside for now. The question is not whether the social is a real object accessible to our senses but how we make sense of certain kinds of experiences which seem to be experiences of the social. In fact, we could go further and argue that any notion of the social that we may have arises firstly through these experiences of the social.

The perception of the social through vision is the most dominant example and is well illustrated in the way the social has been conceived within the social sciences. We do see a group like we see individual things; seeing a group is seeing many things as if they are 'one'. But in seeing a collection of say three things, are we seeing three independent things or seeing one thing which has three parts? There are approaches that argue for the possibility of seeing collections rather than seeing only the parts. For example, the Nyāya philosophical tradition argues that when we see two cows we see twoness in each cow; that is, twoness becomes a quality that is present in each cow.[1] This is one way of understanding what it means to perceive a collection. Sight has the potential to perceive a unity and at the same time retain the multiplicity of the different parts of that unity. The dominance of the visual in our naive understanding of the social is also one that leads to the standard opposition between the individual and the social which is based on the perception of the many and the one. Once we move away from the genesis of the social via sight, there is a rich experiential world of the social available through the other senses. It is our contention that the everyday social in the Indian context is filled with these experiences and it is necessary to first engage with them. At this stage, it is important to reflect on these experiential modes without having to make a commitment to the reality or otherwise of the social.

Smelling the Everyday Social

For those who conventionally associate smell only to a real, physical object it may be absurd to think that something as ambiguous as the 'social' can be smelt or perceived by the senses in any way. We know that things smell, chemicals smell, people smell but how does the social smell? The nature of smell is itself complex and part of that complexity lies in its association with the everyday social. The question that needs our fresh attention is the following: How does the everyday social appear through the sense of smell? Our central argument here is against the grain and seeks to define the relationship between smell and the social radically differently: the everyday social is commonly accessed through smell.

We associate, detect, and define objects through their smell. Smell is not merely perceptive in the sense that it shows the presence of a thing; it is also a source of knowledge about that thing. For example, the smell of an overripe fruit is not only an indication of the presence of the fruit but also of some knowledge about that fruit. Unlike sight, smell is not a sense that is dependent on the spatial location of the object that is smelt. When we see something, we see it as being somewhere. We 'see' the location as much as we see the thing. But in the case of smell, we might smell something without recognizing what that thing could be or where it is exactly located. Thus, the object of smell is not located

---

[1] For a brief account of this approach, see Perrett (1985).

in a thing as clearly as in most cases of sight. We smell the air, smell the sea, smell the food that is being cooked, or smell a flavour. Most of the important examples of smell are associated not with concrete, determinate things but with entities that seem to be immaterial, un-located, spread out, and, perhaps, even invisible like air, space, flavours, and perfumes.

Smell plays an important role in terms of firmly foregrounding in our perception a social that otherwise is likely to remain fuzzy. In fact, smell is a prominent mode of perceiving the social. We smell the social, we smell the collective, as much as we smell the social in an individual. *Or at the least we talk as if we do*. We can either conclude from this way of talking about the social that this is evidence that we sense the social or if this is not desirable, then we should give an account of why we refer to the social in this manner.

Consider the many different ways in which our sense of smell continuously refers to the social. We define communities by con-stantly using our sensory capacity of smell. In the Indian context, the examples are many and endemic to the way we understand communi-ties. India is not just a land of thousand mutinies or a million gods; it is also a land of million smells. The social wafts into presence and travels on the back of many different smells that pervade the social domain. This immersion of the social in smells actually also becomes a way to access, identify, and categorize the social. For example, while the smell of fish seems only to be the smell of things called fishes, it is also a smell that is used to characterize and talk about communi-ties. Bengalis, Goans, and Malayalis are often described in terms of their fishy smell—this smell does not have to be the exact smell of cooking fish but is more a kind of smell, a kind of 'social smell' that ends up as a mark of reference. Arguably, the smell of *hing* or asafoe-tida is a common smell associated with some south Indian groups as this is a smell that can be particularly difficult for some to absorb. Muslims are often associated with the smell of a special kind of per-fume, *attar*. To smell that perfume is often seen equivalent to smelling a Muslim—in a sense, the smell is associated not with the particu-lar Muslim individual who uses that perfume but to the social class of Muslims. (In one Hindi movie *Chalbaz*, Kadar Khan associates attar with Jaunpuri.) Similarly, another strong association of groups with smell includes the association of the smell of coconut oil with the coastal people in South India, that of mustard oil with communities in the Eastern part of India, and so forth.

We do not have to take these associations seriously or get into a debate about such stereotypes. It is not even a matter of whether these associations are true or not. Obviously, using a smell to characterize groups runs into the problem of any essentialism and there are many quick counter arguments against such generalizations and stereotyping. What needs to capture our attention is the fact that our everyday social is continuously filled with meaning-making of the social through its association with smells and other senses. Moreover, the social does not always smell of food or nice things. The smell of garbage is a very important perceptual indicator of a different social. Smell needs an object as the condition for its detection. The scavenging social is defined by the smell of sewage and garbage. Similarly, cooking inside closed houses leaves the residue of smells in clothes whereas cooking in houses which are well ventilated does not have this problem. Smells settle on things and inhabit them. Thus, the natural tendency of the smell to permeate its vicinity with its essence sometimes leads to the consolidation of the particular social. For example, cooking fish or dry fish in the locality which is predominantly vegetarian leads to the collective mobilization against the fish-eating families, such as in the Shiv Sena protest in Mumbai. Smell in this context is a culprit in revealing the social identity of the fish eaters.

Smell acquires its significance only in the conditions of the cultural asymmetries. So, one way to understand this could be to say that smells of individual entities settle on the social composed of these cultural entities. Malls smell, particularly near the places where they cram many eateries. Gujarati owners of houses in Mumbai are notoriously famous for not giving their houses for rent to non-vegetarians. There are many such instances in South India, particularly among the Brahmins or Lingayats, who do not give their houses for rent to those who cook meat or fish. There are similar cases of even the Bengali upper caste being denied houses for rent on the ground that they eat fish. A dominant reason for that is the smell associated with cooking fish or meat as well as complex ontological beliefs about smells, such as the belief that the smells become part of the walls of the house and cannot be removed. Through such processes, groups become 'spatial socials' where people who are associated with particular smells will not be allowed to stay.

Smells gets ghettoized and spatialized much before people are. Smells associated with cuisines begin to define the nature of the community. Orthodox Brahmins do not use onions or garlic in their food and for them the smell of garlic gets associated with Muslims and the meat-eating castes. Communities along the Keralan and Konkan coastline cook with coconut oil and this has a strong smell and an association with communities there. The smells of these are a sure indicator of the kinds of households that use these oils and spices.

It is not only smelling the everyday social that we have to pay attention to. It is also the case that these perceptual modes *create* the social in ways unique to them. The nature of the sensation of smell has an intrinsic and necessary relationship with the social. To understand this, we have to understand the complexity of the sensation of smell. Given the visual hegemony that characterizes our dominant discourses, it is not a surprise that smell as a sense has been much devalued. Although our social is perhaps far more accessible to us through smell, and although smell dominates our social experiences, we tend to ignore its importance. The reasons for this are many but the major one is related to the apparent subjectivity of this sense. Also, in a discursive world where the senses are seen as windows to knowing, non-visual senses play a much smaller part. Although it is true that smells can also generate some knowledge, that knowledge in itself is not seen as useful or meaningful knowledge for the most part, except perhaps in places like a perfumery.

Smell has not been seen as a useful epistemological category in the social sciences. For a science in general, the role of smells, tastes, and touch are quite unimportant. A paradigmatic example is that of chemistry. The world of chemistry is a world filled with colourful objects, compounds, and mixtures. It is a world that is colourful and 'smell-full'. However, although smells are used to describe a multitude of chemicals, they are not epistemologically significant. Smells are descriptive and minimally descriptive at that. We read that chlorine has a pungent odour or that ethers have a sweet odour and that is that. To do chemistry is to go beyond these smells; it is to describe these chemicals in terms of their atomic structure, atomic bonds, and forces. A phenomenological world of chemicals gets converted into a scientific world of the shapes of molecules and their interactions or equivalently, secondary qualities of smell are replaced by primary, measurable qualities. But although the science of these chemicals is devoid of these sensory experiences, the everyday world of chemistry is filled with the experience of chemicals and the effect the chemical has on the nose and eyes.

So it is perhaps understandable that social science as a science is not able to take seriously the sensation of smell. But in the case of the social, it is nevertheless important to find ways to recover the use of smells as a genuine epistemological tool within the social sciences. The first such moment of significance comes when we consider the possibility that smell is a way of accessing the 'object' of the social. Such experiences and understanding of smell is definitely an important marker of the Indian social world and, we believe, of many Asian and African societies.[2]

The understanding of smell in this manner has a long history within the discursive world of South Asia, as McHugh (2012) points out. First of all, unlike the stability associated with an object of sight in general, the object of smell can be unknown and unperceived by the other senses, as well as remain ambiguous. For example, when we see an object in front of us, we are able to identify a stable appearance of an object. When we smell something, the object associated with that smell need not be present before our eyes and may arise from a far-off distance. But there are many cases where we also smell objects in front of us, like smelling a fruit which we hold in our hand. This sense is also sufficiently diffused in that it does not often generate confidence in believing that we know the object of perception quite unambiguously. In other words, the sense of smell is a perfect sense for having the social as its object! The world of the everyday social is filled with a variety of smells. In almost any public space in India, we can smell the different cooking smells from the houses, the perfumes of various people walking by, the incense smell from shops, the garbage smell from the uncollected garbage at the end of the street, the flower smell from the flower seller as well as the continuous smell of vehicle exhaust. There is an unending stream of different smells, each of which carries a sensation of the social.

---

[2] We are not claiming that such processes are not important in the 'Western' world but we are more interested in finding appropriate ways of talking about the social in Asia and Africa. For a discussion on the history of smells in the western context, see Jenner (2011).

However, one might argue that what we smell are individual smells and these have nothing to do with the social. For example, a sudden smell of incense could be traced to a small hotel where incense sticks have been lighted under some photos of gods above the cashier. So one could argue that the smell can be traced back to this particular situation and it has nothing to say about the social at all. But to understand smell in this manner is to miss the point about the nature of smell. It is to reduce smell to the functions of the more dominating sense of vision. The discovery of the origin of the incense smell as well as seeing the situation where it is originating from have little to do with the experience of the smell and more to do with justifying certain expectations about the smell. All smells, and even the particular incense smell, is not a pointer only to the origin of the smell. Rather, the smell is the indicator, a marker, of a perception of something else entirely, an entity which we might call the social or at least, the everyday social. To analyse this claim, we need to understand some other aspects of smell.

First, smell has to be carried by the wind. In a completely windless environment, the sensation of smell will not be possible or, at the least, will be quite different. The dependency of smell on the wind is one that is fundamental to how animals smell. It also has a deep connection to the way the society gets ordered—as we will see later, smells play an important role in the segregation of Dalit colonies within villages. Because of this and other reasons, smell has a deep relationship with touch. Smelling is related to touching and the wind is one mode of tactility which makes this possible. Smelling always involves the act of smelling along with other needed conditions. There is another parallel with individual sensation and the ontology of the world. Smell is often subsumed under the hegemony of sight but when there is no possibility of sight, when there is darkness, the sense of smell becomes extremely important. Along with sound, it becomes the dominant way to perceive the dark world, which is a world of objects that are not visible to the subject. The social is one such paradigmatic 'dark' object and so it is not surprising that the means of accessing what is thought to be the social is often through the senses of smell and sound, as well as touch/taste much more than sight alone.

The question of the order of the senses, sometimes understood as the hierarchy of the senses, has been a core concern for all philosophical traditions. McHugh points out that different philosophical systems like the Nyāya-Vaiseśika, Jaina, or the Buddhist had a different order of the senses and relates this to the metaphysics of their systems (2012: 46). For the Nyāya-Vaiseśika, smell is the first in the order followed by taste, sight, touch, and hearing. The reason for doing so is that the sense of smell is associated with the primary element earth. The other elements such as water, fire, and air have a set of other senses but not that of smell. The power of sight, accepted by the Buddhists, lies in its extensive reach. The range of sight extends far beyond the range of the other senses. Smell, for them, is in between sight and touch: touch is the most immediate and sight can be the most distanced. This privilege of the senses also has important implications for what we can say about the objects of the senses. Obviously, we would think that the object of taste, given its immediacy, is far more palpably real than an object of sight. That is why it is possible to have a category of illusion that dominantly arises in vision. Illusion about objects that are displaced from the experiencer include the sensations of smell and hearing.

Implications

There are many implications of the nature of the sense of smell and the concomitant experience of the everyday social. If the social is experienced, accessed, and constructed through the sense of smell then the nature of this sensation will also influence the nature of the social. In the South Asian context, the nature of smell as discussed above is also associated with many other qualities such as moral and aesthetic qualities. McHugh points out that 'suffering, impermanence, diseases, poverty, foul food, and all the other things people wished to escape in South Asian religions tend to smell quite bad' (2012: 5). Given the dominance of the notion of karma in these traditions, it is perhaps not a surprise to know that 'one's smell indicates one's karmic past and innate Nature' (2012: 6).

The presence of the element of touch within the sense of smell has important consequences. As we have seen earlier, smell is 'carried' by the wind and hence it needs wind for smells to be detected. Wind, thus, is an important propellant that would enable us to classify smell and establish its different qualities: moral, physical, foul, and fragrant. Smell has a moral quality as well, especially when it emanates from the sweat of a labouring body. The smell of public spaces in public buses and trains is a stark contrast to the aestheticized smell of areas like a mall. These smells as such connote moral qualities, not of the individual who goes to the mall or travels in a bus, but of the moral quality of the social which orders the 'smell world' in this manner. So, we could argue that in an act of moral ordering of smell, the sweat of the labouring body that has been treated as foul could then be re-signified as the most valuable asset or as a precious possession of the human being. We have such an insight available in Gandhi, Ambedkar, and Jyotirao Phule who would consider this sweat as the most precious gift of the human body. The moral conception of smell would militate against the particular interest of the free riders or non-sweating bodies thriving on somebody's sweat.

Foul smelling objects disperse their physicality through the wind and this in contact with the body produces the smell. The pollution that arises from touch is also relevant for smell. Thus, it was that smelling corpses, for example, would cause 'ritual pollution' for Brahmins (McHugh 2012: 6). But since smell does not have the immediacy of touch, it causes problems of pollution which are different from that of touch. Touching what should not be touched can be either voluntary or accidental. But in both these cases there is an immediacy which is related to touch, although one can avoid that touch by sidestepping that object. But smell is at the whim of the winds. A smell which is far away can suddenly be carried over to a place by a sudden wind. This nature of smell and its relation to touch influences the way the social (as in society) is ordered. It also influences the way by which our understanding of the social, through the experience of smell, is created.

It is also the case that we often tend to react to bad smells as if they are also repulsive to the touch. For example, when a group of students went to visit a fish canning plant, they immediately came back and had a shower to 'wash' away the smell. Similarly, a group of research trainees who went to study the Walmiki colony in Patna ran away the moment they saw a baby pig kissing its owner, a Walmiki, because of the association of sewage smell with the pigs. Thus, one can understand why there are strong proscriptions in food since many of these are fundamentally related to the association of smell. Even the proscription of onion and garlic as part of Brahminical food is part of a larger meaning ascribed to their smells (although there are other narratives such as their aphrodisiac nature). The relation between smell and taste (both mediated by touch) becomes more intriguing when we consider the pathologies of smell: if one loses the sense of smell, one also tends to lose the sense of taste.

The sense of smell also has a strong relation to memory which releases strong emotions. Smells can trigger deeply hidden memories and thus has significant affective power.[3] The deep moral sense associated with smells is manifested in the way odours were classified: as good and bad, although sometimes a third category of neutral was added. In the medical traditions too, smell was used as a diagnostic tool. It is a common saying in households that bad mouth odour is a sign of bad digestion. In *Carakasamhita*, the major text of Ayurveda, odours are classified as auspicious and inauspicious. They are also used to diagnose the period of death. For example, in this text we can find one of the rules for the diagnosis of death: If there is a permanent smell—good or bad—which does not go away then that is a sign of death within a year (McHugh 2012: 73). This relation between smell and the death of a person is found in many traditions. The addition of values to the factual domain of smells is an important feature of smells that ushers in moral values into the social function of smells.

This complexity of the sense of smell, as well as the deep relation between smell and our experience, particularly of the everyday social, influences the contours of the social in different ways. We have seen above the association of moral values, the relation of smell with touch, the transference of pollution related to touch to that of smell, and so on. Not surprisingly, if the social is accessible through smell, then many of these characterizations will find their way into any definition of the social. For example, with reference to Gandhi, Ambedkar, and Phule as mentioned briefly, we are encouraged to ask the question: How does the sense of morality enter into our experience of the social, particularly the everyday social? What defines our likes and dislikes of certain social groups and practices? While ideology and cultural habits have been offered as dominant explanations for our social actions, we need to take into account the possibility that our experiences of the social co-constitute the creation of the social.

---

[3] McHugh gives the example of Shulman who analyses memory and smell in Tamil and Sanskrit texts and shows the close connection between smell and separation as well as longing (2012: 14).

To re-emphasize the point we have been making: our talk and references of the everyday social are in terms of perceptual capacities. We access a meaning of the social—even if it is not clearly articulated most times—through these perceptual modes. This might mean one of two things: that there is nothing called the social and it is only a way of speaking about a set of experiences, or that the way we perceive and access the social is evidence of some realist commitment to the social. A realist commitment to the social through perceptual categories does not necessarily imply the objective existence of an entity called the social, although it could if our ontology is expansive enough to accommodate non-concrete entities. At this stage, we are only exploring the ways by which the social is articulated through our experiences which seem to suggest that we are indeed talking of an unseen social that seems to surround us. Thus, the analogy with space, as discussed earlier, is still a fruitful one. Our experience of the world is so much immersed in the language of space. Space surrounds us but it also seems to be outside our experiential capacities. However, we can again look to philosophical traditions like Nyāya which argue that space is experientially accessed through sound. So, if the social is analogous to space, then there is a model to understand how it can be sensorially accessed through sound.

One critical response to the argument that the social can be smelt is that it is not the social that is smelt but a person/thing who/which is the cause of the smell. So, one might argue that even if one describes the smell through categories of the social, this does not imply that it is the social which smells and not the individual. Again, we can have two responses to this argument: one is that the smell of an individual is itself social in that the categories of smell and the associations about that smell are all socially mediated. But this argument does not explain what is meant by the social. It just uses the word social as an empty signifier which does too much work without specifying what it really means. The other is to say that we associate a sociality to smell and thus claim that all smells are social—at one extreme, this is equivalent to saying that we smell the social even without the presence of the object that is supposed to be the substratum of that smell. Thus, smells become the objects of the social without any presence of individual beings.

Another way of understanding how the social arises in the context of smell is by taking into account the agency of the wind that is needed for smells to be transmitted. The interesting thing about smell is that it needs an extra 'outside' agency for it to be smelt. We can consider the possibility that the idea of the social is the extra term that is required for any perception to be possible. Equivalently, the social is the 'wind' that carries the smell and it is the extra term that is required for any smell to become perceptible. This view also underlines the importance of an ontology of the social—it is like the analogy of the social as a glue between individuals which arises in the context of understanding social aggregates from the visual perspective.

The belief in the ontology of the social through its access via smell becomes stronger when we consider how smells reproduce the exclusionary social. Even institutions get associated with specific smells which then get identified with them, and down the line the institution itself reproduces that smell. One simple way by which this happens is the use of smell to nonverbally communicate specific socialities. This is true of religious spaces but also true of places like a mall where certain kinds of 'global smells' (very often global fragrances related to globally produced things) are used to say something about the social status of the mall and through extension, the social status of those who shop there. By doing this, these socialities derive and sustain their social meaning through the medium of that smell. It is equivalent to declaring that it is so by transmitting the smell. This is as much true of institutions as it is of groups and communities. They do this by appropriating various smells within themselves—smells of particular incenses, perfumes, specific fragrances of food, and so on.

On the other side, smell becomes a social stigma because the smell is separated from oneself. There is an anecdotal story told about Gandhi. In his Sevagram ashram at Wardha, a social worker wanted to work. Gandhi asked him to go and clean the toilet. After the man cleaned the toilet, Gandhi asked him whether there was a foul smell in the toilet. The man replied in the affirmative. Gandhi asked him to go back and clean it again. And this continued till the man lost the sense of smell and could encounter the toilet without its association of the foul smell. The removal of the gross smell would have been quite easy—first through cleaning, then through the use of toilet fresheners, and so forth. But what Gandhi was asking the man to do was not just to remove the smell by replacing it by some other 'nicer' smell. Gandhi wanted this man to undertake a metaphysical exercise because smell is much more than the materials associated with the smell. So one has to overcome the very idea of certain associations related to particular smells and not merely reduce the smell to the substance that is thought to produce it.

Such a metaphysical position about smell informs the understanding of smell in the everyday social world. For example, there are communities who even when they do not work in scavenging (and therefore are not associated with that smell) still retain that stigma. It is no longer 'olfactory smell' but a 'social smell' which has nothing to do with the olfactory sense. In fact, from these examples, one could argue that smell becomes the vehicle for encoding, sustaining, and transmitting certain notions of the social. For example, certain groups traditionally associated with scavenging sometimes are treated as if they continue to carry that smell even when they are well-to-do citizens doing various other jobs. One could claim that they carry the smell as part of the stereotyping and the attempt at humiliation. But this is to miss the more important aspect of a particular form of social action which uses smell as a marker of the social. When people use smell as a category to categorize communities, they are in essence saying that the group comes into being as a group because of the 'social smell' associated with that sociality.

At the metaphysical level, smell is a moral menace and hence its warning is issued through the sound of the bell or a whistle. Sound communication differs in different contexts. In one context, it may involve an element of the aesthetic while in another a sense of repulsion. For example, classical music or folk music will communicate to people an aesthetic element when it is in the right context and the right performative space. But garbage collection announced by a *Ghanta Gaadi* (which is the garbage cart or vehicle which collects garbage from houses and announces its arrival by ringing a bell or a whistle) involves a deep sense of repulsion, particularly at the level of its reception by those who are not the garbage collectors. Through this sound, the sense of smell travels faster than the sound of the bell or the whistle. This can be easily seen on the faces of those domestic servants or women who make repulsive signs with their faces when they hear this sound. What is registering through the sound of the garbage cart is the repulsive smell. The unpleasant gesture on the face of this person (ironically the one who is creating the garbage) connects the foul smell with the garbage-collector's body or figure which is taken to be either dirty or decomposed like the garbage. The early arrival of smell makes some of them spit on hearing the sound of the Ghanta Gaadi. The spit is an expression of disgust towards the person accompanying the garbage as much as the garbage.

The tactile source of smell is in the morphology of space: segregated and non-segregated. In fact, the foul smell has its origin in segregation. The moment we segregate different kinds of dirt from our body we begin to develop the sense of foul smell. Garbage becomes a site of sickness and a danger to public health, as well illustrated even in places like Bengaluru whose garbage has led to serious illness for villagers outside Bengaluru near whom the garbage is dumped. It is the logic of segregation that converts the human settlement into a site of foul smell or garbage depot even if such human settlements do not emit foul smell from their physical location. For example, Dalitwadas are first segregated with caste morphology and then condemned as the source of smell. Dalit colonies are many times near the open defecation ground. They create the ground and then the community is condemned as the source of the smell. The irony of this is that the Dalits are segregated, and they are also forced to sit on judgement about which garbage is more foul smelling than the other. The segregation of garbage in the social space becomes the segregation of garbage within houses.

The source of foul smell forces the upper caste to put in place certain kinds of village topography. They, in order to avoid the foul smell, force the Dalits to build their houses typically on the eastern side of the village because the wind flows from the west to the east. They use the natural flow of the wind in order to order the social. Thus, there is a re-signification of the foul smell—smell can be functional only in the porousness of the social. If the social is completely covered with fragrance, there is no notion of a foul smell. People now routinely use ACs in their cars and close their windows when they come near a garbage truck. What if the social itself has a foul odour which is not palatable to its occupants? They insulate themselves from the social since all social is dirty and smells. So the everyday power of the smell involves re-signification of what is condemned as foul and what is elevated as more pleasing. (The globally common 'pleasant' smells in malls across the world connotes social experiences of comfort, pleasure, subservience, desire, and so on. Ironically, these pleasant smells are artificially produced through chemicals which would be more harmful than garbage!) The re-signification of smell can be explained through the action of fisherwomen who, in the local Mumbai trains, use the smell of fish to disperse the density of commuters and get easy passage into the local train. They shout out, *machli, machli* (fish, fish) and disperse the crowd who run away from the idea of the smell even though the smell is not there.

Smell (as in food) is one way to draw the boundaries of the social. This is extremely important because the concept of the social is often seen to be homogenous and does not have any specific forms which can individuate different socials. (This is a lot like space—all space is homogenous, and we cannot distinguish one part of the space from another, since space does not have parts like objects might.) However, such homogenous socials are not experientially found. There are many socials, and smell and sound, for example, give a concrete shape to these different socials. Our argument is that we need to engage with these complex ways of engaging with the experience of the everyday socials if we want a meaningful account of social processes in India. For example, there has been much written about the denial of rental houses to those who have different food preferences compared to the owners of these places, as we have mentioned earlier. While the responses to this are most often expressed in terms of prejudice and so forth, these are not enough to give a social theoretical foundation of these and related actions.

Hearing the Social

Sound expresses the first urge of humans to communicate, intended to announce their existence to living creatures outside themselves. Sounds communicate this existence and the arrival at the gates of civilization. Once it arrives there, sound has different operational functions. It functions through a constructed morphology. Arguably, sound has a capacity which is natural. Normally people have vocal cords and they use it but untouchables are not allowed to announce their existence at the gates of civilization. Their living essence is outside themselves: The corporeality of their sound gets transformed into the materiality of music, as if they are not allowed to produce sound from their vocal cords. In fact, they are forced to announce their arrival by using bells or the sound of the drum. They are forced to use their musical instrument not for their own aesthetic needs but for organizing the sociability of the *agrahara* or upper caste society. They are supposed to produce variation or layers in their sound. For example, they are not supposed to shout when they are in the upper caste public sphere. They can do so only in their colonies, which is then called chaotic and noisy. Such morphology of sound which tends to bind the texture of society in space and time ultimately provides organizing conditions within which the morphology of sound has to play out either into high decibel sound or complete silence. The category of space and time tends to coordinate the morphology of sound. A sound folds into itself when it enters the high-caste public sphere or is transformed into music or replaced by another sound of a drum. In this social life of sound, an important difference between sound and music occurs. When sound travels to Dalitwada, it becomes freedom and begins to flow freely from the Dalit body leading to cacophony. It plays out with full freedom without being choked or blocked. Drums played in the Dalit colony thus produce the possibility of a new social within which one could redeem the unbounded freedom. The sound of drums travels across time and space. Sound is social through its communicability. Many of these processes are as much part of the larger world of the poor today in increasingly 'prosperous' societies all across the globe.

Sound, like smell, is an important perceptual component of the social. The social can not only be perceived by sound but it is also the case that our basic experience of the social is also formed by sound. It is only by hearing many things that we think of the social and this is deeply imbricated in the possibility of language and music. Sound is perhaps the most important element in the experience of the social. Sound creates/experiences the social in a way that is not possible in vision. Groups are formed not just by individuals standing next to each other (a visual collective) but by creating sounds together. This insight is an integral practice of community binding and is ritualized in many rural communities even today. When NGOs organize programmes, many of them often begin with music sessions where they all sing together. Singing together creates as well as makes one experience the social in ways which cannot be done through other perceptual modes.

Social experienced through sound is qualitatively different from that experienced through vision or action based on the social as an aggregation. It also has a deep relation to an important philosophical concept of Indian philosophies, that of *vyāpti* (pervasion).[4] This comes from the possibility of understanding a collection not through numbers of individuals who belong to it but by a sense of the social which pervades all those who are part of the social. This means that to have an experience of the social it is not really necessary to have many individuals within it. In a way, the claim that individuals are already social is only one way of expressing this pervasiveness of the social. The social experienced through sound is really not a social which *has* to be a multiplicity. The multiplicity, even if there is one, is unified into sounds. The nature of sound supports this unique engagement between the social and sound. A sound as an auditory experience is not made up of parts as in a visually perceived object. We hear a sound as a unity of many elements but do not, as a general practice, distinguish the elements which go to make up this unity. This experience is another paradigm of the social and is best captured through the relation of pervasion. In the tradition of logic in Indian philosophies, we can see the conceptual power of this terminology. When these logicians discuss the inference of fire from seeing smoke, they describe the relation between fire and smoke in terms of the pervasion relationship by arguing that a necessary relation between smoke and fire is nothing other than saying smoke is always pervaded by fire.[5] The use of this metaphysical framework to understand the social is best exemplified by the experience of the social through sound.

One of the most powerful and important ways by which this is accomplished is through the use of music. Singing together is not only to make music but is also a way of creating an experience of the social. To put it more starkly: if there are a group of people who are together, there is no simple way by which this group can create an experience of the social. They could be a group of strangers in a bus stop or in a theatre. Their common intention already 'binds' them and, in a sense, they are already social or at least proto-social. Or, at the least, they exhibit the potential to coalesce; what we could call as 'socialesce'. Coalesce originally meant to 'grow together' and that really captures the sense

---

[4] See Sarukkai (2011) for more on this concept.
[5] See Matilal (1998) and Sarukkai (2005).

of 'socialesce' since the social is not just putting together but coming together, a particular kind of coalescing together. But they do not create an experience of the social for a person who joins that group in the bus stop or in the theatre. The social that has the potential to be created still remains as a potential and is not actualized.

Consider the situation where a group of people come together for a common purpose. The individuals in the group are strangers to each other and their capacity to 'socialesce' is very limited. Then, imagine the scenario where they begin to sing together, maybe as an exercise or spontaneously. Singing together makes them a different group than the group which just stood together but how can we characterize this difference? What we are suggesting is that singing together creates a sense and an experience of the social among the individuals and also at the same time becomes a way of recognizing and experiencing the sociality of the group.

There is this sense of mystery about music which is transmitted to the idea of the social. Prayer calls are one classic example. Consider the call for prayer from mosques. The 'Pak' or pure, sacred call is a piece of soothing sound which resonates early morning announcing the arrival of dawn and the end of darkness. It is not a mere call to prayer—that could have been accomplished by a statement 'Come to the mosque now for your morning prayers'. Instead, it is a 'song', a call that captures the common experience of the human and the divine. The devotee hears the divine, 'touches' the divine through sound and music. Some of the greatest music in Indian classical and popular music are religious songs. The sociality of religion draws enormously from the capacity of music to create an experience of the social unlike anything else. The sounds in the public spaces of India are filled with these sounds from places of worship and each time one hears these sounds we are experiencing particular socialities through them.

Everyday prosaic sounds create powerful experiences of the social. Public life in India is characterized by sounds which bring the social into one's home. The sound of the cooker whistle from neighbouring houses every morning (like the smell of cooking from other houses throughout the day), the sounds of children playing and talking on the streets which mingles with the call of the vegetable woman and that of the person collecting old newspapers, the exhaust sounds of a vehicle or the cawing of a crow—these are not just sounds but are the sounds by which we experience the social, which gives us a *first awareness of our own belongingness* in that social.

Sound is created as well as heard. Animals can hear the arrival of danger and then accordingly produce sound that communicates the warning of danger to other animals. In the case of animals, warning sounds may be for protecting the self and the community but this also is a warning that can be shared by other animals. In the warning, the sound becomes a moral act. Creating the sound involves responsibility but this responsibility assumes a privileged position—the monkey on top of the tree, for example. Similarly, a human being is also the recipient of the information of the danger but has to now share this with other humans for social purposes (for example, information about riots). Monkeys have no choice to remain silent because their own existence is at risk. They cannot decide or afford to be silent in the face of danger. But although there is no hearing impairment for humans, they can nevertheless go for socially induced hearing impairment. Hearing loses its natural quality particularly when it is on its way to becoming a 'classified' social. What is a classified social? It can be understood in terms of making a set of people hear something which may not be in the cognitive interests of others. For example, the social gathering of the Babas (Hindu 'religious' leaders) when they promote militant Hindutva. It also loses its naturalness when a sound becomes an individual property. In this sense, sound is fundamentally social and when it is individualized/privatized it goes against the meaning of sound itself.

Another example of a classified social can be Vivekananda's Hinduism but the receptivity of this social at the level of hearing is not a matter of conviction but of curiosity. Whereas when Ambedkar's message is being heard by the Dalits, it is taken as a matter of conviction. Or the 1917 call given by the peasants of Champaran to Gandhi was heard by Gandhi as a matter of conviction. In the case of the American audience, Vivekananda's classified social, the sound appears to be spiritualizing but there is also a tragic dimension to it. An apt example to illustrate this is the cry of sati (Muranjan 1973: 129). In the Indian context, Hindu patriarchy converts the genuine cry of a sati to a dead silence. Conversely, patriarchy tries and puts its own voice on silence mode. Or some of them actively use technology to put the human cry to silence—first, they use drugs to silence the cry of the woman, then they will fence the pyre so she does not run away, then there will be a layer of security guards, and finally the creation of the counter-sound of drums to muffle the sound of the woman.

The counter-sound becomes a necessary social condition to organize hatred, arrogance, and authority against the enemy. As examples we could consider the patriarchal arrogance against sati or minority person as the object of hate. In military training, sound becomes a power. A soldier has to create a primordial sound in order to conclude his violent act of killing the enemy. This sound contains intense degree of rage and hatred against the enemy and it acquires a social character when the group of people get energized by saying slogans before such actions. On the other side of the spectrum, a sound contains a deep sense of repulsion. For example, when orthodox Brahmins cannot hear the sound of a Dalit as it is considered defiling or carrying pollution, particularly during the rituals of Sandhya. The sound as natural resource is converted into a socially compressed fact. The language of (music of) the soul therefore leads to unconditional expression of sound while the caste of mind leads to the compression of sound. The language of mind, in contrast, through its ideological embodiment, leads to the act of selective hearing, not hearing, withdrawing, and so forth.

Thus, the Hindutvavadi does not want to listen to the secular voice and they try and douse it off through the strident noise created by them through social media. Yet, it is necessary to hear what is human and what is reasonable. We have no freedom to remain silent and are also accountable for what we speak. We have a freedom to hear what needs to be heard. Such a necessity to hear others has to go beyond individual choice: *Sun na padega* (we have to listen). It has to go beyond instrumental utilitarian consideration and should not even be out of social obligation. Hearing the small voices of history is a social need because it is also self-liberating and is not therefore social obligation. Hearing out of social obligation lacks genuine commitment and unconditional intellectual and moral involvement. For example, listening to complaints from the marginalized, or one's subordinates, can make the privileged develop some kind of cynicism, and cynicism is anti-social. Thus, to prevent oneself from becoming cynical about reasonable complaints, some morally guilty persons can use social obligation of hearing the others. Cynicism is necessarily a negative aspect that can cast aspersions on the body or personality that is perceived to be canonized. Hence, a person adopts social obligation of hearing others as a moral condition to keep her personal body canonized.

Those who are not heard, whose sounds do not enter other ears, need to speak more. Socially impaired hearing becomes a deliberate mode for those who refuse to hear and they grant authority to themselves to refuse to hear. Or they retain the privilege or authority to speak all the time. Speaking all the time instead of listening to others is not an individual problem of hearing but a reflection of social hearing. Some might call this as talking-down instead of talking-to. In India, there is a topographical condition within which this talking-down takes place. For example, in many Indian villages the socially dominant people always speak to the lower castes from the structures that are elevated, like *gadhi*. When there is a need to call people of the lower castes, these people would shout from the heights of the gadhi and not come down to the same plane as the workers. This physical 'talking-down' is converted into symbolic talking-down of various kinds, thereby going beyond mere functionality. It is not a surprise that such structures are reproduced in various social institutions, ranging from the legislative, law enforcement, and even in the everyday practice of schools and other institutions.

Sound and Taste

In our social world, there is an interesting connection between sound and the mechanics of the creation of sound through the mouth. Because of which, a materiality to sound through spit is generated. How does one understand the phenomenology of utterances, the words uttered through the mouth? Some people who are obsessed with the idea of pure body would always avoid uttering the words that have a defiling element around them, such as 'untouchable' or '*achut*' (in Hindi). The moment they are in a position where they have to utter the word, they, instead of producing the word in the mouth, will just spit the word out. And if this particular word lingers longer on their tongue or in their mouth without it being uttered, it is bound to 'decompose' into a bad taste or an unbearable repulsion. Hence, it has to be spat out. For example, the phrase 'I am not an untouchable' is spat out and is not uttered.

Words thus are converted into a dirty substance; a spit is an explosion of dirty substance. The well-entrenched discourse on spit (*jootan*), also related to leftover food, is so much a part of the everyday social. There are elaborate dos and don'ts with respect to spit as it relates to contact with food, vessels, cups, and so on. There are very strict codes of not touching something with the same finger which touches one's own mouth, particularly among the Brahmins. Spit, in other words, becomes as much a social product as a natural body secretion. Moreover, in a certain sense, the dissolution of words in the mouth suggests the loss of human capacity or ability to understand or produce a speech act that can harness a constitution of a sentient being or self. Conversely, the words released from the Dalit mouth tend to acquire a foul taste for the upper caste. Words thus get the foul taste of jootan. The moment the utterances of 'bad words' fall on the ears of the upper caste, his or her otherwise ritually integrated self gets disintegrated.

Music has a power to break the rigid social in ways which words alone cannot. For example, the upper caste women are nowadays quite receptive to the tune of the music that is played even in the marriages of Dalits and by the Dalits. These women come out of their houses to watch the marriage procession and also dance with the music. Dalit music has become a rage in Tamil movies and are now routinely played in the weddings of Brahmins. Music also democratizes the spaces that are organized around hierarchy. This is a radical change over the social that existed 30 to 40 years back, where women from the upper castes neither participated nor listened to music that is 'popular'. The influence of film music and through it the 'performance' of various castes have become a part of upper caste marriages in Chennai and other places.

How is it possible to understand this radical change in the social practices of these groups and the changing social face of reception of different types of music in India? This can possibly be explained by the mediation of this music through the market. The performative idiom of music has undergone a change in the sense that it has become more spectacular in terms of its presentation, organization, and its background conditions. This is not without the force of market and the market functions as the invisible social. But it is more than the market forces alone for it also speaks to the formation and experiences of new socials. Sound is most importantly an agent in these formations and experiences. Socialities associated with this phenomenon can also be seen in family aspirations and public ambitions that need to be redeemed through the spectacle. Earlier it was done by offering a big feast—food was the social in this sense. There was no participation but there was some kind of social transaction. But here, with music, there is participation. Even the religious has become a part of the modern social where music induces upper caste women to dance in the streets, in public functions organized to celebrate initiation ceremony in cities like Pune.

Touching the Social

Touch is another way to perceive the social and is an important way by which the social is experienced by us.[6] The sociality of caste is primarily through the sensation/repulsion of social touch. When the people of the same caste touch each other there is a different sense of touch which may be love and care. But when the upper caste touches the lower caste, what is the quality of this touch? There are many illustrations of touch/untouch that go to form the experience and narrative of the social. Notions of untouch range from not touching some human beings to not touching museum pieces. The private is defined through contact and touch, thereby leading to notions of personal space in public areas and buses. One could say that the idea of aggregation or collection is in a tension between being together as a group but not touching each other since complete touch, complete unity through touch will break their multiplicity. Touch is the fulcrum around which the social remains a social.

The collective experience in many Indian situations has a lot to do with the nature of touch. Consider the following common experiences that one would encounter almost every day: People are far more comfortable not shaking hands and prefer to keep their distance; touch between men and women, even to shake hands, is largely absent except in some work and professional contexts; physical contact between fathers and daughters as a social practice is quite infrequent; the phenomenon of untouchability still has a powerful presence in the society; and so on. In the Hindu tradition, greeting someone with folded hands and not through handshake works out very well according to the social expectations of the upper caste. They, in the name of following the

---

[6] See Guru and Sarukkai (2012) and Jaaware (2018).

'Indian tradition', can avoid touching the defiling Dalit. Performance and non-performance of touch creates social asymmetry in which an upper caste has the power to withhold the initiative to touch the defiling Dalit. Hence, touching involves power and its exercise regressively moves from the natural to the social. It, at the social level, compels the Dalit to be dependent on the willingness of the upper caste to touch the former. Again, one can see this being reproduced in various situations between the richer class and the poor and working class.

Consider the handshake. Why do we shake another person's hands? Why do we do it as a form of greeting or when sealing a promise? Shaking hands also seems to be a way of accepting who socially belongs to our own communities—these communities can vary. Our community can be marked by nation, religion, caste, profession, place of residence, or even being an adult. We do not shake hands with those who do not belong to our communities in the same way that we do with those who do belong. We do not shake hands with children, for example, the way we do with other adults. We may not even want to shake hands with beggars or in the Indian social context with people who do not belong to our caste communities. Shaking hands is a form of touching the other and in the very act of touching there is a social sanction. We would not shake hands if we did not have social sanction to do that. One could argue that greeting people by folding hands is to politely express unwillingness to touch the other. Shaking hands is already performing a social act, one that is not only driven by social conventions but also one which reinforces how the social is touchable in various ways.

Other phenomena related to touch add to the complexity of these functions of social touch: The closeness of people to each other in public spaces, the immediate availability of strangers to physically help an individual, the use of language as a form of contact/touch, and the sharing of food among friends and strangers. It is not possible to understand these and many other social phenomena only in terms of the actions, motivations, and desires of individuals or by reducing the social touch into touch of embodied particulars, such as other humans or objects. The phenomenon of social touch is based on an ontology of touch. In the everyday social, this occurs in so many ways. It is exemplified in Hindu religious practices and syncretically in other religious practices too. This has to do with the practices and rituals around touching idols of gods or other embodiments of the divine. In orthodox temples, particularly in South India, touching the idols is proscribed and touch has to be performed through various intermediaries. In many temples in the North, as well as in thousands of roadside and small temples in rural areas, devotees can actually touch the idols. It is not a surprise that these practices of touching the divine are also isomorphic to the caste practices that are dominant in those places of worship. Equally important is to note that ontologies of touch, as a touch of the non-embodied (whether the divine or the social), are often internalized through these everyday practices. The multiplicity of these sensations of the social associated with touch has to be understood before we can formulate an idea of the social in the Indian context.

Collections and aggregates are defined as much by touch as by other sensory modes. The collective becomes a collective only through a shared sense of touch. A football team is a social entity and becomes a team through modes of touch that reveals the social. In a football team, members do not touch each other like they would if they were only two individuals. The social of the team, that which makes a group of players into 'one' team, is defined by their sense of social touch. One of the 'shared-touching' is the ball. It is the common object that is 'shared-touched' by all the players. Great football teams exemplify an important facet of touching: for the Barcelona team of recent times, the game of football was essentially not about scoring goals but in keeping the ball as much as one could within the team members. The social of football arises through this form of touching. In other words, touching the ball is one way of touching the social that defines the football team. This shared-touching cannot be reduced to the touching of the football alone. Social manifestations of this abound in all sectors of the society. For example, touching the dead leather is not a ritual taboo for an upper caste football player but this player avoids touching the lower caste player; hence the Dalit is a goalkeeper.

The example of personal/public space between people is an important social phenomenon in India. In public areas, including in public transport like buses, people are invariably pushed close to each other. But what is important to note is the ease by which men, in particular, feel comfortable even when other men are much closer to them as compared to some western nations. The space which is referred to as the personal space around each individual in a public space is quite shrunk in the Indian context. There is also a clearly defined grouping of the social where people get immediately uncomfortable about seeing somebody very close to them. One can understand this by claiming that as individuals we like a space around us which is not violated, although in some cases we are open to this violation. This explanation psychologizes a social act without explaining why this reduction should first of all be done. Consider the social act of being together, even as strangers in a bus. If the situation is conducive to a sense of belonging-ness that arises in the bus at that moment, people begin to explore the bounds of closeness. This is not to violate the personal space of another person but should be seen more as a perceptual searching for the social which is communicated through the sensation of touch. That is, even when we do not touch the other directly, by coming closer we come within the boundaries of touching. Most importantly, we sense the other through touch and not merely through sight in such cases. The shift from sight to touch is really an important transition point towards discovering the sociality of such groups.

Friendship is another important social phenomenon where we can see the importance of touch. Among both men and women in India, it is still a common sight to see members of the same sex holding hands or even lying in close proximity to each other. But given the caste-ridden society, such touching normally takes place only within a narrow social context. It is necessary to understand this phenomenon because it clearly demarcates how ideas of friendship work in many Asian societies as compared to the European or the Anglo-American ones. This form of touch-sociality defines norms of friendship, and gives a different way of understanding how the social performs in acts of friendship. Denying the importance of this act by describing it as a cultural act special to some cultures misses the point about how touch functions in the formation of the social. But these forms of social touch are not always in friendship: the touch becomes instrumental when Dalit women touch upper caste women when they help them during pregnancy and birthing.

So too does the absence of such forms of friendship in some societ-ies say something about the formation of the social in those societies. Indians who have lived abroad, particularly in the US or some coun-tries in Europe, often talk about the notions of friendship that are so different with different social groups in those countries. So what really is the difference? Is it only a difference of how friendship and private spaces are understood there? Such explanations miss the possibility that forms of social touching are ways of exploring the nature of the particular social that characterizes friendship. That is, the sociality of friendship is different from other forms of socialities. What we mean by this is that the way we are a group among friends is different from the way we are groups among other groups of people, such as in the cinema hall or among work colleagues. And we discover these different socialities through our sensations—we perceive these forms of sociality through sight, touch, smell, taste, and hearing. We eat differently, wear different clothes, look different, and speak differently with these groups. We do this because these are the modes by which we create and perceive the special sociality that defines each of these groupings.

Often, one can see this quite starkly in university hostels where men hang out together in ways that would be quite surprising in many other societies. This has often been called as male bonding that is quite strong among Indian men. What kind of a process is male bonding? Is it a kind of culturally sanctioned way of being closer together? Or is it actually a particular form of discovering the sociality special to these forms of friendship? We would argue that male bonding actually manifests the special sense of touch through which the social is actually experienced in such groupings. Equivalently, the touching experience of male bonding allows a different experience of the social nature associated with this experience. We can definitely have notions of male bonding—such as sharing drinks and watching a game which are typical experiences of heterosexual male bonding—which may not have these forms of touch experience. We would not claim that these alternate modes cannot be called male bonding; all that we can say is that the social which forms the foundation of that experience of bonding can be experienced through all the sensory modes and what those men watching a game might be doing is experiencing it through other modes and not through touch, as it might happen in the Indian case. This is not really very different from experiencing an object through the many perceptive modes. Some might look at an object with more care instead of exploring it through touching or smelling. These are different ways of engaging with the object. Similarly, we engage with the entity called the social in different experiential ways and these mark out the uniqueness of social groups.

The sense of touch as 'touching the social' is manifested in so many other practices that are part of the Indian social experiences. One very important way in which the social is experienced is through the sharing of food. The materiality of food as well as its sharing illustrates another powerful way by which the social is touched. The sharing of food is endemic not only to many functions and rituals, but it is also a form of practice which binds certain people together as a special social unit. It is powerfully manifested in school lunches where children who form groups among themselves are those who share their lunch with each other. Typically, these groups sit separately and what maintains them as a group is the sharing of food which each of them bring. Social practices such as in some Muslim communities where groups of people eat off the same plate or the *prasadam* given in temples are experiences of socialities that are mediated through the corporeal and embodied experience of food.

A common social phenomenon in India is the role of dance as a form of being together socially. Dancing is an extremely important component of the social space of India. Dancing brings together individuals in a special way. The mode of sociality that is catalysed by dance is different from other modes of togetherness. In fact, for many communities dance is the way people come together thereby defining the possibility of their being social. In contrast to understanding dance as a cultural product of a community, we could also see dance in some cases as the agent which creates the group. As a cultural practice, dance becomes incidental and contingent but when seen as a necessary component that creates the social, dance plays a fundamental role in creating that social. For example, the participation in dandiya raas during Dassera in Mumbai apartments by people of all communities (and not just Gujaratis), the ubiquitousness of bhangra across India, or dancing to Bollywood music. Such social practices have become so common that these dances happen not only in marriages but also at every religious festival!

Dance is an excellent example of 'social touch'. What is different from a group of people standing together in the bus stop or walking together in the streets or dancing together? The mode of being social in the last case is qualitatively different from the first two cases. In this case, when people dance together they are 'in touch' with each other, even if they do not physically touch each other. The body movements are primarily about sound and touch, and movements capture the space beyond which they will not go or beyond which they cannot touch. Dancing in communities takes many different forms. There are dances where all the families join in, including the men and women. There are dances where the non-dancers participate not by dancing but by doing various things around the dance, including participating in some rituals or cooking food.

One of the best illustrations of this difference is captured in the phenomenon called 'flash mobs', where a group of people who are part of this impersonal collection of strangers suddenly start to dance in a coordinated manner. They dance and they disappear, leaving behind a special experience of sociality. A sociologist working on alcohol consumption in Kerala described another interesting manifestation of the 'flash mob'—groups of men congregate around public alcohol outlets in Kerala and suddenly come together as a collective mob wherein they each contribute some money to buy a bottle of alcohol which they then share.[7] They come together at that moment and disperse after the act of social drinking thereby creating a particular form of socializing. In some tribal societies, it is very common to come together and indulge in collective drinking of country liquor, both in a marriage as well as at death rituals. Such instances of coming together illustrate different forms and functions of the social, ranging from the social as anthropological to the social as modern, thereby leading to the need to distinguish the social as sociological and anthropological, from the social as modern.

Social-touch thus is not the touch of one individual on another, not the touch of one hand on another; it is the touch of the social on us and our touch on the social. The way the social touches an individual, and makes that individual experience the sensation of that touch, is very different from a person touching another. We feel the social touch—the feeling can be comforting or be oppressive, but nevertheless it is a sensation of touch.

What are the implications of our claim that we experience the social through the sense of touch, just like we experience it through the other senses? There are different ways of understanding this claim. We can begin with an analogy to colour. We cannot touch a colour in itself,

---

[7] Personal communication with the researcher, Manoj N.Y.

that is, it is not possible to touch brown. However, we touch brown things and in touching them, would we say that we have an experience of touching brown? Or equivalently, why would we not say that we touch brown when we touch brown things? It is not that the social is given to us as a readymade object/body. It is constructed through our experiences of the social. There are unique experiences that are of the collective and these experiences are read as experiences of the five senses. From these experiences we reconstruct the social body as one that generates these experiences.

Untouchability as the Social Touch of Caste

It is ironic, therefore, that given the immersion in the tactile experiences of the social in India, the best exemplar of the experience of touch in experiencing the Hindu social arises through untouchability. If there is one marker that defines the foundational principle of caste practices in India, it is untouchability. This idea functions as the organizing theme for the social structure of castes.

We can start with the claim that the experience of caste in terms of its sociality is through a tactility that is not fulfilled. If touching is seen as a process and not as an end result of grasping something, then it is possible to see how untouchability as a practice is a form of touching which at the end does not grasp the untouchable object. But neverthe-less it is a practice of touching and has all the elements of awareness that constitute touching. It is an active form of not-touching that con-stitutes this practice.[8] This active form of not-touching as a form of touching is a defining moment in the social corresponding to caste. The sociality of caste arises in many other ways—by this we mean that the sociality of caste is perceptually experienced in different ways and untouchability as an active form of not-touching remains at its base as that which makes the caste-social unique.

It would not be an exaggeration to say that the sociality of caste arises through this mode of touch. Proscriptions of caste are primarily about touching and not-touching. The injunction against inter-caste marriages are also a manifestation of this proscription of touching, a touching which can lead to the formation of the social. By denying inter-caste

---

[8] See Guru and Sarukkai (2012) for more on this.

marriages what is being denied is the possibility of discovering a social that is defined and unified through touch between different castes.

So also the proscriptions on the cooking of food and the sharing of food. Questions of contamination and pollution are material and based on the act of touch. These proscriptions based around touch define the boundaries of the social and thus are an essential part of the construction of the social through the sensation of touch. The denial of entry into temples is as much a reflection of the practice of social touch at work. There is a difference between food grain and food. Food grain production is a social phenomenon in two fundamental senses. In one, the food grain is produced through the formation and involvement of a particular class into productive labour. This labour produces food grain that is socially necessary in the sense that different classes in society consume it. Food grain also has a function to reproduce the social class of labourers who produce food grain. Food grain is also necessary for its social distribution among different classes and this is done through the public distribution system (PDS). Cooked food marketed through the food service industry is also a social, inasmuch as it is catered in order to meet social needs. The social arises through the creation of taste as against merely eating food as nutrition. It is taste that becomes the embodiment of the social; and we should not forget here taste's intriguing relationship with touch.

The manifestation of social touch characterizes caste in the following complex ways. How do the other castes treat Dalits? , the others treat a Dalit's back as quite spacious and as an open dumping ground. They can dump their burden on this back. At the social level, this reduces the Dalits as those who will carry the social burden of carrying all that the others do not want to carry. The disproportionate amount of Dalits who are labourers and scavengers today suggests that the sense of social touch that operates here is not a touch of affection or care but as a surrogate to carry one's burden. The logic of this sense of social touch operates in many interesting ways, one of which leads to the view of caste as carapace.

Caste as Carapace

There is a dominant feeling among the upper castes, and even among some of the Dalits, particularly those who dream of capitalism, that the latter have a vested interest in perpetuating caste consciousness. For example, the repeated claims about caste identity in the context of the recent Rohith Vemula tragedy, when they claimed that Rohith was not a Dalit, voices this narrative repeatedly. According to this argument, those who see the presence and operation of caste in the suicide of Rohit are, in fact, perpetuating casteism. At one level, such thinking seeks to insulate the upper castes from their responsibility in perpetuating caste. It also denies the fact that caste as a first order evil resides in some of the upper castes. Although using caste as carapace is a second order evil, it is counterfactual since the Dalits do not really want to carry this burden but are forced to carry it; this sense of touch becomes morally heavy. It is almost tragic on the part of Dalits to use caste as a carapace to protect them from different kinds of social assaults on their morally integrated self. Dalits have to struggle to not be Dalit and yet cannot avoid being a Dalit. Most of them seek social and moral protection either through the legal codification of caste reservation or through certain punitive provisions. Hence, the 1989 SC/ST anti-atrocities act becomes a carapace for them. The denial of the right to touch and also right to be touched ultimately assigns the sense of the heaviness of touch. This is heavy as its denial tends to corrode the very moral essence of the human being.

Caste has moved from one meaning to another, creating different vocabularies each time: from Untouchable in Ambedkar to Harijan in Gandhi, in S.M. Mate from *asprusha* to *asprustha*. This approach to a history of caste is based on the processes of meaning-making. Scholars of caste tend to make the meaning of caste. This is against the concrete experience of caste discrimination. It is the discourse on caste that dominates the thinking of caste rather than discovering caste as a reality. These discursive efforts seek to confuse the concrete meaning of caste which has a history to it. This confusion is produced out of the necessity to absolve oneself of a feeling of guilt. Even an academic narrative on caste sends a painful reminder of one's own caste history. Caste identification and over-identification become the ontological status of caste. In how many different ways does one get chained to the caste reality? Such questions remain unanswered in the groundlessness of caste. Groundlessness has to be understood in terms of radical fluidity of meaning which seeks to replace the need to understand the existence of caste practices. How does one make meaning of caste: by rendering it ambiguous? One may argue that there is an advantage with the concept of ambiguity. It can be enabling and can generate multiple meanings of caste. However, one can entertain this view only at the cost of ignoring both ontological as well as moral burden that the caste reality brings to bear on the Dalits. Protection from caste atrocities becomes a moral burden for them. The vocabulary of ambiguity can confuse the concrete meaning of caste as a lived reality, which ironically sits on the back of Dalits as a protection from the high-caste Hindus. Thus, caste in all its incarnations becomes a carapace on which the inauthentic social or a social in the grotesque rides for its own glory taking the form of a public display, the 1989 anti-atrocity act for instance.

Caste honour as the repressive or inhuman or barbaric form of the social tends to trump or override the normative conception of the moral. In the case of the Dalits, it is the power of honour that is used for protection. Dalits also use their caste to defend themselves. Caste as social reality thus contains the same instrumental reason but serves two different purposes. The upper caste imposes the consciousness of inferiority within the Dalit in order to tighten the hold of their social domination. At the same time, the Dalit has reason to carry the burden of caste just to seek create redressal protection through legal intervention. Thus, caste as social has two different ontological significances.

Here the social is inseparable from the ethical. Caste as carapace is already overburdened by the weight of other forms of the illegitimate social. One is compelled to carry caste as carapace as self-protection. The moral compulsion needs to be understood basically in terms of the gross deficit of social trust in Indian civil society. The social could be understood in terms of passive injustice that has its roots in the upper caste indifference to the dire Dalit question. In fact, the upper castes need to stand with the Dalits, the concrete or tormented social beings who are an embodiment of the question, who are born into the question. This standing-with would be constitutive of active justice done to Dalits.

The social acquires moral quality only through certain virtues such as generosity. Generosity happens through the moral capacity or willingness to share the natural resources, both human as well as physical. Social control of natural resources, particularly in the Indian context, acquires meaning which is beyond the market transaction. In fact, caste beats the rationality of the market, particularly in terms of the transaction of water. Generosity mediated through water gets replaced by parochialism linked with caste. The social sense of generosity dries up, particularly when it is on its way to reach the bottom of the caste hierarchy. In the Washim District of Maharashtra, the Dalits were denied water and hence they dug their own well. Tajne (a Dalit) and his family were the residents of Kallambeshware village and his wife was denied water by the upper caste from the village. Bapurao felt humiliated and to avoid this he dug the well in just 40 days.[9] It is in this sense that the social acquires its restricted meaning which betrays the wider sense of generosity. But when it climbs bottom up, it tends to become morally expansive.

In Sasaram, Bihar, in the village of a prominent Dalit leader Jagjivan Ram, the Dalit well had plenty of water even during scarcity. He showed generosity and welcomed the upper castes to draw the water from the Dalit well. Similarly, in Kasbe Talwade in Barshi Taluka of Sholapur District of Maharashtra, there is a borewell in Dalitwada which has plenty of water. All the upper castes draw water from there. Interestingly, the well is at the same location where Babasaheb Ambedkar had organized his meeting in 1942. In one case, the Dalits are much more generous on humanitarian grounds to distribute water among the needy but in another case it is the caste that kills your generosity.

The Cartography of the Social

Caste as social has both wings and legs. The papers of the transfer of a Dalit might reach later but what reaches first is her caste. The social travels fasters than the material. At the analogical level, caste becomes a rumour. Such rumours, of course, have wings, but they also have legs. In the olden days, the socially powerful caste dominated even nature and Dalits were pushed beyond any social interaction. Since they were unseeable, untouchable, and even erased from the social imagination, they were socially segregated, thus disciplining the dominant forms of the social through a legal mechanism. But paradoxically, to discipline the social requires caste as carapace.

As mentioned above, Dalits require caste as legal protection from the social hostility of the anti-social upper caste. The social is forced to carry the caste as carapace and one is forced to protect oneself by

[9] *Times of India*, Delhi Edition, 8 May 2016.

using the cover of caste. The social and the anti-social castes are both social and anti-social; its inner dimension is social whereas its outer dimension is anti-social. The caste label or name used by Ambedkar in the early 1930s had this inside-out conception of the social. The inner dimension of the social was universal while the outer expression of the social was particular. The social of the dominant does not have this tension between the inner and the outer. It is the same in its essence and also in its expression. Similarly, the inner dimension is persuasive while the external is constraining. There is some kind of pragmatism involved in the adoption of the particular, and the social adopts a more universal form depending on the dissolution of many particular socials into a universal solidarity. For example, the social which is hierarchical, arranged into many fragments, would be organized into a solidarity.

The social in India is built up around the moral axis which involves the ascending sense of gratitude of the lower caste to the higher one and the descending sense of gratitude of the higher caste to the lower caste. There is no reciprocal sense of gratitude. They do not exchange the word 'thanks' on an equal moral basis. The lower castes have to be grateful to the upper castes. The following two examples illustrate this very well. In one of the villages in the Vidarbha region in Maharashtra, some Dalits helped an upper caste douse the fire that engulfed the house of the latter. But the Dalits were prevented from touching the earthen pots full of water which they wanted to use for extinguishing the fire. Ultimately, the Dalits defied the opposition and saved the house by touching the earthen pots. The Kunbis (the OBC caste according to the Mandal characterization), instead of thanking the Dalits for saving the houses, started abusing the latter on the count that they had polluted their water and earthen pots. Gratitude, which is social, finds a lack of reciprocity due to caste.

We can use the above discussion on caste to illustrate how the social arises as touch. Caste appears as a social entity and is perceived through sensory modalities like touch, smell, taste, sound, and sight. Here we argued for the tactile sense of the social. Following the arguments given above, we can say that we touch caste and that caste touches us. Caste is available as a tactile sense and our expressions of caste also manifest this tactility. It is not an accidental fact that untouchability is the core idea that supports the notion of caste in Indian societies. Tactility of caste is manifested in many different ways. We can consider one example discussed above, namely the idea of generosity. Caste's relation with generosity is extremely important and compelling. But what is the nature of generosity? We can reduce the notion of generosity to a linguistic description of what it means to be generous. But the sociality of caste is not a description but a particular experience. Caste envelops you, it surrounds you, it hugs you. It does everything in excess. It can suffocate as well as support. Generosity as a social act is a tactile act of the social.

Social Touch and Sports

The conception of belonging is not an abstract experience but is a concrete experience. One can experience this sense of belonging through the feeling of corporeal touch. We have discussed in an earlier work (Guru and Sarukkai 2012) the philosophical complexities of touch but in the present context touch is defined in terms of its moral power to forge inter-subjective relationships among the people. In this context, the conception of touch plays a crucial role in deciding the contours of the social. Touch thus takes a lead in producing the positive expression of the social. Conversely, the absence of touch would then mark the difficulty in producing the social with a positive expression. In the Hindi film *Lagaan*, touch produces a social with affirmative expression. But in actual life, certain kinds of sport systematically shun the corporeal touch and ultimately supplant the possibility of associative social, the social as ennobling experience. One good person can ennoble the social, but in a caste-society ennobling hardly has any chance to succeed.

In India, sports are not free from the norm. Seemingly, the game of football fails to generate the sense of belonging among the players. Here is an anthropological account of touch that is mediated through different forms of sports through a narrative of the Dalit footballers' experience in Odisha. The idea of touch rules out the participation of Dalits in sports that involve different degrees of physical touch. Thus, they may be permitted to play either hockey or cricket but even now it is difficult for them to get to play in games like kho kho, kabaddi, and football, and most importantly, in wrestling. These are Indian sports which involve substantive physical as well as rhetorical touch. As the history of sports show, the upper caste wrestlers refused to wrestle with those with the social background of untouchability. In such adversarial conditions within which the untouchable wrestlers were confined by the caste system, a historical lead was taken by Shahu Maharaj of Kolhapur, who gave these untouchable wrestlers upper caste names as part of a strategy to promote skill among the untouchables (Pawar 2001: 87). But this was not aimed at annihilating the caste system. As mentioned above, football is supposed to involve a rhetorical or mild touch and even this is not tolerated by the upper caste football players. In the Odisha case, the upper caste players could not drop an untouchable player from the team due to the pressure from the management. He was given the position of a goalkeeper so that they could avoid touching him. In this regard, it is interesting to note that the sport writers in India find the repulsion of the lowest caste negative but also as a useful reference point to underline gender discrimination in Indian sports. So comparison to the treatment of women in sports to that of low castes is common such as this statement in a newspaper report: 'Today Indian sport women are akin to lowest caste in the game arena.'[10] It is quite natural on the part of such writers to lament that in sports women are treated like the lowest caste, but their sense of egalitarianism stops at the discrimination of women and does not extend to Dalit women. If it had, they would have lamented the complete exclusion of low caste women from the field of sports.[11] There have been many comparisons of the role of African-Americans in sports such as basketball and American football, and the Dalits' participation in sports. It is generally accepted that the overall success of desegregation in sports in the US as compared to India is also linked to the politics of touch.

The conception of touch in the Indian context has got an evaluative function. The idea of pollution continues to dominate other spheres such as that of sports. Hence, caste refuses to remain confined to the local level. Or it does not fit well into the fragments of social relationship. Let us explain this by citing some illustration from sports that were organized in the early twentieth-century India. The English used

[10] Sidartha Saxena, 'Discrimination of Indian Sportsmen at All Levels', *Times of India*, 13 July 2010.

[11] In recent times, there have been quite a few tribal women who are leading in fields such as archery and hockey but as far as Dalits are concerned, the situation is not very promising.

desperate methods to teach football to Indians and they almost succeeded in their efforts.[12] When an English missionary tried to make Brahmin boys play football, they refused to touch the ball because it was made of leather. The Brahmin boys would stop the school in order to escape playing football. This seems to have happened in Tyndale-Biscoe school in Srinagar. The missionary school teachers would take the lead in introducing the upper caste boys to the game of football but could achieve little success. Some things may have changed from then but some have not.

Thus, a Dalit football player belongs to the sport but not to the team. He is a goalkeeper so that he can touch the dead skin of the ball but not the 'live skin' of the upper caste players. Conversely, for the upper caste players, it is alright to touch the dead skin but not the live skin of a Dalit player. Even in *Lagaan*, Indian players do share the spirit of the game but not the human touch. In fact, caste ideology has been structurally inbuilt into the very rules of the football game. Touching football with the hand is a foul and this works out very well for the social need of the upper caste players! Football has to be kicked with the foot and kicking the ball with the foot does not jeopardize the ritual purity of the upper caste players. Therefore, for them, there should not be any difference between the leather shoes and the football because both these articles acquire their essence through their corporeal association with the foot.

The social is an embodiment of virtues, like friendship, generosity, and other emotions. These virtues are formed into social and historical conditions but a social system consolidated by caste is closed. The social conditions such as isolation and dissociation are produced and reproduced historically. In the Indian context, it has become quite natural to belong to a caste. The caste-based social is like a prison and continues from historical time. The social is a site for agency, activity, and struggle since it has to be reconfigured from within. The social struggle of the Dalit needs to be viewed form this angle. Being at peace with oneself through isolation is a-social if not anti-social. The Dalit will corrupt the *agrahara* and hence needs to be kept away, perhaps in perpetual isolation, both physically and socially.

As far as Dalits are concerned, they cannot seek any fundamental break from the caste-based social which becomes a moral burden to

---

[12] The Unholy Ball, *Sunday Times of India*, New Delhi, 26 June 2006.

them. They are forced to carry it on their back across time and space. Thus, as discussed earlier, for Dalits caste identity becomes a carapace. Their association with a stigmatized Dalit social is a conscious attempt to defend themselves although their fondest hope is that they want to develop a self-image independent of their caste identity. Caste as carapace inheres in it the unhappy consciousness of the Dalit. Dalits are not able to put their inner life in moral order as they find it difficult to appear in the public without the burden of carapace. They find it increasingly difficult to acquire a generic identity which would enable them to appear in different spheres of life with different identities. Would a Dalit earn recognition by remaining in isolation of his society? Would her desire for individualism or a disembodied self fulfil her desire to earn recognition from other equally disembodied selves? The answer to this question is largely in the negative since a dominant Indian social is yet to be reconfigured along a radical line.

In the caste-ridden society, people are anti-social as they lack sociality as a condition. Unseeable, untouchable, and unapproachable are some of the symptoms of the social atrophy. It is only in the modern condition that one becomes social but that too only in a negative sense. The social as modern has contradictory dimensions to it. It acquires a Janus face: one side of it is benign and the other, malignant. The benign side can be seen in terms of cognitive generosity while the other side could be socially ungenerous. There are scholars in universities who would share some ideas with the Dalit but would not support the reservation policy. Similarly, there are some scholars who would support reservation but would not be cognitively generous to Dalits. They would support reservation but would refuse to guide Dalit students. In fact, for Dalits, social generosity is the precondition to be ready to receive the intellectual benefits that flow from cognitive generosity. Social generosity is important for building the intellectual confidence of Dalits.

In this chapter, we began with showing how the everyday social is experienced sensorially, which is captured in the way the social gets associated with sight, smell, sound, touch, and taste. Any construction of what the social is must begin from this point just as we begin to understand what an object is from the sensory experiences that we have of it. However, in the last part of the chapter, we also saw how the idea of touch gets expanded in many ways in the caste-social, leading to the discussion on caste as carapace. At one level, this process illustrates a significant point about the relation between the senses and the object of the sensations. In the case of biological touch, the act and experience of touching is not really changed by the object of touch. What happens in the case of the social is that the sensations themselves get modified and sometimes become part of the object of experience, namely the social. One might argue against this claim by noting that we are perhaps using terms like smell and touch in a metaphorical manner. Our response to this would be to suggest that the distinction between the natural and the social, or the literal and the metaphorical, do not really hold good in this experiential domain of the social, as our examples clearly show.

We conclude this chapter by making two observations. First is the consequence of explicitly grounding the social in experiences. The significance of this can be seen when socialities associated with human societies are contrasted with that of the new socialities associated with digital technology. Social media is not social in the way other socials are since they lack the richness of the experiential domain of the social. Social media is not really social as far as the sensory experiences of the social are concerned and this has consequences, including deep problems of social alienation, loneliness, addiction, and so on. Second, there are also other experiences, other than those directly related to these modes of sensation, which are essential to the experience of the social. The experiences of belonging and becoming are defining experiences of the social. They are also related to questions of self and identity, since where there is experience there is a self that is needed to unify and order them. The themes of self and identity are an important consequence of the sensory experiences of the social. The next chapter discusses some examples of the everyday understanding of social belongingness related to Indian experiences. To make sense of this conflict between the ideas of self and that of the social, it is important to understand the ontological connection between the social and self-identity, which we undertake in the chapter following the next one.

4 Belonging and Becoming

While we tend to use the term 'societies' as if they have same or similar meaning for all the societies in the world, it is often the case that the difference between these 'societies' is stark. The universalization of some objects of discourse is essential for constructing a scientific discourse. A term like 'molecule' has universal applicability in the way the term 'society' does not have. A molecule, however complex it may be, can still be universally defined in terms of its atomic structure, the bonds between its constituents, and other such characteristics. What is really universal about societies in India and Germany? And even within India (which is not a social term but a political one), what is common to a society in rural Tamil Nadu and one in Sikkim? The search for universalization of a term that can become the object of discourse of the social sciences leads to a restricted view of society. This is not a problem in itself except when this highly restricted meaning comes to exert a dominant influence on its other meanings. The instability of the meanings of society and the social is a potential problem for the social sciences since they would challenge the possibility of grand theories of the social world. Unless we believe that the social as understood, described, and analysed by scholars such as Weber, Durkheim, and contemporary theorists across the world have a core commonality, the nature of social theory itself would have to be rethought. If not rethought, we must at least embark on the task of theorizing from alternate conceptions of society and social that are not naively universal. In this chapter, we will consider some simple examples of the varied socials in the ordinary, everyday life in India. We will then build on the earlier conceptualizations of the social along with these instances to describe the social from the next chapter onwards.

It is obvious that the social world is different in different places. The society of Mumbai or Kolkata, made up of countless 'dense socials', offers an experience of the social that is so different from the more well-to-do suburbs in these cities. Chawls are a very good example of a social world that is perhaps not duplicated in any other social setting, including slums. Between the chawls of Dadar and the slums of Dharavi, Mumbai offers a multitude of socials that are characterized by the diverse experiences of socialities. In villages, there are other unique socialities that may be catalysed by caste social practices, gendered socialities, and so on. To believe that the excess of such social experiences can be captured through some universal structures in social theory would, in our opinion, be hallucinatory at best. The cities and villages of India (and many other places in the 'non-West') are not like those in the societies that produce dominant theories of the social. The fact that this has not been critiqued as it should have been is also due to the absence of other approaches to the social that can capture the uniqueness of these societies. We do not imply, therefore, that it is impossible to theorize the social; all that we claim is that unless the categories of experience and related cognates are taken into social theorizing, such theories will only speak of dominant societies and their preoccupations.

The term 'Indian society' is commonly understood as something more than the collection of some individuals in it. This might be based on a belief that there is something in common with all these members and there are some properties that they share which defines membership to Indian society. The membership of a society can be defined in various ways: Ascriptive identities such as caste, religion, race, and ethnic or acquired membership of different clubs such as in sports. The membership can be defined in these other ways too: Identity cards like the Aadhaar card, passport, voter card, and so on. The latter largely fall under legal identities that are legitimized under a legal regime. The former have a non-legal sense of membership but both (and other forms if present) share the property of bringing individuals into the domain of the social. However, it is possible to make a fine distinction between these forms of creating the social: the membership to a society based on legality involves the process of becoming, while the membership to a society based on non-legality involves the process of belonging. So, in general, one 'becomes a citizen' (legitimized by legal processes) but 'belongs' to a caste, religion, or a group.

When asked what constitutes 'Indian society', all the 'Indian people' can be pointed to or it can be defined independently of its members (extrinsic and intrinsic definitions). In the case of the latter, it is identified with some essential properties so that 'Indian society' gets defined in terms of some qualities. Thus, the idea of society and the social can either be material (like in the collection of real individuals) or abstract (like in the essences of being Indian). The terms society or social are often used with both these meanings without clarifying the difference between them, which often leads to confusion.

Belonging and Becoming

The sense of belongingness is perhaps the most fundamental experience of a human being and it manifests the sociality intrinsic to individual persons. Perhaps, the right way to say this is that only the social is given to us and we have to form the individual from it. Modernity is the process of discovering the individual under its social covering; however, in doing so it has gone to the other extreme of reifying individuality. We could begin with a hypothesis that every social collection is defined by its own unique sense of belongingness. We belong to a family, to a community, to a religion, to a caste, to an organization, to a nation, and, perhaps, to the world. But in each of these cases, the nature of belonging is different. We belong differently to our families as compared to the organization we work for. For example, instead of belonging to, we become the member of an organization. We belong in a different way to a caste group as compared to a club. In contrast to caste, we become the member of a club. Our belongingness to a language, culture, and tradition are all uniquely differentiated.

What are we attempting to say when we say that we belong to something? The meaning of 'belong' in each of these expressions is complex and varied. A common meaning of saying 'I belong' is 'I am'. The statement 'I belong to Islam' is often equivalent to 'I am a Muslim'. But note that even in this simple example, belonging is not the same as identity or merely stating who that person is. One belongs to Islam but not to a Muslim. Belongingness to Islam makes one a Muslim. Similarly, it might be thought that the expression 'I belong to India' is the same as 'I am an Indian' but just as in the previous example, belonging is not the same as the identity as an Indian. India—as a geographical entity—is different from the many different senses of being Indian. Becoming, on the contrary, is part of the acculturation of a kind. One becomes a citizen.

Language is another interesting example, particularly in a richly multilingual society like India, which can explain the concept of belonging. Although we do not say 'I belong to Hindi' or 'I belong to Kannada' we often mean that when we say, 'I am a Kannadiga'. Like the differences between India and Indian mentioned above, the difference between Kannada and Kannadiga is quite marked. To be a Kannadiga one does not have to belong at a particular moment to the state of Karnataka or to the tradition of that place. There are Kannadigas who do not even speak Kannada. Moreover, a person living abroad might still claim that she is a Kannadiga although her practices may not be the same as those living in Karnataka. Even within Karnataka, being a Kannadiga has different meanings in different regions. However, there is nevertheless a great sense of belonging to language as such and many would argue that truly being a Kannadiga is to live in the world of that language. In India, language too becomes ontologically related to the process of becoming and belonging.

These examples briefly illustrate the important role of the ideas of belonging and belongingness in social life and social relations. Most importantly, these terms seem to be an expression of a special experience of belongingness. Psychologists have extensively written about the importance of the sense of belongingness to human life. They have argued that this is the basis of social relations and trace many pathologies such as alienation and suicide to problems arising from the lack of a sense of belonging to something or the other.

In this book, we are not following the psychologists' approach to belongingness. We do not want to look at belongingness exclusively in terms of psychological states such as emotions. Instead, we consider belongingness as an existential term that is at the root of any idea of the social and thus focus on the spheres or layers of belongingness that lead to different kinds of belonging such as belonging to a family, nation, institution, religion, caste, gender, and so on. We are interested in explicating *how* we belong to something. Understanding these types of belonging can lead to a better understanding of how we belong to each of these entities. In each of these cases, it is the sense of belongingness that creates the sense of the social and the sensory experiences through which the social is accessed become the route to the experience of belonging. Therefore, the experience of being social in each case is different.

It is important to focus on this experience of belongingness since many other influential ideas such as identity, pride, discrimination, fairness, justice, rights, duties, tradition, customs, and so forth, are all intimately related to this experience. We can, as many have done, think about these ideas in terms of non-personalized descriptions (primarily in terms of society and its structures) but our argument here is that in doing so we neglect to factor in the experiential and this leads to a major misunderstanding of these notions. This misunderstanding, in the Indian scenario, is also reflected in the growing gap between 'ordinary' citizens and the academics who produce specialized knowledge about these societies and communities. Their theoretical descriptions many a time do not seem capable of engaging with the lived experience of the social; instead, they focus more on structures of society such as the government, law, social institutions, and so on. One might argue that there are important social structures to which members of a society might not have a sense of belongingness. For example, an individual may not have an experience of social belongingness to the community of the police. But this claim would be a limited understanding of the experience of belongingness. Moreover, this structural way of understanding the social is also dominantly influenced by the experiences of the modern West and very often this approach cannot capture the nuances of the socialities inherent in Asian and African societies. So, while the emphasis on impersonal structures of the social is extremely important to understand societies, it cannot become a dominant epistemology of the social.

However, there is no one experience of belongingness, one notion of what it is to be with another person or with a group, and so different groupings tend to have different experiences. When people come together as fans in a cricket stadium, suddenly there is a sense of belonging 'together'. They come together, they become 'one', in a particular sense. What is this state—strangers before they come to the match and strangers after they leave the match—where they suddenly bond, scream, and shout together? This experience of relating and belonging is found essentially in all domains of human action.

However, we want to highlight a different phenomenon that is special to the coming-together of humans. The coming together of humans is characterized by a peculiar reaction that arises when people form a group. This happens even when two individuals pass each other on the street. When strangers become aware of one another, already a new event is taking place that illustrates the processes of the social. As two people approach each other, one might begin to notice the other which in turn will catalyse a host of questions such as the following: Do I know this person? Is he coming towards me? What are his characteristics? Could I be in any danger from him? While many of these questions might indicate the mental state of the individuals, many of them revolve around this experience of relating to the other individual. For example, when one recognizes the other as a friend, as a teacher, a student, a neighbour, or a relative, the whole demeanour of the person undergoes a change. The recognition of the other as belonging to a particular category leads to the sense of belongingness which will characterize how this person views the other. For example, the moment a person recognizes the other as a teacher then this person's behaviour and demeanour changes. These two individuals remain no longer as two individuals but become one social entity at that moment. Even if the two just pass each other and go on their way, the presence of each alters the state of the other at that moment. And when they pass each other and go beyond their 'social' boundaries, they become two 'individuals' again or more precisely, inhabit another social domain. The coming-together of human individuals is, therefore, quite different from a mere collection of things. These modes of interaction are extendable to animals also.

Many important debates revolve around the spaces of the social, around this spatial experience of passing each other or coming into the domain of the other. One of the most prominent ones is between Gandhi and Ambedkar around their understanding of villages. For Gandhi, the village is the most important unit of a society and his vision of India was built around village economy, village politics, and village sociality. On the contrary, Ambedkar was wary of the village, primarily because of the nature of sociality of Indian villages which, for him, was a loci for inhuman caste practices. The spaces of crossing-over of individuals are quite different in the urban settings. Ambedkar's hope for the urban milieu over that of the village was also the hope for a sense of anonymity for individuals who were otherwise the target of exclusionary sociality practiced in village communities. In the contemporary vocabulary, giving a person her/his 'space' has become a popular expression of the dynamics of coming together. Visitors to India often point to the lack of 'personal space'—the physical space around them—when they travel in a bus or train. People in India, we are told, tend to be much closer together as bodies and they more easily enter into the personal spaces of another. For many, this intrusion into what they see as their private space around them causes much distress but at the same time it is this intrusion into the common space between people that also characterizes affection and love, or even a sense of friendship when two people hug each other when they meet.

There are many questions that will arise in this approach of focussing on relations, particularly that of belongingness. The first point is whether something beyond the two individuals, which we can call the social, arises in these moments of interaction. Should the social be something beyond and outside the individuals? If the *moment* of the social is an experience these two individuals have when they cross each other, where is the social to be found? Within each of our individual experiences?

There are two quick answers: one is that the distinction between the individual and the social has various presuppositions. Today, the privilege is to the individual—the world revolves around the autonomy of individuals. The goal of human existence is seen as an assertion of the individual will, their will to power and to desire and this succeeds in creating the category of individuals in opposition to society. It leads to individual thinking and merit as pure characteristics of individual virtues such as intelligence, hard work, and so on. But this view of the individual forgets the essential sociality that is central to our being, to our thinking, and even to our desires. Even the act of thinking, which one might believe is private and belongs only to the person who thinks, is social in a profoundly significant way. The ways by which one thinks, the languages in which they are thought, the concepts that are used, are all derived from the social. The shift to the rhetoric of the autonomous individual—the individual who supposedly can 'dare to reason' a la Kant—has been overplayed and in so doing, the basic sense of sociality that defines individuals has been displaced.

Second, the sense of belongingness is fundamental to the experiential inter-subjective needs of an individual. And the experience involving these needs is basically catalysed as a response to the social. The sense of belongingness is so acute that even extremely individualized experiences like solitary explorers often find a fulfilment of this sense not with other humans but with animals and nature. Today with the flow of hyper-technologies, this sense of belongingness is with technologies of various kinds. People today can live without the company of other people, but they cannot do so without technologies that bring the social into their private space. The sociality of Facebook and the Internet are strikingly different from that of the physical space inhabited by other people. In a sense, these experiences of the social through technology is just like the experience of playing games through computers. It has become so common to see children play field games like football, hockey, and cricket in their video machines—they are the only players, the screen is the field, and they develop a relationship with the machines in lieu of real people. So, it is not that these are isolated individuals or that they illustrate the preference to individualism. Rather, they have become hyper-social and not hyper-individual since their social has expanded to include all kinds of virtual entities. The claim that these solitary modes of existence show the significance of the independent individual is deeply mistaken as the fundamental experience of the social in terms of belongingness is very much within these people.

A simple example might help illustrate these ideas. Untouchability as a social practice is about the relationship between two human beings, one who refuses to touch the other. Consider the situation when a person of a particular caste meets a person of another caste coming towards him. If the latter is somebody whom the former considers as an untouchable, then the behaviour of both of them radically changes. The untouchable in such a situation would often have to move out of the path, make sure that he is not seen by the other, and so on. Now, one might say that what happened in this case was that two autonomous individuals see each other and act according to some social norms. Or, another way of looking at it is to say that the social permeates the two individuals and their coming together catalyses certain responses due to the prior existence of the social. The two individuals act according to the rules of this social in which they are both immersed. They do not act like autonomous individuals at all. We do this all the time, when we walk on the streets, go to a cinema, or eat on the roadside.

Thus, the sense of belonging is not merely a psychological state. It is not a state that arises psychologically as responses to the situation of our lives. One can see this clearly in cases of non-belonging. Many people feel like they do not belong, like they are not welcome. They may feel that they do not belong to the community they live in, to the nation, to their own caste groups, to their institutions, and many even to their families. Poor people in big cities often are excluded from the sense of belongingness to many better-off areas. In fact, the poor in the big cities 'exist' without an address. The phenomenon of gated communities is a powerful example of how contemporary societies view sociality. These communities create a sense of fear and insecurity about the larger public. Through this fear they define the social as a space that is constantly in need of protection. But such communities cannot escape creation of socialities of their own. They build a society that consists of people who are like each other in some sense or the other. It could be in terms of their jobs and money they have, or as is happening increasingly in recent times, it could be a collection of people belonging to the same caste, or same sectarian groups, or same religion, and so on. In all these cases, people decide to reduce their sense of the social and limit it to only those who are like them in some sense or the other.

It is the sense of belonging that gives people the feeling of authority, ownership, and ease when they enter into places, including public spaces like restaurants and parks. Those who feel that they do not belong to such places are often hesitant, uncomfortable, and totally uneasy when they find themselves in such places. The feeling of not-belonging is pervasive: one may feel that one does not belong to a family even though she is a part of it, or not part of their organization or their community like others are. The feeling of not-belonging to a larger social is often the cause of dissatisfaction, alienation, and violence. These experiences of not-belonging are not psychological aberrations of the individual but a reflection of the experiential structures of the social that exists prior to their responses. Perceiving the social in this manner removes the excess of impersonal rationalizations of society. It also speaks of the social in the way all of us experience and not as an abstractly removed entity.

Social Performance

The social behaviour of Indians, both within India and abroad, often draws scathing comments from other Indians, particularly those who live in or are exposed to other cultures. It is said that Indians try to avoid meeting other Indians while travelling abroad, cringe when one of their own starts speaking loudly on the mobile in the London or the Boston metro, or when they see an Indian family open their food packet in a mall. All these become markers of social practices of a community which are at odds with the practices of another community. In such cases, the social is a source of embarrassment. The personal becomes a way of escaping this embarrassment. Teenaged children often express embarrassment to be with their parents in a social space. Teenage sociality is often a reaction to their own place within larger social groupings and is a struggle to understand the nature of their belongingness to family, to friends, to an anonymous society, and so on. The social as embarrassment is also seen in comments we make about our surroundings or even the country. Some are embarrassed at seeing poor people around them, or to see people who do not dress like them or eat and look like them. While these examples may point to the problem with the very notion of the social, they are also primarily consequences of some notions of belongingness that underlies all these responses. Within India, these acts play out every day in our public spaces.

It is often remarked that India is a land of enduring contradictions. One of the most important sources of these contradictions is the difficulty in clearly distinguishing the individual and the social, and related notions such as the private and the public. Railway travel in India exemplifies these tensions and is a microcosm of similar contradictions in the society. Hordes of people will suddenly enter a reserved compartment, particularly in the day time, and will want to share a reserved seat. The person who has the reservation is put under moral pressure because if he does not share his space then he seems selfish. Without saying anything, the people who enter reserved compartments seem to say that they too are travellers like the others and that the common act of travelling together entitles them to something, at least the edge of a seat which they can sit on. If the person with the reserved ticket gets angry it is mainly because he thinks his reservation entitles him to something which is his alone and not meant for sharing with others. At the same time, there are many passengers who gladly share their space with the unreserved travellers.

Another common occurrence in trains is when a family shares an elaborate meal and then throws the garbage outside the window, on the railway platform or under their seats. When groundnuts with shells are sold it is common to see the shells strewn on the floor of the train. The sense of the collective and the social here is more complex. The person who buys the groundnut will offer it to his or her co-passengers and then they all start chucking the shells on the floor as a collective action. A passenger who is conscious of the notion of private and public space, and of certain modes of acceptable social behaviour, also soon ends up throwing the shells on the floor.

A recent advertisement campaign by Aamir Khan was about social behaviours which was directed at all the people in India. This was about not dirtying the public space by spitting or urinating where one pleases or throwing garbage from moving cars on to the road. Along with the constant barrage of advertisements for Swachh Bharat (Clean India), these are attempts to inculcate a sense of the public in Indian citizens. The fact that such lessons (of what constitutes acceptable social behaviour) must be 'taught' so late in the history of the nation should be a matter of some puzzlement.

But at the same time, there are other manifestations of public action such as the increasing community violence against those who marry across castes (particularly if one of the spouses is a Dalit), actions of Khap Panchayats which go against the basic grain of public space, heightened hate talk that incites public passion, and so on. Politics in India today is far more about 'private goods' than 'public goods'. The political leadership has also become hereditary in almost every political party. There are innumerable examples of how the public nature of political representation has been transformed into actions of private families and elite collectives. These examples go beyond any accepted social norm for democratic countries and violate decent social behaviour.

There are innumerable examples of public behaviour that often makes one think that a sense of the social—which acknowledges at the least the presence of another—is missing among the people in India. The difficulty in maintaining bus queues (with notable exceptions such as in Mumbai), the common practice of people throwing garbage in their neighbouring area, jumping signal lights as a matter of habit, not giving way to ambulances and school buses, speaking loudly on the mobile phone in music concerts and film theatres, constantly finding ways to 'beat the system' are constant reminders that our sense of a social space, of what it is to be a part of society, is one that is different from some other societies and from what has come to be accepted as 'global social norms' or at least norms of some dominant countries of the West.

Many believe that somehow all this is related to an inability to distinguish between the individual and the social, and related distinctions such as the private and the public. However, this claim would not be wholly correct since an account of the meaning of the concepts of the individual and the social is first needed. From where and how are these concepts of the individual and the social formed? In a contemporary global society, we are told that the notion of the individual gets formed during the period of Enlightenment in Europe as an autonomous rational being. This picture of the autonomous individual is used to legitimize the freedom to decide for and by oneself, to understand the liberatory power of an emancipated thinker as well as the grounds which legitimize the right to satisfy one's desires to a much larger extent than conceived of before. In claiming that such is the form of European Enlightenment, its proponents over centuries have privileged the individual to such an extent that any idea of the social is always subservient and in contrast to it. The very idea of freedom has often been reduced to freedom of the individual from the constraints of the social and this is perhaps best expressed by the phrase: 'be all that *you* can be'. This relation between the social and the idea of personal freedom is extremely important and influences the suspicion towards the social today. In this view, the social, mistakenly synonymized with the public, is seen as a space for freedom, a place where one can do what is not possible to do within the confines of the family, religion, or caste. The social through this mutation into the public becomes a space for individuals to have the freedom to pursue their desires. This easy slippage between social/ individual to public/private is deeply problematical and often hides the motivations which privilege the individual over the social.

Consider some examples to motivate these counter-reflections. Along with the intrusions into the space of the individual, there are also other social actions that we need to account for. Let us go back to train travel. When people travel together, it used to be the case that a family offers the food it ate to strangers sitting around them. There are so many instances of complete strangers in a train going out of their way to help newcomers to their city. Thus, in a train journey, other passengers, complete strangers, may intrude into this unknown quality called the 'individual space' but they also function as food-givers, story-tellers, travel guides, psychoanalysts, playmates (groups that start playing cards, for example), debaters, and so on. A train is a social space where a particular kind of sociality, a sense of togetherness, 'happens'. It is true that these common practices in a train journey, as well as the ways by which we behave with each other, are changing (particularly because of digital, personal technologies) but they point to an important and complex, sometimes confused, mode by which the individual and the social relate to each other. Such practices and mores of social behaviour are common across Asia and Africa.

Contrast this with a train journey in Europe or the USA, at least in 'advanced' parts of these societies. Unless there are special circumstances, travellers do not talk to each other. To see strangers sharing food or even shelling groundnuts together would be a miracle. To listen to life stories of strangers, to have children running up and down a train, or somebody even picking up your newspaper to read—these are quite impossible to imagine in these societies today. There, the train is really made up of monads—either individuals or couples or a few families—who function as if they are retaining their individuality which is marked by privacy. Most times they would not even look at another person directly. At the same time, this monadic behaviour also leads to very polite behaviour towards one another ranging from not shouting on the mobile phone to being courteous towards other passengers. Such impersonalized social behaviour arises due to a particular cultural way of understanding the individual and the social.

The social is thus 'performed' in many different ways in India. In meetings at villages across India, especially those of activists, we can see a robust sense of the social exhibited in an egalitarian sitting together, cooking and eating together, and playing music and dancing together. These are not cultural events but serious meetings in which the exhibition and creation of the social is primary to their purpose. There are thousands of such gatherings across the country.

In describing the primacy of the social, we are not suggesting that the social is all about singing, dancing, or eating together. The social is also a contentious site, a place of exclusion, discrimination, and humiliation. Groups are not allowed into other groups; hierarchies are established between them. Social formations in public spaces, including trains, are often inimical to women. In the case of a train journey too, there are these problematical cases. During periods of religious conflict, we knew of cases where Muslims were very worried about using their name for reservation since the chart of passengers would exhibit their name publicly. In these cases, as well as in instances of riots, one cannot really predict what a group will do with its moments of sociality. However, the point is that the way the social is imagined in, say, a Dalit group, has various similarities to the way the social is imagined in a dominant caste group. Sociality is experienced and imagined in many similar ways across groups. Is there a consequence of this commonality between widely differing groups? Is that available for political purposes?

The important point here is that the social acquires meaning in many different ways. One is through ideas of aggregation and collection. Another is through notions of meaningful action. Yet another, which we have described in this chapter, is through notions, and kinds, of performance. There is a lot about the Indian socials that is strikingly dramatic and many times theatrical, whether in public behaviour or even conflicts or celebrations within homes. This theatricality pervades the trading zones—the market spaces as well as the institutional ones. Social performances through religious practices too are endemic and pervasive. The very idea of performance does have a sense of the social within it as a necessary element, but this is not to reduce the experience of the social only as an experience of performance. Nevertheless, the kinds of socials that are available to us, and those that mark out the uniqueness of many societies in Asia and Africa, are perforce intrinsically linked with the force of the sociality of performance.

Family

It is impossible to make sense of the Indian social without finding new ways of understanding the family. While this is a very large topic today, we restrict ourselves to a brief discussion on the nature of belonging-ness to a family, and its relationship to the social.

How does one belong to a family? Why do we believe that we actu-ally belong to a family? The experience of belonging to a family is extremely important as it has great influence on the way we socialize with others. It also illustrates a long-standing tension between the idea of the social and the natural best exemplified by this problem: Is there a 'natural' affiliation to one's family? If so, what distinguishes belonging to a family in contrast to belongingness to society, religion, tradition, and so on? Is the family more 'natural' than other group formations?

Our notions of belongingness to a family influence our idea of belongingness to other entities such as the workplace, the nation, and so on. One of the major problems of institutions in India is they often function as a familial space instead of a 'professional' one. In fact, in India, the constant intermixing of the personal and the professional is rampant and can be found everywhere: from small institutions to large government-run organizations, in politics to governance. Many institu-tions and leaders of these places 'personalize' relationships within the workplace. To personalize a so-called professional domain is to use those markers and habits of belongingness within a family in the pro-fessional space. Typically, older men begin to function like fathers, for example, by exhibiting undue concern about younger employees. This often leads to clashes, especially when they bring their family values into the judgement of the lives of younger people, particularly women. So, such behaviour typically begins to exhibit patterns of patriarchy. This is one of the main reasons why Indian institutions—ranging from public ones to private and the academic—can rarely engage with or even understand disagreement and dissent, since familial notions of disagreements and means of dealing with them are often brought into the workplace. So, terms like hurt, disappointment, and trust enter into the professional discourse very easily.

Just like the carry-over of the notions of the family into the work-place, the idea of the natural is often brought into notions of cultural belongingness. Many things are more easily accepted the moment they are presented as being 'natural', or when they are naturalized in a particular way. The idea of naturalness is ascribed to characteristics of gender, caste, and religion and naturalization is used to stereotype communities and cultures.

The family is a very complex entity. First, the family is an exemplar of that which is both 'natural' and 'social'. It is natural in that there are biological relations between the members of a family and social in terms of the experiences of a group. Thus, a family stands for the possibility of both natural and social coexisting at the same time. Second, the family defines how the other socialities are to be understood, even if it is only through comparing and distinguishing from a family. Third, the family also becomes an important model of the natural—as biological, as genetically transmitted, or as exemplifying natural traits of human beings. Thus, historically, we find that heredity is often used as a naturalistic claim to subjugate certain sections of the society, as, for example, in caste and race. A natural biological process like motherhood is often invoked to put women in their 'place' and used to make claims that women are more emotional than rational.

Fourth, the family also exhibits a prototype model of a social organization. That is, the family is the first example of how you can live and relate to others. It is all the more obvious when you consider the large joint families in India. Even if all of them no longer live as joint families, the familial relationship is joined in ways that are not seen in many Western societies. For example, cousins are often referred to, and seen as, as brothers and sisters and the relationship between a person and her cousin is often as strong as that between her and her biological brother, if not stronger. A joint family in this sense is a stronger family but also a stronger social entity. It has a looser naturality but there is still the presence of a biological relation, often described as blood relationship.

Fifth, the family sustains social orders like caste and is the locus of the survival of cultures and tradition. They are the agents of the continuity of these social practices. Festivals, rituals, and ceremonies all belong to the domain of the family. When these are taken out of the family due to various reasons, including the nuclearization of the family, then new imitative modes of performing rituals and festivals appear in the social space and these carry the practices that are unique to families and not that of larger communities.

Sixth, the family is both a protective and conflictual space. There are many families that are dysfunctional. The naturalness of motherhood—characterized by care and sacrifice of a mother to her children—has been strongly and effectively challenged today. The psychological distance within family members also challenges any ideal notion of family. Many times, individuals find friendship, support, and solace outside the immediate family. When family members fight, it can often be worse than fights with non-family members. So, the question of belongingness within a family is not a simple matter.

However, the notion of naturalness does distinguish the sociality of a family from that of other groups, at least in the way most people understand the family. Some might argue that there is no social within the family and a social can arise only from certain kinds of grouping not related to the family. But then why do we routinely distinguish a family from any group? If a family is distinguished on the basis of a natural relation as against a social group, then what really is the significance of naturalness within a family and how can that have any bearing on the experience of belonging? This issue is very important because when some socials create a sense of belonging modelled on the family, then they are forced to introduce some aspect of the natural. For example, when the nation is seen as a family, some notion of a natural belongingness to the nation will also be necessary. The public discourse on anti-nationals, a disturbing trend in India today, illustrates this propensity to view nationalism as a 'natural' relation between the nation and its citizens.

A family itself arises out of a particular kind of sociality marked by sexual behaviour. Two people come together to procreate. Given the importance of naturality to the idea of a family, it is extremely important to describe the origins of a family also in natural terms. So mating is naturalized (as if the couple have no choice but to do this). So is love. Both love and sexual desire are often described as consequences of 'natural' forces. If they are not accepted as such, then we will have to consider the possibility that a family itself arises out of some form of sociality. In this sense, the social is prior to the family. The growing voice of transgender and other classifications of gender has led to an important rethink on these traditional ideas of family. But at the same time, It is important to note that while the expanded notion of gender is dominantly a product of a global social movement, attempts at legitimacy of the spectrum of genders often invoke the idea that these dispositions are but 'natural'—thus putting them also within the structure of a 'family'.

A strong critique of the notion of the natural as being essential to notions of family can be developed from marriage practices in India. Both arranged marriages (which still remain the norm and is getting more consolidated in recent times) and 'love' marriages are afflicted with the social more than the natural or the individual. It is often remarked that marriages in India are not between individuals but between families. Many also consider marriages as something divine. Both these expressions of marriages as bonds between families or a relationship with divinity are attempts to negate the possible belief that a marriage has only to do with two individuals. Marriage, for a very large population in Asia, Africa, and the Middle East, has less to do with the expectations and desires of just two individuals. In many cases, families choose the spouse, decide how the marriage is to be conducted, and sometimes even decide on the future of the couple.

Love marriages do not escape this either. It is almost as difficult for two people who 'fall in love' to decide to get married. They have to deal with not only pressures from the immediate family but also from the larger caste and religious communities. The consolidation of khap panchayats, growing caste-based killings of young inter-caste couples, the difficulty posed both by the religious organizations and the State for couples belonging to different religions—all these reemphasize the sociality of marriage and also love. Ironically, the conversion of marriage into an exhibition of desire has not only led to huge expenditure in the conduct of marriage but has, in the guise of having a marriage according to the wishes of the couple, increased the stakes of the social within marriage. The guest lists have become longer, there is a multiplicity of food choices, and the marriage is an exhibition of consumerist desires. Most families run into debt after conducting a marriage because of 'social pressure'.

So a family in India is a product of social complicity and is perpetuated under social duress. Like in many other societies, the idea that marriage is a means for procreation remains dominant in India. Pressure to beget not only comes from the immediate family but also from the extended family, from neighbours, colleagues, and friends, and many times even from strangers. Often couples who either decide not to have children or cannot have children are put in a position to socially defend and explain this 'lack'. Even the sexual production of the couple and their place in society are dictated by the demands of the social. Much of this is often forced through a construction of mother-hood and the necessity of being a mother. At the same time, mother-hood is presented both as an intensively personal domain but also as a social responsibility. So, we find that in India there is a proliferation of In Vitro Fertilization (IVF) clinics as well as new corporate hospitals to cater to a new image of mothers as autonomous consuming agents. There are countless examples of women, particularly among the middle and the well-to-do classes, choosing the Caesarean as a less painful form of birth. Maternity hospitals are caught in a unique form of socialization—in between a hospital and a hotel, between being a home and a shopping mall.

All these are very good illustrations of the complex interrelationship between the notions of the individual, the social and the natural. As we mentioned earlier, much of our ideas of the everyday social can only be understood by looking at the triadic relationship between the social, the natural, and the individual. Given this model, we hope that it is clear why the family is such a central fulcrum around which our conceptions of the notions of the social, the natural, and the individual are developed.

We began with pointing out that belonging and becoming characterize important elements of the social. In the context of the family, what does it mean to belong? This question is frequently not asked because the natural often functions as a synonym for 'belong'. If there is a natural connection between two things, then the question of belong-ingness does not arise. The notion of belongingness is needed to make sense of strangers coming together. In societies, which do not have a meaningful model of why and how people should come together, there is a need to give an account for this phenomenon.

But if the family is itself socially mediated then the question of belonging within a family is meaningful. Belongingness is not sym-metric in a family by its very structure. Since the children need care and protection initially, there is already a structure which places the parents in a different role. The fundamental issue in families is whether this role remains a hierarchical one. In India, it is common to find the father still exerting a strong influence, if not control, over grown-up children. The role of the father gets to be defined both in his relation to his children as well as to his wife. The family also illustrates the problem of any group—how does a member recognize what the group is and how does she understand her relationship with that group? The problem about groups is primarily this: The father has a relationship to his wife and his children as a unit, but also to each of them separately.

'What' belongs to 'what' in a family? The father does not belong to the mother, the children do not 'belong' to their father or if one insists that they do, then a clearer idea of what it means for a human being to belong to another human is needed. This problem is compounded by the fact that a human who belongs to another is seen as a slave. But all of them, parents and the children, belong to the 'family'. They all have a sense of belongingness to the family which is different from the individual relationships they have with each other: that is, even if they do not 'belong' to each other, they do belong to the family. The family creates the 'one' out of the 'many'. It is a collection, a set. And like the empty set, it can exist without any members. The family has an existence of its own and members of a family come and go—but subject to a 'natural' constraint. Thus, we could say that families have an independent existence of their own and members of the family are in a relationship of belonging to it. All members belong to something which is 'outside' each of them—that is, the mother, the father, and the children do not belong to each other but belong to a new entity called the family. In principle, this belongingness is democratic and symmetric—each member belongs equally to the family. The father does not belong 'more' to the family when compared to the children. Although he may have more authority over others, as far as his belongingness is concerned, all members 'belong' equally.

Although they all belong equally, the sense of belonging can differ. The experience of belonging to the family can vary in intensity. The father or the mother may take ownership of the family and this may heighten the sense of belongingness. Responsibility, duty, ownership, and sacrifice are different forms of cognitively expressing the experience of belongingness. These are also the reasons why a family can never be a set of immediate biological relations. A family, as an idea, is always more than the immediately biological, and so we have joint families, extended families, families with adopted children, and so on, leading to the view that organizations, community, society, and the nation also become families in certain contexts.

We have focussed on the family here in some detail since many of the characteristics of the socialities of caste, religion, as well as gender roles in society are very strongly dictated by the experience of the family across India (and in many other societies in Asia, Africa, and the Middle East). The family is also a good example to understand some of the experiential aspects of the social. But we should note that there are deep problems when caste or society in general are modelled on the family. Families are closed systems because not everyone can decide to 'join' a family. In the traditional model, a family is not open to membership—there is no coming together, no assemblages that can happen with families. When caste is modelled on such a structure, it mimics at least two aspects of the family: one, the biological relation in the family becomes hereditary relations in caste, and two, the closed membership of the family translates to the position that one cannot decide to join a caste or drop out of it just like in a family. However, given the new social meanings of families derived from adoptions, same-sex couples having children, and transgender families, there is a radical possibility of rethinking the idea of a family without giving up on deep socialities. In other words, the escape from the family is not necessarily a society of single men and women but a social group with more fluid notions of the natural and the individual.

So far in this book we have argued for an ontology of the social which is experienced both sensorially and through experiences of belongingness. These experiences are similar to the experiences of the individual and can perhaps even be reduced to individual experiences. For this to happen, a notion of the self is needed. The question then is whether it is possible to think of a social self like that of the individual self. Are the social experiences unified within a social self? The next chapter will explore this possibility.

5 Social Self and Identity

In this chapter, we will argue that the idea of a social self is at the origin of much of the everyday understanding of the actions of the social, including that of identity within groups. In the next chapter, we will see how this social derives the capacity for authority which is related to the ways by which identity gets consolidated and sustained.

Social action has become an important framework to understand the social. The Weberian classification of the types of rationalities and types of social actions is one good example.[1] However, in general, there is too much investment on meaningful actions and meaning-making which reduces the locus of social action to individuals. Unfortunately, the forced relation between the individual and the social is based on a fundamental suspicion about the social; it is almost as if anything done as a group has less value than that done by a 'rational' individual. However, social actions are not only about individual intentionalities and meaning-making—these reduce the totality of social action to specific types of individual actions for all purposes. What we want to do here is to explore how the social can itself act, and not how certain acts by individuals can be seen as social actions.

So far, we have seen how the notions of the social arise in the everyday. Individuals in a society invoke the social and talk about it in various ways. They use this term to make sense of a variety of acts and also to use it to order the way they act in their daily interactions. It might

---

[1] See Kalberg (1980) for a detailed analysis of Weber's types of rationality.

appear that every individual has a clear meaning of the social, but this is not the case since the social they talk about, refer to, and which influences how they act is a shared, collective social. But how can the social causally effect human agents, especially if is not a concrete entity? Even if the social were to be an abstract term (and in the earlier part of the book we have shown otherwise: the social can be experienced in various modes), it is possible to understand its causal potential. There are three simple examples of entities which share some characteristics of the ontology of the social but are also seen as causally efficacious. The first example is that of numbers and other mathematical entities. Modern science is not possible without these abstract (non-spatiotemporal) entities and it seems as if these entities have a deep causal impact on the concrete (spatiotemporal) world. The other two common entities which are also useful to consider in this context are space and time. In fact, many of the ambiguities in talking about the social are reflected in our talk of space. The invocation of the term 'social space' is an indication of how the social shares many of the characteristics of space. Philosophically, there are many points of similarities: The claim that space is not experientially accessible is the same claim about the social; the relationship between objects and space is similar to that between individuals and society; explaining causal action (or inaction depending on the theories) of space on objects has similarities with explaining the causal action between the social and individuals. Thus, causal processes in nature and society do not all have to be reduced to causal connections between concrete, embodied entities. Extending the last point, we could ask if the social can interact meaningfully with social actors—this includes not just human individuals but also the larger domain of 'actants', including animals and technological objects.

At one level, it is obvious that something like the social influences individual acts all the time. This is what it means to say that everything is social and that the social pervades everything including family, individual decisions, and activities such as science and music. But when we say that the social pervades everything, we have to give an account of it. Is it one 'social' that is being referred to? Is there one such unified 'social' or many different socials? Do we mean that the social acts as a causal agent? That the social influences the nature of that object or that action? Or is it a part of that thing? For example, when it is said that even personal choices in dress are social, it could mean that some entity called the social influences the personal choices of what dress to wear. Such references to the social are endemic in the everyday life. Is there anything meaningful about such statements or are they merely a habit and a way of talking? We would argue that even if they are a way of talking there is a reason for doing so, a good reason why this becomes the default mode of expressing our everyday life. Moreover, by repeated use of such expressions, they get consolidated and actually become an agent of action in various ways, to the extent that we would find it very difficult to make sense of our actions without using the idea of the social.

The everyday social seems to function as an actor and an agent. It influences, modifies, and is the cause for many things to happen. But when it is described in this manner, what is being presupposed? Does this capacity lie in its status as a concept or as a 'real' entity that somehow has causal efficacy? One might say that if there is a causal power to the social, it arises through its material manifestation—the society. The social can act through society—or representatives of society, including individuals and institutions. While this is generally true, it is also the case that the social can act in ways that a material society cannot. It can act as a social even when a society is not present. Some might say that the notions of agency and structure precisely perform this task. In a sense, structure when counterposed against individual agency is merely a stand-in for 'social agency', the agency of the social. It has also been argued that structures are only the conditions for action and the legitimate site for action still remains the individual. How is it possible to imagine the action of the social not through individual surrogates but as autonomous action in itself?

In this chapter, we will approach the question of the social by drawing upon the articulations of the everyday social. How is it that individuals invoke concepts like 'We' to describe certain kinds of processes and experiences? Is the use of 'We' similar to the use of 'I' when describing experiences? Is the idea of the social to be discovered in the ways by which the we-consciousness arises and is sustained? Is the first experiential mode of the social available in the origin of this consciousness?

We will begin with a simple argument: There are good reasons to acknowledge the existence of the individual self, which are similar to those which support the notion of the social self. We will argue that the philosophical themes around the idea of the self are very useful to motivate an understanding of the idea of the social through the notion of social self. Most importantly, the argument that we propose is that the social self is phenomenologically real. The everyday social is constantly informed by the experience of this social self and influences social actions based on this experience. The formation of the many socials is deeply dependent on the formation of the social self. As discussed earlier, the experience of belongingness is an extremely important marker of the social and this experience is intrinsically linked to the social self. The phenomenological existence of the social self, one could argue, is one of the essential markers of the many everyday socials. In this sense, this self is the internal nature of the social, and in the chapters that follow, we will explore the external relations that characterize these socials.

Arguments for the Self

There are many arguments for the self and its extension into the domain of the social. But in what follows we will focus on one essential aspect of the self. Arguably, the most consistent reason for invoking the idea of the self is in making sense of a certain kind of experience—the I-experience. But that alone is not sufficient for an ontological argument for the self—among other things, this experience has to be distinguished from the other experiences that can be located in and reduced to the body, mind, or the senses. First, consider the I-experience. The argument is that we have experiences that are characterized by a sense of oneness as also a sense of belongingness. This sense of belongingness also leads to expressions of identity about oneself. This experience is not like other experiences in that the other experiences refer to and are grounded in the I-experience. We tend to believe that experiences 'happen to me and I feel it'. Moreover, this experience of the I distinguishes one person from another, although these different individuals may be having the 'same' experience.

The reasons that have been given by philosophers for the existence of a self are also the ones which can support the idea of a social self. In saying this, we are not saying—at this moment—that there is 'something' called the social self but only pointing to the ways by which the notion of the social self gets repeatedly invoked in the experience of the everyday social. Notions of identity of a group as well as experiencing common emotions and feelings of unjustness, humiliation, betrayal, and harassment, for example, are based on a phenomenological experience of the social self. Not only that, they are dependent on the language as well as the characteristics of a social self, which, not surprisingly, seem to be based on the characteristics of an individual self. Many social processes illustrate this claim. For example, how it is that women who may not have had particular experiences of harassment or humiliation can experientially feel what another woman has gone through? Or how is a Dalit able to experience in some sense an atrocity done to another Dalit? How can we give an account of such deeply felt experiences of a social self without reducing it to psychological states or to individual proclivities?

Some of the arguments for the existence of a self are based on giving an account for a special set of experiences that we have. There are different modalities of perception such as seeing and touching but it seems as if it is the same self that sees and touches. The feeling of oneness of diverse experiences, the unity of past experiences as if they are connected, the feeling that all these experiences are happening to the same person, and notions of unity and personhood have all been seen as evidence for the presence of a self.[2] Memory raises a new set of issues related to the self since memory implies the need for an agent who has the experiences and who also has the capability to remember them.

But the idea of the self is not enough to capture the complexity of our social experiences. This alone is not enough to understand the unique experiences of the everyday social that pervades not only our talk of the social but also our actions. We believe that such an approach is particularly relevant for the Asian and African societies where the notions of the social are played out in completely different ways from that of the technological West.

As we saw in the earlier chapters, the sense of the social is experienced in different ways. But equally important is action, the capacity to act together, to act in a social manner. We should recollect here our earlier argument that belonging to a group is not based on merely

---

[2] See Bhatt (1962) for an excellent discussion on some of these issues.

articulating certain views associated with that group but to have a lived experience of the 'unchoice' as well as a new condition—that of acting according to the dictates of the social to which they belong. How does this approach help to understand a wide range of social processes or how a social self is formed through collective action? Or how a social is reduced to the authority of a few or even the authority of an individual? Is the social formed as a conscious action of an autonomous individual? Is that primarily an ethical action that is needed in the formation of the social? For example, it can be argued that the Rashtriya Swayamsevak Sangh (RSS) negates an ontological social self by dissolving it into the individual nationalist self. Rohith Vemula, a Dalit student from the University of Hyderabad, was accused of being anti-national by such forces. The enlarged conception of the social then comes under siege, thanks to the narrow understanding of nationalism by the right-wing forces in India. Answers to the aforementioned questions need a formulation of what a social self could mean, which is what we will attempt in this chapter.

There is yet another argument about the social self in the context of India today. Some might argue that social self acquires its concrete shape only in terms of its space and time dimensions. Without time and space, the social self might remain empty. We will use two examples to explain the conception of an empty social getting its concrete shape in terms of time and space. Lakhs of Neo-Buddhists from all over India conglomerate at Diksha Bhumi, Nagpur, (Maharashtra) every year on the 14th of October. This conglomeration is a kind of testimony to confirm Dalit allegiance to the normative emancipatory philosophy of Buddhism. This is a benign notion of the social which is mediated through the reconfiguration of space and time. But there is also a malignant conception of the social: Right-wing outfits gather with the purpose of attacking minority localities or Dalits, or imposing social boycott against Dalits. For example, Dalits and Muslims came together in June 1988 in Panchgaan village in Akola District of Maharashtra and defended collectively against the Shiv Sena menace. Their problems were common in the sense that both these communities were being threatened by the Shiv Sena but for different reasons. Dalits were threatened into giving up their struggle for Gairan land (common government land) while the Muslims were threatened as they were buying the land from the local Marwari landlords. Sena activists came together from different villages and tried to attack the Muslims. In Lohari, they came from neighbouring villages.

These incidents show a twofold process of the social: one, the creation of a new social among the Dalits and Muslims, and the other, the mutation of the social self of the Sena which gets its sense of masculinity only in the context where they feel they have been reduced to the position of subordination by the Dalits and the Muslims. The social self of the Sena thus emerges in the inversion of the masculine self which defines the very existence of the Sena.

Arguments for Social Self

First of all, we can begin with a striking similarity between the discourse of the individual (I-self) and the discourse of the social (we-self). Communities have an identity like individuals do. They even name themselves and construct memories of their collective experiences. Collection of people—communities or nations—have experiences similar to the I-experience: A feeling of oneness of a community or a group, unity of their experiences, having an identity like the experience of belonging to a country, and having a collective identity which is so strong that often the personal self dissolves into this collective identity. This we-self is private to the group to which it belongs and those of another group cannot experience it. In this sense, the we-self is as private as the I-self. We will call it the 'social self' for various reasons. But does this mean that there is such an entity? Even if it is believed that human individuals have a self, can nations or castes or religious groups have their own, one homogenous self? What can this even mean?

The themes of identity and memory which seem to be central to the category of the self occurs repeatedly across certain kinds of groups, which we can here call 'societies' as a general term. Not all collections, such as flash mobs, an arbitrary audience in a film, or a passing crowd in a railway station, exhibit this property. Certain aggregations develop a sense of the 'We' and this collective, through this experience of the 'We', begins to accrue memories, identity, and narratives around the 'We'. For the other cases like the cinema audience or the flash mob, there is no stability of experience to let the 'We' experience arise. So, when does a collection become a social? As we argued earlier, the social is experienced through the sensations of smell, sound, taste, touch, and sight. Just as the individual self is the substratum on which all the individual sensory experiences are united, so too does the social self function as a substratum of these different experiences of the social. Thus, the different modalities of the We-experiences are all united in the We-self, the social self. These are experiential qualities that characterize the qualities of the social. So, if the idea of the self is invoked to explain all those experiences then so can the notion of the social self be invoked to make sense of the experiences of sociality. Philosophers have made a move towards this most famously through the structure of the self and the other. But we will argue that this is not enough; the other alone is not enough to create the social. Something else has to happen.

The social self is not really in opposition to the individual self. There are two ways through which we can approach this issue. One is from the psychological and sociological understanding of the self and the other is through the growing importance of narrativity in studies of the self.

Sedikides and Brewer (2001: 1), from a psychological perspective, point out that 'the self-concept has three self-representations: the individual self, the relational self, and the collective self'. These three are the ways by which a person makes sense of their self-experiences, namely through personal features that characterize the individual self, through dyadic relations with others, and through group membership. While the individual self differentiates itself from others in terms of its unique characteristics, the relational self shares a binding with others and is 'based on personalised bonds of attachment'. The collective self arises through membership to larger groups and creating unique groups which can be differentiated from other groups, and is 'based on impersonal bonds'. These authors start from the presumption that all these three self-representations are present in one individual and that all these three are *social*. We can see now how the idea of the social self arises not as a self that is common to a group but as an intrinsic element of a self that belongs to an individual. Some psychologists would agree for the primacy of the individual self, but there are also interesting arguments that the social self is the primary one and subsumes the individual self.

Such studies are also complemented with neurobiological studies, including the burgeoning new field of 'social brain science'. This is a field that draws on evolutionary theories and neurobiology to under-stand the neurological basis of social behaviour (Heatherton et al., 2004). Some of the arguments of this approach are as follows: group living and group behaviour are necessary evolutionary mechanisms that protect the human race. For example, cheating and lying behaviours would be socially unacceptable because they threaten the survival of the group. The brain too has parts which are coded for social behaviour and damage to them results in damage to 'social competence'. These authors point out experimental studies that show how the brain gives special status to humans in recognizing and processing objects, which is a reflection of the way the social is encoded biologically. They begin by acknowledging that the self has an obvious experiential dimen-sion but look to medical imaging technologies to throw some light on the self. Experiments have proved that brain response with regard to memory was better if there was some reference to the self ('does happy describe you?' as against 'does happy mean the same as optimistic?'). The point in such approaches is to understand how the social is so fundamentally and essentially inscribed in the personal, or in other words, how the self is already a social self.

There has also been a growing literature from narrative theory which offers some insights into the nature of the self and its relation to sociality. First of all, there is a growing acceptance of the impor-tance of narrative for constructing any idea of the self. As Brockmeier and Carbaugh (2001: 15) note in their introduction to their edited volume on narrative and identity, 'what these studies ultimately sug-gest is that the very idea of human identity—perhaps we can even say, the very possibility of human identity—is tied to the very notion of narrative and narrativity'. There are various ways through which this relationship can be exhibited. We will just choose two from among the many in their volume: autobiography and the different kinds of selves that Harre talks about. In the case of autobiography, as Bruner points out, contrary to our assumptions about autobiographies, the referents of autobiography are not really the past (he notices that autobiographies have only around 70 per cent of past-tense verbs (Bruner 2001: 29) or the self (if it means only the individual self). He argues from a study of autobiographies that self-making, which is the point of autobiographies, is not only one's understanding of their self but also shows the influence of how others see the self.

Unlike traditional accounts of the self as private, he shows how it is inter-subjective and distributed like knowledge (2001: 34). He goes on to add that 'autobiography (like the novel) involves not only the construction of self, but also a construction of one's culture—just as Geertz (1988) assures us that writing anthropology also involves a kind of autobiography' (2001: 35). The fact that self-making is a conscious process which uses language in all its richness and complexity only makes the social more prominent, which allows us to suggest that the individual self is already social, not in terms of self-other but as a discursive and narrative self—it is language that is social and there is no self without language.

Rom Harre, from the perspective of narrativity, suggests that there are three selves which are all formed through narrative. He begins by agreeing that the sense of the self gives the notion of personhood but asks how this comes about. In this context, he suggests that there are three types of selves which we use. Self1 is in the context of perception—'only persons perceive' but the self plays the major narrative role in this interaction (Harre 2001: 61). Self2 is a reflection on oneself as a person and Self3 is the self as manifested to others like in autobiographies. We would extend this to argue that in this essential narrative mode whereby we tell ourselves to others and vice versa, there are two elements: one is language and the other is concepts into which we place others—for example, we do not normally believe that we form a social group with trees and rocks (when some do, it is only because of a world view which places humans on par with other natural things). Thus, the social self is created through narrative and language in its diverse manifestation. However, for Harre, none of these three selves are entities, so there is no ontology associated with them (2001: 64). This is significant since we find that in all these approaches to the social selves, the ontological significance is only with the individual self. The social arises as features of the individual self and thus is at the most only an epistemological characterization of one ontological term, Self.

The above discussion shows how the complexity of the nature of the self essentially involves the idea of the social. Although language and its relation to the self seems to imply that the self is a social entity, it still does not challenge the ontology of the individual self, one that is individuated 'within' persons, which is accessible only to a particular person, and which supplies the substratum to make sense of one's life, memory, and experiences. None of these views allow an easy and automatic transition to an ontology of the social self as a self of the social—where one would like to assert the existence of a self that is common to some individuals.

While the next section will try and address this possibility of understanding the ontology of the social self, in the larger context of social ontology, we need to consider some important parallels between the experiences of the individual and the social self. Consider one argument, mentioned earlier, that the self is different from the body since the body dies, changes, and decays but none of this happens to the self. The process in a society is similar: If the society is understood as something more than merely the set of individuals who form that society, then that society continues to exist even when those specific members are not present. It is fair to say, for example, that even when specific individuals who formed a community are no longer alive, the community nevertheless continues to exist and, in fact, might exist almost exactly the way it was then. Families which have names of houses (as in Kerala) continue to exist even as its members pass away; the family name itself, and not individuals who belonged to it, becomes the unit of the socially real as far as these families are concerned. Even when no individual is alive in that family, the family name remains.

We can extend this observation to take into account the other arguments for the existence of the self. The first point to note is that the body is a collection like a society, except that there seems to be a natural unity for the body. Across cultures, the body as a model for society, including the much-discussed model for the caste system, has been influential in understanding the structure of society. The parts of a society have to be in harmony with each other like the parts of the body. Like a body has a disease, so too can society. The diseases of society have to be cured, have to be removed out of the body-politic. Society has been modelled on the body as a unified object and also on the body as an organism. Marginalized groups are often referred to in terms of a disease like a virus, infected, a plague, and so on. The description of communities as parasites is another example of the organism metaphor in order to legitimize certain actions on them. Society also takes on individual characteristics: The colonial discourse illustrates how societies are described in terms of individual properties like being lazy, intelligent, angry, and so on. Just as the 'evidence' for the self was based on the unity of perceptions, Charles Taylor (1989) invokes the idea of the self to make sense of the stability of enduring cultural beliefs. But we should note that this argument by Taylor is about cultural memory and the person who remembers, and not really about the social self.

The social also exhibits a similar structure of memory as in the individual case. Remembered experiences of an individual which are unified together under the self are replaced by group experiences which are unified together under the social self. The set of body, mind, senses, and so forth, is already the first model for the social which is made of different things. But the central problem is to explain how this unity is possible in the case of the social.

When we invoke the social self in terms of the we-experience, we are primarily attempting to distinguish the difference between the I-experiences and the we-experiences, in a way that does not reduce the latter to the former. There are certain experiences that are radically challenged through the special nature of the collective experience. Sports is one good example: The experience of watching a match with friends is a qualitatively different experience than watching the same match on one's own. Sports need a collective since its essential experience for the viewer lies in the experience of the we-self more than the I-self. In other words, just as the awareness of the individual self is catalysed by certain kinds of experiences, such as remembering that something had happened sometime back, so too is the social self catalysed by these collective experiences. In fact, it is only because that there is a shared sense of self—in exactly the same manner as the individual self—that we can even experience such collective experiences in watching sports and other group events. Among other things, the caste experience too is in this sense a collective, social experience.

But why should this experience lead to the postulation of the social self? Just as the individual is both the experiencer as well as the agent who remembers that experience, so too is the collective experience. When an individual watches a game, she not only remembers what her experience was earlier but often she will remember it also as 'our' experience and not purely as 'my' experience. We use expressions like 'we were shouting', 'we felt dejected', and so on to remember those experiences rather than 'I was shouting' and 'I was dejected'. This is not a communicative act but one that truly expresses our experience. Moreover, collective properties are different from individual ones and their nature cannot be reduced to the properties that describe the individual. The social has an intelligence which does not belong to 'pure' individuals. We need to invoke the social self in order to make sense of the 'life of the social'.

Having said this, what could it mean to invoke the social self? First of all, any claim to the existence of an entity that is shared across individuals already stretches our vocabulary. We should also note that many accounts of the self tend to make an eventual shift to the transcendental albeit in different ways—ranging from Sankara to Husserl. But rather than venture into those troubled waters, we will instead conclude by recollecting some relevant arguments about social ontology in general.

Social Ontology of the Social Self

We have discussed some core aspects of social ontology earlier. Here we will relook at this theme through the idea of the collective mind and collective identity. The general question of the ontology of the collective is quite independent of the questions of the social. The best analogy is that of the metaphysics of sets. Our naive understanding of collections and aggregates is suffused with the terminology of sets. A set is a collection of members; technically, any member is allowed into the set. The question then is whether there is an entity called the set which is over and above its members? Equivalently, if all the members are removed, does an entity called the set remain? As we know well, such a situation arises in set theory in the form of a null set and, as some philosophers point out, the null set is really the most important ontological term, and perhaps the only entity to which there can be an ontological commitment.

We will begin with two examples to give an idea of how to think about the collective from two entirely different directions. First is the idea of a group mind and the second is through the linguistic analysis of 'we'. Given that the mind is private and individuated, just like a self is, it is useful to see how work on the collective mind shows us the possibility of understanding what a social self could be. Wilson (2001: S263) states the group mind hypothesis as 'groups of individual organisms can have minds in just the sense that individual organisms themselves have minds'. In evolutionary biology, this approach is a paradigmatic attempt to explain how groups adapt for evolutionary reasons as well as for survival. Drawing on the view that groups can get so integrated that it will be difficult to distinguish the contribution of an individual, Wilson argues that the 'group could literally be said to have a mind in a way that individuals do not, just as brains have a mind in a way that neurons do not' (quoted in 2001: S263). Examples include not just bee behaviour and decision-making in buffalo herds (on voting to decide the direction of movement) but also in human decision-making. As Wilson notes, this claim is the extension of biological group level adaptation into 'cognitive or psychological processes'. He also illustrates how this hypothesis was held by influential founders of social psychology and social sciences, such as Durkheim. These approaches were largely about group psychology and the impossibility of reducing it into individual psychology, and so are what Wilson calls the 'collective psychology' tradition. The other origin of this hypothesis is through work on social insects and the idea of the superorganism used to refer to certain creatures where it is the group which functions as the fundamental unit of action. For example, individual ants, bees, and wasps function 'more like organs' or parts of a larger body unit.

While emergence is an idea that is often used to explain such group entities, there are also other ways of describing it such as the multi-level hypothesis that would accept the existence of the mind at both the individual and group level. This is unlike the superorganism case where the mind is only a group trait (2001: S265). Wilson also suggests another possibility, referred to as the social manifestation thesis, to make sense of this group behaviour: it is that such group behaviour are only manifestations of individual characteristics that arise in group situations. Moreover, manifestations of group thinking in humans can be reduced to individual minds such as in Wilson's example of voting. The fact that group thinking, from the perspective of evolutionary biology, is so closely related to better survival strategies reduces group thinking as a purposive response to some situations. The argument that eventually such group decisions give advantage to individuals is another counter to the possibility of the group mind.

The debate on the possibility of group minds is yet another support for ways by which we can think of the social self. The case for the social self is stronger than that for the group mind. As we saw above, there are some basic questions about the group mind which includes the social manifestation thesis as well as the individual utilitarian argument in the case of humans. In the case of the mind, the emphasis on the cognitive as well as the emotional leads to the constant possibility of reducing group mind to individual minds. However, in the case of the self the situation is quite different. If we go back to understanding the reasons for the existence of the self, and remember the arguments for the social self through the notion of the we-experience, then it is easy to see that the social self does not arise like the group mind, although metaphysically they share the same structure. The experience that calls for the social self does not arise through deliberation and through cognitive strategies for survival. It is purely a kind of experience but is only collectively experienced, in the presence of others. It does not matter how many of the others are there—for example, an individual might have a similar experience in watching a game with three of her friends or six of them. It is the experience that is made possible by all of them watching that game; the intensity of this experience might vary but the nature of the experience is the same.

Another way of approaching the ontology of the social self is through the analysis of the use of the term 'we'. Vallee (1996) begins by pointing out that by and large linguists understand indexicals like 'I' and 'you' as being directly referential not in a Fregean sense since every utterance dictates the truth value of the same statement like 'I am tall'; as he notes, 'Fregean senses determine a referent with no regard to the context of utterance' (1996: 212). He goes on to add that the plural counterparts of I and you will also be referential (with at least two objects) and context dependent. He further argues that any account of 'we' should take into account the intuition that every utterance of 'we' should include the reference to the 'I'—if I am not part of a group, that group has no referential force as the 'we'. He also suggests other common meanings that 'I' and 'we' share: both do not express 'what a description would express' (1996: 221), both are context-sensitive, both cannot be co-referential, and neither can 'be a bound variable' (1996: 222).

But there are also differences between I and we: 'we' does not fix the reference like 'I' does (normally 'we' will stand for 'me' along with a specific group of people even for only two people); 'I' is 'intention-proof' (cannot make the intention change the reference of the I) whereas in the use of 'we', the intention of the speaker can change the reference; 'we' does not pick out the referred set from a collection (say a group of people around an individual when she utters 'we'). From this, Vallee suggests that 'we' is not an irreducible indexical and that it can be reduced to 'I' and demonstratives like 'they' and 'you' and thus reduces 'we' to a set of I and you/they/s/he and so forth (1996: 226). But this conclusion is not necessarily warranted, particularly because of the ambiguity of how the We is formed from I and other terms. In particular, what is the account of 'and' here since that is really the crucial point—'and' is the special character of 'we'; it is not the terms 'I' or 'you' that matter but the way they are put together. Thus, it seems after all the work done to decompose the 'we', Vallee ends up with a circular argument. Moreover, such a linguistic analysis does not distinguish between the 'we' that is used in talking about a specific group of people with a specific relation between them. It cannot distinguish the 'we' of a caste group from the 'we' of a family or a 'we' of a group of office colleagues and larger collectives such as the nation.

But there are other ways by which 'we' is used in our speech acts that should be noted. One of the most important functions in the use of 'we' does not lie in the function of referring to a group. It is the mode by which an individual speaks on behalf of others. When one student in a class says, 'We feel that the class is tough', she is not necessarily only speaking on behalf of others in a quantitative sense. That is, she is not speaking on behalf of all, or of the majority. It is enough that she feels that she can speak on behalf of others, others with whom she forms a we-self. In this function, the we-self functions just like the I-self, for, after all, the I speaks on behalf of oneself all the time. It is that function of the individual self that should be understood in order to understand what we could mean by the social self.

Social Self and Social Action

How does all this matter to the experiences that characterize the everyday social? How does it matter to the everyday social actions by countless individuals? How does this approach generate insights about the various social processes in India, including those that have led to major social conflicts? It is often remarked that today identity politics have become dominant in any social process. Identity politics is largely based on the functions of a social self, whether explicitly expressed as such or not. Collective identity experiences mimic, very often, the individual experiences described in terms of the self. So, understanding and dealing with identity politics needs prior clarity on the presuppositions that makes such identity politics possible. This issue is also closely related to that of social action. When an individual acts, the action is driven by the self. We define our action in terms of saying things like, 'I am typing', 'I am doing this or that'. In the case of many social actions, we tend to invoke a sense of the social self that is often the unspoken agent of action. That is, when an individual is part of a mob, he is not saying, 'I am attacking this person' but 'we are attacking this person'. So, a sense of the social self is necessary for social action or at least for action that an individual thinks he is doing on behalf of others, or with others. Even when there are individual actions such as choosing a bride in the 'arranged marriage' system, they are legitimized by some notion of the social self. Although these actions look like they represent the autonomous act of an individual, they can as well be understood as actions that are performed on behalf of the social. That is, it is not only that 'social pressure' directly influences an individual's action but it is also that an individual acts on behalf of the social; one of the senses of such an action is that the individual is merely a medium for the action of the social.

One might be able to accept that the social influences individual action but might not want to accept any notion of the social self. But then we need to give an account of how the social influences individual action. Why does an autonomous agent, an individual who is following certain codes, decide to act in that manner even when it is not to her well-being? And what exactly does it mean to say that the social influences an individual's action? Calling this 'socialization' does not help since we need to understand why we get socialized so easily. The way in which our everyday social makes sense of this action of the social is by describing it in terms of a social self—identity and belongingness is one of the central elements of this. We, many times, act on behalf of others; similarly, we act on behalf of the social we belong to. And it is this belongingness to a social that is often manifested as the self of that social. So it becomes important to know the nature of this entity as well as its interaction in order to have a more meaningful understanding of social action that is not always reducible to an individual's intention, motive, and reasons, most of it concerned with forms of meaning-making (Mantzavinos 2010).

We live in a time where human autonomy has been privileged in various ways and yet we also live in a time in which our actions are more zombie-like in that they are dictated by so many other forces including identity, market, and so on. Holding on to naive notions of individual action and the privilege of the autonomous individual can only be self-delusional and it is necessary to understand how these social mobilizations and group actions take place. What is the rationality that drives groups towards hatred and contempt leading to an 'ugly social'? How does this social get consolidated within a few? How does this 'invisible' social even act on many individuals so as to make them function like machines? Romantic views of individualism cannot help. In a society where thousands of students choose their subjects of study based on the invisible pressures of the social or when most social practices are often described and legitimized in the name of the socials people belong to, it is no longer possible to depend on the binary of the individual–social to make sense of these actions. As mentioned earlier, there is a lot in common between this invisible working of the social and the working of the market. We must recognize that the market is in itself a social and belonging to the market means to act in accordance with it. The market-social functions in such a way that individuals are made to think that they act autonomously and make their own choices within the market! Individual action in the social domain is a lot like that—we think that we act autonomously but without the recognition that the choices we make in society are as much an illusion as we make in the market. In the next chapter, we will see one way of understanding how the social exerts authority and through it influence actions of individuals.

But this view also has a serious problem, which is that the social is an ambiguous term which can become totalitarian very easily. This worry is genuine, but it is also based on a misreading of the idea of the social. What we are talking about are a multiplicity of socials that are active and experiential, and which constitute the everyday social life. It is not a unified, stable, and imposed hegemonic social. The very nature of these socials has forms of resistance within it. Hegemony is primarily the task of having one homogenous social manifested through its social self and related qualities. But the social in its very formation has always a potential of breaking into many smaller socials. The everyday social is really a space of these many socials. It is the formation of these many socials that really enable a resistance to the hegemonic social.

One example is that of the formation of socials as forms of resistance. For example, the formation of the social self could be in terms of purpose. In this context, the formation of the social self has to be viewed in terms of collective perception, collective thinking, and collective action. Paulo Freire's cultural action for freedom or collective action for creating conditions of un-freedom constitutes one such example. We can consider social protests about Nirbhaya or Dalit women (victims of sexual assault) or Rohit Vemula (victim of caste discrimination) or Junaid (victim of communal hatred), and the ontological basis of this social formation. The similarity of experiences was one important binding force in these social formations. Morally tormenting experience of people from the North East, that of battered Muslims, or the devastated tribals is similar and hence creates the possibility of shared socials. The formation of such a social self is not an easy process. In fact, those forces which have been desiring to create a homogenous Hindu Rashtra have been trying to deny the ontological basis to such a self. Such forces seek to dissolve such a self by making a link between the individual and the nation. This kind of deontological connection between the nation and the individual makes it easy for the Hindutva forces to beat some with the stick of nationalism. Rohit Vemula was the victim of such a beating. Individualizing nationalism, thus, provides the basis of condemning some as being anti-national. Hindutva forces, however, arrogate such legislative power to decide who is national and who is anti-national. On the other hand, within the series of 'rabid socials' that we find in such authoritative formation, there are some who do not require normative authority as they invoke their own authority as the final authority. But we need to understand one thing clearly: these outfits may enjoy autonomy in carrying out their explosive action against the historically battered social groups but such actions happen within the regressive norms of a larger social which is constitutive of the Hindutva design to create one social order based on hierarchy. So, the authority that the Shiv Sena invokes when they impose bandhs or force Hindus to observe certain cultural practices is only an attempt to mimic the authority of the larger socials. The Hindus who attacked the Dalits in Una or those who attack Muslims in the name of protecting the cow are those who express a sense of belonging to a social and create their own authority to do so. These are people who do not have knowledge of textual authority or of belonging to a world of practice. Rumours, Facebook, or social media become the authority for such a social self.

The Social Self of Caste

According to Hannah Arendt, the social exists between the private and the political (Arendt 1958). The private, according to her, is an intimate and exclusive sphere which cannot be regulated by an *outside authority* such as the political or the legal. If we take her argument into consideration, then we cannot consider the practice of untouchability as constituting a crime even though it has been practiced in the private sphere such as the family and the home. But in the Indian context, the private is the source of evil and it is much more astonishing to see the private extending to the public thereby contaminating the public with the practice of untouchability. Let us consider the first argument about the family as the source of untouchability and caste. Untouchability as a social ideology, which finds its salience in the public, is practiced by women from a touchable caste with utmost rigour. The higher caste woman is often seen as the main custodian of caste and untouchability. Why is this the case?

The everyday enmeshing of the social into the private and vice versa has many instances. In most Indian cities, we find the *chaturvarna* (the four types of caste order) system reproduced in the private sphere. For example, in Delhi's rich locality and houses, maid servants are employed to do different jobs as prescribed in the chaturvarna codes. Thus, a woman from an upper caste would do the cooking, an Other Backward Classes (OBC) woman would clean the vessels or do baby-sitting, while the Dalit, walmiki woman would do the toilet cleaning and mopping. In many houses in Delhi, a tribal maid is lucky enough to get at least three jobs in one house except the cleaning of toilets. It also works out to the advantage of the woman who hires since she does not have to make inquires that are considered as unpleasant with regard to the social background of the maid. These inquiries are already made by the agencies that supply maid servants. The high caste, affluent women can outsource these unpleasant questions to the supplying agency. Why is an adivasi women preferred over a Dalit woman? Because maids from the adivasi community are considered to be physically as well as ritually clean. If one further decodes the hidden intention of the upper caste urbanites, one would find that these hiring families treat adivasis as ritually clean as the latter do not form a part of Hinduism. They are outside the fold of Hinduism. Secondly, tribal women are preferable to Dalit women as they, in the upper caste perception, are clean by virtue of their hailing from the clean forest and not from the dirty Dalit ghetto. Dalit women do get domestic work but only the sanitation work and not the 'clean' work. Thus, the caste division of labour at the domestic level is reflective of the chaturvarna system. A particular social infected by a virus of caste gets reproduced in the private thus erasing the difference between the private and the social.

In the rural areas, by and large, it is the women, particularly from the peasant caste, who seem to be very particular about observing caste rules through the practice of untouchability. Here, we would like to make a central argument that untouchability as a social phenomenon acquires more resilience when it is pushed from the public sphere into the private. In the private, it is high caste women who become almost the sole custodians of protecting the thick social (caste infected). The social also acquires some degree of thinness on account of the disappearance of untouchability from the urban interpersonal interaction and other market-based social practices.

One might argue that the density pressure of the urban is leading to emptying out the space between the private and the public. But this space has been filled with an element of anxiety and curiosity which is expressed in the following question: With whom am I interacting? The space between the two particulars which needs to be organized around the unrestrained relationship devoid of an element of anxiety or suspicion denies the social the advantage of acquiring a 'pure' character. The space between the two particulars gets occupied with hidden hate. Those who operate in the space do not operate with a free mind and this siege of the state of mind gets confirmed when the upper castes take a bath in order to purify their body that in their perception might have been touched by the co-presence of the crowd of untouchables in the common space. The sceptic might always say that they take bath not because their bodies became 'polluted' with the presence of untouchables, but they do so in order to clean their body from air and dust pollution. However, those who exist only from one air-conditioned environment to another also take a bath. Thus, the seemingly anonymous space gets overdetermined by the caste social that has its habitation in the domestic.

But in the domestic sphere in urban areas, it is the upper caste women who take major responsibility in terms of nurturing the caste social. These women map the caste social on to the domestic space. This mapping results in the fragmentation of space on the scale of the ritual hierarchy. Thus, Dalit women are allowed to enter the houses only from the backdoor and to the toilet and not beyond whereas the touchable women can enter the kitchen. In their everyday interaction with the untouchable women, these upper caste women follow the socially sanctioned caste rules that do not allow any transgression in regard to social exchange of either cooked food or water. In the urban setting, the caste practices followed by upper caste women tend to reproduce the chaturvarna as mentioned earlier. Those who argue for the social divide between the rural and the urban are mistaken as caste is common in both the urban and the rural when it comes to the private sphere of the domestic. The informalization of the economy further sharpens the rough edges of the social burdened with castes.

In the rural context, there are no obviously accessible common drinking resources and the strangers who are on voyage from one village to another have to approach the upper caste household and make a request for drinking water. It is the women from these households who decide whether to give water or not. In many cases these requests are turned down, or Dalits are given water but not in a glass as they are supposed to drink water that is poured into their cupped hands. Such practices are not only inhuman, but they are also deeply humiliating. Ironically, the everyday practice of untouchability by upper caste women initiates the social death of Dalits.

What is the logic in the social discrimination practices by high caste women, both from the urban as well as the rural context? Why does such a person become the custodian of caste through everyday practices of untouchability with perfect sincerity? Is it because she also has her share in producing the caste person? Obviously, the larger structural role of patriarchy cannot be dissociated from these actions. It would be unfair to blame the woman and not the structure. Some would explain this by saying that the woman finds some kind of individual power in practicing untouchability and has a subsidized satisfaction in the little sovereignty she enjoys over the kitchen which is the most sensitive part of the house as far as she is concerned. In this regard, it is Gandhi who does not listen to Arendt who maintains the view that public rules cannot be imposed on private life or the family life. On what ground can we defend this view of Arendt? The family interaction is limited only to intimate families. It is an exclusive sphere that is not available to everybody. If this is the case, is it social at all? Transgression is the precondition to create a new, modern, seamless social, and there is no pressure on the part of these urbanites to follow this condition. They can put one foot in the caste-ridden social and the other in the party culture, thanks to the cheap labour that is made available through migration from urban to rural areas.

The private is extremely important and is the social protection for the upper castes. Gated communities built around caste and class, which are growing in number, are a 'public' extension of this protected private. The socialization of these ideas cultivates a particular primordial consciousness among both men and women, socializing the latter into accepting the limits and working within the limits. Socialization into caste leads to the internalization of the ideology of pollution which in effect does not generate, for example, urgency among the OBCs to transgress the limits of caste. Many maids from the OBC caste refuse to work in the Dalit household in the urban setting. The social based on reciprocal recognition stops at the door of the upper caste. Reciprocal recognition as the threshold of human interaction gets blocked at the threshold of the door of the upper castes and now other caste Hindus. The socialization into the ideology of pollution necessarily smothers the language of legality, but much more importantly it negates the possibility of being decent to each other in a reciprocal manner. The civil law of India does not uphold the claim of a person that it is her right to enter the house of an upper caste person. Thus, the social is more a matter of moral ethical significance rather than legal enforcement. The upper caste 'flows' in the public but folds himself or herself into caste as soon as s/he enters the private, intimate, sphere.

The inability of a lower caste person to transgress the boundaries of the caste social tends to fortify the fence that has been raised by the high caste Hindus around themselves. Caste acquires the image, and plays the role, of a rooster which remains within the compound of caste/religion that encircles the home. The social as interpreted in terms of the sphere of freedom finds itself compressed by the logic of caste, patriarchy, and religious bigotry. In effect, the social that is driven by the logic of caste leads to the compression of freedom. The upper caste male members may have genuine desire to invite the untouchables inside their home but will find it difficult to exercise this freedom as they feel constrained to extend the invitation. One is prepared to acknowledge that they have genuine desire for sociability, which they are unable to practice at the social level. This is because caste plays the role of a rooster which lingers in the compound of the home. The upper caste individual is overpowered by the repressive caste structure and its socialization, and human agency is reduced to a mere carrier of the overall caste structure. The upper caste takes off his social mask as soon as he reaches the threshold of his house and does not participate in creating a new social based on universal values of dignity, friendship, generosity, and compassion. Caste still provides a sustained source of belonging and selfhood which replaces the need for belonging elsewhere. The threshold of the house or the compound of the house does provide the upper caste a moment to free oneself from caste and eliminate the fault lines based on caste. It provides an opportunity to be at a crossroad rather than be in the confines of caste. But caste is produced to corrupt the seamless, the quality of being social.

A Dalit in the interest of fashioning out a new seamless social takes the moral risk of getting humiliated on account of facing the inhospitable atmosphere that prevails in the upper caste house. Dalits sustain the moral injury but they do so in the larger epistemic interest of detecting the limits that are internal to the upper caste notion of freedom. The question that one needs to ask is this: Why should one insist on getting into somebody's house? Will it not result in intrusion of the private spheres? What about the violation of the private? This logic of private–public dichotomy is untenable in the Indian context when the upper castes convert the public into private in barring the entry of the untouchables or a Dalit into their houses. Thus, the social becomes imminent in the political. The social is the reciprocal return of the ethical such as friendship and not the generosity shown to a destitute or a needy person. The mutual interaction between two persons has to be unconditional as a Dalit does not expect the upper caste to

treat her as an object of sympathy or pity. The human need is to annihilate mutual hatred and fill the social with some degree of *Manuski*,
humaneness and dignity. This would add an egalitarian content to the
ethical relationship, liberating the physical space through an invitation
into the house. Caste pride as the essence of the social gets replaced by
the ethical.

It is important to realize that exclusion and its legitimization by
using the private–public dichotomy is not specific to caste experiences. The recent events around the denial of entry of women in the
age group of 10 to 50 at the Sabarimala temple is another illustration
of what we have discussed in this section. Both in the case of access
to Dalits and access to the Sabarimala temple by these women, the
larger social was acting against explicit constitutional values and legal
judgement. As also in the shameful instances of manual scavenging
in India. The justification given by the men and women, not surprisingly, invoke these same notions of the family, pollution, private,
public, social identity, and so on. These are the currencies of the
everyday social and what we have tried to do here is to analyse how
they catalyse social action.

Thus, what we see is that the operation of caste and gender is
dependent on qualities of everyday socials that are not only sensorially
perceived, but also operationalized through a unity of experiences that
is the hallmark of the self. In the next chapter, we will see how such
socials get associated with the fundamental question of authority.

6 Authority of the Social

In many of the uses of the idea of the social in everyday life, the social is used as a term of authority. Authority may need individual agents to enforce it but the notion of authority itself is independent of enforcement. Law as authority functions in a similar manner: a particular law is an authority of a kind and is present only as a linguistic statement which has been legitimized as a law. Those who enforce that law, like the police or judges, transfer the authority of the law to themselves at that moment. But the authority of the law transcends its empirical performance. Social authority is also very much like this. But what are the contours of authority that are special to the social? How does the social get its authority? Or is authority an intrinsic and necessary part of the idea of the social? Is the most salient property of the social its authority? In this section, we will discuss the notion of authority and posit the authority of the everyday social through the discussion of the authority of the natural.

There is more than one implication in the use of the word 'authority'. It is used in the sense of giving permission, controlling actions, and as a decision maker. It is also used in the sense of being a ground of, that which validates something else. It is used to refer to a wide variety of agents such as texts, books, ideologies, individuals, government, society, and culture. Authority can be vested in this diversity but in this very possibility we have to find the meaning of authority. First, how is authority grounded or vested in something? Is it granted to that entity or is it self-granted? The authority to govern, for example, can be legitimized through democracy, as well as in dictatorship, in very different ways. Authority can thus be located in a diversity of actors but as we will see in what follows, it can also function without a specific agent. Authority in society is often operated through humans but there is also a powerful sense of authority encoded in certain texts that have a prominent place in that society. These texts can be religious, ethical, or even the Constitution. Is the operation of authority through texts and humans different? While these and similar questions are important to understand authority, we are primarily concerned with understanding how the social gets its authority.

Authority is grounded, as well as articulated, in different ways in different disciplines. One might say that in philosophy it is manifested through texts, scholarship, and certain forms of reason; in science through evidence, experiments, and mathematics; in religion through religious texts and the representatives of these religions; in ethics normally through a set of codes. In all these cases, authority in its most essential form is something which justifies something else, something upon which certain types of actions are legitimized and validated. Therefore, authority is something that can be evoked without agency or grounds when the structures of legitimacy override these elements. Authority is that which grants and permits (but not necessarily enables) something to be done. It is a sanction which allows actions. In the case of human action, we often look to certain forms of authority and these forms are embodied in various ways: kings, political leaders, religious leaders, State, court, police, God, and so forth, but in most of these examples, the embodied form of authority is nothing more than the enforcers of authority and are not the authority themselves. So, the State, court, and police are only enforcing set of strictures which are already available to them; the legislature creates a set of laws that are already within another given—the Constitution; the Constitution itself is based upon a core set of principles. Even the authority of kings was based on certain texts, tradition, and codes that regulated their action. While the authority of science rests with the scientists as enforcers or actors, the ultimate authority for science becomes nature (more on this in the following sections). And in ethics if there is any justification for moral action beyond texts it rests on the idea of moral authority, on some notion of the nature of the human self.

In this chapter, we are interested in exploring the relationship between authority and nature, and through this reflect on the nature of the authority of the social. We will explore how nature gets its authority, how this authority influences not just the critique of (human) authority as a fundamental principle of science but also consolidates the principle of nature as authority, how this view catalyses the critique of political authority as a fundamental impulse of modernity and, finally, how it supports and promotes various versions of naturalistic arguments which today play an important role in the legitimization of authority.

We have seen how the everyday social becomes a real term of engagement in everyday life. We talk about the social in these everyday interactions as if it is around us, as if it can be seen, smelt, and experienced in various ways. These forms of invoking the social suggest that our engagement with society is in terms of a multitude of socials. While this may seem equivalent to saying that a society is made up of many communities, we have argued earlier that this picture is quite different in that the many socials are not reducible to communities or individuals. In this chapter, we will discuss the nature of authority by which the social influences individuals who 'belong' to that social.

One of the intriguing aspects of the everyday discourse of the everyday social is the invocation of the authority of 'society'. A notion of authority as the invisible hand of the social is quite pervasive and powerful in many social actions and is explicitly acknowledged as such. The pressure of the social as authoritative norms on individuals and families is so strong that life-changing decisions, including education and marriage, are often dictated by the compulsions of the social. Or such decisions are at least sanctioned and legitimized by the social. In societies such as India, and many other non-western societies in Asia, Africa, and the Middle East, the social functions as a silent and strong authority figure. The fact that this invisible authority figure is often seen as patriarchal is only one form of hypostatization of the social, that is, one form of making the social real.

There are some features of this account of authority that mediate social action as well as individual action. One is that it is almost always invisible, in the sense that there is no specific representative of this authority. Although there is constantly an attempt to locate the authority in an individual or group, the power of this authority lies in its capacity to transcend embodiment into individuals or groups. So, in its most important sense, this authority is non-agential, unlike authority in politics where authority and power are directly invested in individuals or institutions. This also implies that in politics, authority is answerable in that there is at least somebody or something that is answerable. But in the case of invisible authority, like tradition, while we may discover agents of authority, they are nevertheless fluid and incomplete. When people invoke the authority of the social as a reason for their actions, ranging from buying something (like a vehicle or a house) or sending their children to particular schools or choosing the spouses of their children or demanding that the members of the family behave in particular ways, they are acting as if they are under a genuine authority, except that this authority is not embodied in a specific form. This authority functions in multiple ways: as causal, as guidance, as motivation, as justification, as legitimization, as pragmatic, and so on. These are the meanings which attach to what we recognize as social authority.

But what can a disembodied form of authority really mean? What could it be? How can it act to so profoundly influence individual action? When millions use the idea of the social as a form of persuasion or an agent of action, are they using it as a form of description of an authority exerted by an individual? As we mentioned earlier, we may want to rearticulate the experience of this authority in terms of individual or agential authority but to do so would be to miss this essential point about the social. In fact, tradition itself is a notion that functions as a non-agential authority. While people will do things in the name of tradition, there is no specific agent who stands for tradition and who stands as the locus of its authority. The authority of caste which runs deep in the Indian society is another example of authority which functions as a social non-agential authority. There may be attempts to convert this into agential authority by invoking texts or leaders of caste groups or religious heads of that caste. The very attempt to do so, as well as the multiple locations of this authority, immediately suggests the anonymity as well as the non-locatedness of this authority.

How can we possibly understand this form of authority? Does it seem like some invisible, spooky force that makes humans act according to its diktats? Does it even have a set of diktats that we have to obey? In what follows, we will give two powerful examples of non-agential authority and the effect they have had. One is the example of the notion of natural in the natural sciences which exemplifies many of these characteristics of the authority associated with the social and the other is the 'authorless authority' that legitimizes the Vedas. The social seems to operate on members like the natural operates on objects; thus, the idea of authority in the experience of the everyday social seems to function a lot like the way nature does. The naturalization of the many socials is a consequence of this intrinsic relation between the natural and the social. In particular, the authority associated with the social is very similar to that of the natural. This is intriguing and points to a larger process in which non-agential authority becomes a hallmark for social authority akin to natural authority.

The Problem with Authority

The question of authority is somewhat passé in academic circles, it seems. While authority is still a term that incites strong reactions in a democratic society, the notion of authority seems to have become less and less important for academic study. In sociology, for example, Furedi (2013) points out that although the founding fathers including Durkheim, Weber, and Mosca, engaged deeply with authority, contemporary sociology does not consider this concept to have the same significance. He points out that contemporary sociologists including Bourdieu, Bauman, and Giddens have argued how the nature of authority has radically changed (advertisement and consumerism have 'displaced the necessity for authority', 'authority has become redundant', and 'we live in an age of multiple authorities' respectively). For example, the question of the authority of the past, which is in a deep relationship with the authority of tradition, does not really hold in most societies today. It is clear that these sociologists are talking about authority in their own societies, for the authority of the past and tradition are really the core problems about authority in India and countries in Asia and Africa. Furedi (2013: 11) goes to the extent of suggesting that arising from modernity, 'society faces a crisis of authority' and that 'authority based on a normative foundation has become very weak'. On the face of it, such a crisis is fundamentally engendered by modernity's focus on the autonomy of reason and through this the critique of textual, political, and religious authority. However, we must also note that there is a legitimization of the autonomy of reason and it is within this legitimization that modernist ideas of authority emerge. These include concepts such as freedom, autonomy, legitimacy, and so on.

The sociological approach to authority focusses on its relation to the ideas of order and trust but these, according to Furedi, suffer from 'their detachment from history'. However, he also points out that Durkheim, Weber, and Mosca's theories of authority were part of a larger awareness of the past. Analysing authority naturally leads to the question of foundations or grounding or discovering reasons for certain legitimations, and the problem of foundation is that all the instruments of authority such as laws have no 'intrinsic authority' in themselves. The ultimate source of social legitimation may be a self-evident one that needs no further justification, but the fact is that authority seems to be always grounded in something like tradition, 'divine command', monarchy, and so on. The Weberian approach is also illustrative of this 'problem of foundation'. As Furedi points out, although Weber understands authority as having 'different sources of legitimation', he nevertheless does not analyse the relationship between the notion of authority and the source, thus tending to conflate the two (2013: 7).

When we look at authority in the manner described above, we can see that it is essentially a relational concept and the major image that influences a model of authority is one of the rule by parents or the authority of parents over their children. If we look for authority as the foundation, then it has an ontological status, but this will shift the focus to how authority is created rather than how it is received and sustained in a society. Furedi suggests that this Weberian view does not take into account the relational aspect of authority, a view that influences later writers, including Foucault. The relational aspect illuminates the relation between authority and power, since authority operates through power to make people obey, follow, persuade, motivate, and so forth. But if authority is seen to be distinct from power then it is the relation between them that matters. One approach then would be to suggest that authority has to be understood in both these foundational and relational aspects.

The other dichotomy of interest is that between the autonomy of authority to have the power to act on its own as against a subject who decides to follow authority or even be persuaded based on his or her choice to follow authority (as discussed by Hannah Arendt). Here the question is the location of the site of authority: whether it should be located in the authorial figure or in the subject (who decides on) following authority. In the case of the social, it is often remarked that the social either forces people to follow its rules (for example, tradition) or that individuals can be persuaded by the authority of the social and decide to follow it based on their own autonomous decision. Whatever be the case, the social presents itself as something which is capable of having authority and we would like to explore how this is possible. Natural science is an excellent example where authority and autonomy clash in subtle ways. We will start with the analysis of nature as the central authority for science but the natural is not an agential authority. It is scientists who really act and do the job of science but in the ultimate analysis they are not the authors of the knowledge of nature but mere 'transcribers'.[1]

Authority and Science

One of the most intriguing outcomes of the story of science's opposition to authority is not the rejection of authority per se but only the rejection of certain kinds of authority invested in humans and institutions like the Church. Interestingly, it is not that the idea of authority was given up by science, but it was merely displaced from human, agential authority to nature. Science functions, even today, under a very powerful idea of authority but this is one which is located within nature. It is only the dictates of nature that matter to science. But this leads to an odd situation: nature is the final authority for science, but it is quite unclear as to what 'nature' really is or how this authority is invested in or operated by it. Nature has authority as a non-agential authority—that is, an authority which has no agent to perform it or be answerable to it. But this shift to nature as authority is a consequence of a particular reinterpretation of nature by scientists.

This approach towards authority and the way by which nature becomes the figurehead of authority for science is extremely relevant because the way the social exerts authority also seems to be quite similar. When a practice of the everyday social is explained by saying 'this is what society is' it is a lot like a scientist's statement, 'this is

[1] See Sarukkai (2002).

what nature is'. Both nature and society (or the natural and the social) provide legitimacy for certain actions, are not agentially embodied, are not answerable to the subjects who follow this authority, are not locatable in any specific sense, and are experienceable in many interesting ways. We will see below that not only are the natural and the social non-agential authorities, but such a process arises in the ancient debate on the authority of the Vedas. These are fascinating examples which explain how it is possible to make an ontological commitment to the social.

It is often claimed that the Age of Reason and the Enlightenment marked a decisive shift in the way humans conceptualized the world and themselves. The origins of modern science are often conveniently tagged onto this historical moment and by isolating the claim that science arises through a rejection of religious authority, the idea of science gets associated with society and politics. A good example of this view is the argument by Judd (2009) that considers 'questioning authority' as the defining 'ethic' of modern science. Although the relation between science and religion is far more complex than captured in the simple accounts of challenging the authority of the Church, it is nevertheless useful to note the influence of the development of science on thinkers like Hobbes and Locke, who in turn deeply influenced modern political theory.

Judd begins by arguing that modern science should be primarily seen as an activity that privileges the questioning of authority, and as a process this 'influenced the evolution of modern political thought and practice' (2009: 1). She also suggests that natural science and political thought led to three major aspects of enlightenment—autonomous reasoning individuals, questioning authority, and the legitimacy of political resistance. She begins with Francis Bacon's view of nature and science, and more importantly the questioning of authority that he practiced. Bacon was not really questioning the authority of religion; instead, what he did was to question the authority of the Scholastics and the hold which the 'wrong' Aristotelian philosophy had on the practice of science.

The argument for the influence of the practice of science on political authority is traced through Hobbes and Locke. Thomas Hobbes was deeply influenced by Bacon and the new science. He was Bacon's secretary before Bacon's death, and had met Galileo. Science was the model not just for studying nature but also for politics and ethics, which for him emulated physics and geometry. Judd's argument is that natural science combined with political theory gave rise to classical liberalism (2009: 4). So also, was the case of John Locke, who was, in addition, a member of the Royal Society from 1668. His influential works *An Essay Concerning Human Understanding* and *The Second Treatise of Government* were, Judd suggests, 'analogous to Newtonian physics'. In this sense, politics was deeply influenced by Bacon and Locke who in turn used science as their new model; particularly, the character of questioning authority which was to be the leitmotif of the new science.

Judd argues that this attitude of questioning authority drawn from the scientific view 'resulted in the evolution of three key Enlightenment ideas': (*a*) the autonomy of individual reason which supports the idea that humans can also govern themselves, (*b*) questioning tradition which leads to the superiority of the secular over the religious, and (*c*), the recognition that 'political resistance is a legitimate act' (2009: 41). She finds in Hobbes the strongest and first link between natural science and modern political thought. He was, like many after him, enamoured by the notion of the scientific method and thought this approach could be used to study society by breaking it into its constituent parts and discovering what he called the 'constitutive causes'. By categorizing politics as a science (both deal with consequences, the former of 'politique bodies' and the latter of 'bodies naturall'), he brought them together not only in terms of method but also in the hope that both were to be considered as desirable for mankind.

Hobbes' invocation of scientific imagery is more: His model is a utilitarian one balancing liberty and authority, and this balancing is done through rules like arithmetic and geometry; even liberty is defined scientifically as 'nothing else but an absence of the lets and hindrances of motion' (quoted in Judd 2009: 53). There was yet another important aspect of science that influenced Hobbes and served as a model for political societies: the notion of the laws of nature. He repeatedly describes liberty and various other concepts around it in terms of laws and rules. For example, 'the safety of the people is the supreme law', 'the general law for sovereigns' is a 'law of nature'. For Hobbes and Locke, 'reason is the law of nature' (2009: 55). Although these laws seem to be laws of human behaviour (for example, his first law of nature was about man's attempt to be in a state of peace), they are nevertheless related to the philosophical presuppositions of natural laws. Moreover, by invoking such laws, Hobbes was going against the entrenched idea of divine laws and invests the capacity within humans to make such laws.

John Locke too was deeply influenced by science. Not only was he a collaborator with Robert Boyle, he was also a member of the Royal Society, studied medicine, and was influenced by scientists. Even his conception of power was in terms of active and passive power, reminiscent of Newton's classification of gravitational powers. There was a strong influence of the scientific tradition on his ideas of power and liberty. The new conceptual understanding of nature needed for the practice of modern science began to be of great influence in conceptualizations of power and authority. The influence of scientific descriptions of nature led to one important cultural phenomenon. Increasingly, the authority of nature was being invoked to explain moral behaviour as well as scientific descriptions of the world, a trend that continues till today.

But what exactly is it to claim that nature has authority? What are the implications of believing in this authority of nature? If nature is made up of many elements, what exactly is it that contributes to the authority of nature? The answer to these questions begins by recognizing that nature is not just a pre-given and that nature had to be reconfigured by science in order to do the job—of exerting authority—required of it.

Spirn, in writing about landscape architecture, begins with the idea of nature that is inherent in designing gardens. Designers, she writes, 'make ideas of nature central and explicit, citing nature as authority to justify decisions to select some materials or plants and exclude others, to arrange them in particular patterns, and tend the result in certain ways' (Spirn 1997: 249). She goes on to add that designers equate nature and divine authority, as famously exemplified by Frank Lloyd Wright who equated nature with the 'body of God'. But what exactly is the idea of 'nature' here? Writers have pointed out to the complexity of the meaning of nature; one lists over 60 meanings of the word as used over time.[2] Raymond Williams calls this word the 'most complex word in the language' (quoted in 1997: 251).

What was special to the late eighteenth- and early nineteenth-century views on nature was the influence of science and, in particular, the view

[2] See Baindur (2015) for conceptualizations of nature in Indian traditions.

that nature was governed by natural laws (Daston 2014). This view arose from the seventeenth century's reinterpretation of the meaning of laws. Starting with Descartes and Newton, the notion of laws as the defining idea of nature begins to become popular. Its impact was such that the idea of laws, originally referring to divine laws or mathematical laws (as in thirteenth-century optics), suddenly became a common metaphor in the study of nature as well as of societies. Laws—whether that of nature like the law of gravity or of society—were 'constructed as divine edicts' (2014: 583). Daston suggests that for the Enlightenment thinkers, nature was to be seen as 'an aspiration rather than an inexorable reality' and thus, although this imparted authority to nature, it was more 'as a utopian project' (2014: 585). But, Daston argues, by the mid-nineteenth century, nature had become more conservative, had become something which could not change. By the nineteenth and twentieth centuries, all values had been removed from nature and it no longer was the ground for moral values but was dictated solely by physical necessity thus leading to the position that 'the natural and the moral belong to different ontological categories' (2014: 585).

But these views of nature were not created outside a historical and social context. The picture that we are given is that an essential component in the making of science was the emphasis on questioning authority. What exactly was the authority questioned by the early natural philosophers? One could argue that the prime target was not even the Church, and definitely not religion in its entirety. The disagreement was on specific aspects of the natural world such as heliocentrism which was a matter of dispute between the 'scientists' (remembering that the word 'scientists' is a nineteenth-century coinage) and the Church. The reaction was also against scholasticism, particularly Aristotelian scholasticism. Hobbes' reaction against scholasticism gave him a model for incorporating Bacon into the method of natural philosophy. For both Bacon and Locke, religion was still accommodated but in terms of 'nature' it had no place. Hobbes took a stronger stand against religion and was often ridiculed as an atheist. But for all these thinkers, the critique against the Church and scholasticism was not against them per se but only against them because what religion claimed about the world did not match observation and evidence. In other words, it was an epistemological judgement about the truth and falsity of claims by the Church and earlier philosophers. But to do this was not to merely critique religion and philosophy, but to also actively create a new entity called 'nature'. The reformulation of the concept of nature by Bacon and those who followed him is also at the heart of the project of the creation of modern science.

One of the most important consequences of this approach was that Bacon and others did not really challenge authority or eradicate the concept of authority. They only displaced it into other domains—for example, the domain of the individual who has the autonomy to reason. As mentioned earlier, this belief in the possibility of the individuals to be the final authority through reason was primarily about shifting the locus of authority to the individual from other larger structures. In fact, this shift to the authority of the individual, we would argue, actually makes the question of authority more important—that is, authority becomes more important in a metaphysical sense but gets diffused in the political sense. The eradication of the concentration of authority in one individual or one institution succeeds in distributing authority to many and hence the impact of the authorial figure becomes less. But this process in no way dilutes the centrality of the concept of authority. In the final analysis, this project of distributing authority among autonomous individuals cannot be a scientific project. Its real project is to invest authority within a recreated nature. For science, only nature is the ultimate authority and its authority is exemplified by these paradoxical entities called 'laws of nature'.

Ruby (1986) traces the origins of scientific law to Roger Bacon's use of 'law' (lex) in the thirteenth century and his use of the 'law of reflection/refraction' in optics. She also points out that the notion of law was not used in a metaphorical manner. However, the real impact of the use of 'law' comes through Descartes and primarily through Newton's use of laws of motion (1986: 357).

Henry (2004) has a different argument about the origin of laws in nature and points out that the notion of the laws of nature originated in its modern form from Descartes (and not from Roger Bacon) who derived this idea from mathematics. But given that mathematical laws are not causal, Descartes grounded these physical laws in God. Henry distinguishes natural law and the law of nature as follows: Natural law is used also as moral law, and had been in use much before, and are essentially laws which are obvious or arrived at through reasoning (2004, fn: 74). Descartes's conception of law in *Principia Philosophiae*

(1644) and Newton's in *Principia Mathematica* (1687) are the first examples of the new conceptualizations of law (2004: 80). Henry points out that Ruby's claim that Roger Bacon's laws of optics made no reference to god is a mistaken one since these laws were mathematical laws. Optics and other mathematical sciences were seen to be inferior to physics, following Aristotle's view about the secondary nature of mathematics in comparison to physics/natural philosophy (2004: 93). For Descartes and after, laws of nature were the entities that could explain mechanistic motion and thus become the foundations of all physics that followed. But the defining relation between morality and science, as seen in the contemporary understanding of science, originates at a later period.

Daston (2002) discusses how the moral authority of nature gets constructed. Her argument that the naturalistic fallacy is modern is an argument to show how the idea of nature was changed in the nineteenth and twentieth centuries to remove any notion of value, moral and aesthetic, in it. She argues that the moral authority of nature arises from three different conceptions of nature: First, nature as specifying the kind that marks out an object for what it is, the second refers to the idea of nature as in the local, the fauna and flora, whereas the third conception—which is modern—is that nature is 'comprehensive, uniform, and universal' (2002: 375). According to Daston, what really distinguishes these types of nature is the distinction between custom and law, where law as universal captures the modernist conception of nature. She further notes, 'In the course of the eighteenth century, the notion of natural regularities modeled on customs gave way to that of regularities modeled on laws. This was a momentous metaphorical shift' (2002: 383). All these complex processes actually work towards a very important and defining moment in modern science, namely the investing of authority in nature. This is an authority which arises from this unique process of naturalizing the natural through ideas such as the laws of nature.

Laws and the Authority of the Natural

Laws of nature are fundamental to the practice of science. Galileo not only recognizes the importance of the laws of nature but also relates them to a metaphysical presupposition about language. The way science conceptualizes nature is very similar to the way it conceptualizes objects for scientific analysis, and this is to reduce an object to a collection of measurable properties. Thus, the sun becomes an object for scientific analysis when it is reduced to a set of values of properties of mass, temperature, size, and so on. Literally, the sun is nothing more than this collection. Newton's method which consists in replacing objects by a point located in the centre of the mass of the object was a great revolution in that it made it possible to do mathematics of physical objects. The claim that nothing is 'really' lost when an object is reduced to a point, although it retains its value of mass, is an important meta-physical claim about the nature of objects. What is important to realize is that what science does for objects it does for nature. This means that nature is first of all conceptualized as an object which is characterized by physical properties. In so doing, the human is kept outside nature and yet brought into nature when needed. But for nature to be a scientific object, as nature and not as a set of natural objects alone, it is necessary to describe it in terms of essential properties that cannot be dropped in idealization of objects (such as mass). Thus, when nature becomes a proper scientific object, it too is idealized and reduced to its essential properties. And the most important essential property that stands to characterize nature is the set of the 'laws of nature'.

The laws of nature, for science, are far more important than the objects of nature. Laws are fundamentally relations and they explain the order of nature. They explain why objects behave the way they do, and many influential scientists hold the view that laws govern nature: objects in nature are governed by natural laws in a manner similar to the way people in a society are governed by social laws. These laws of nature are very specific, and they can describe and explain a wide variety of phenomena. For a scientific description of nature, particularly in the way it was conceptualized in the early periods of modern science, the whole of nature is ideally reducible to a collection of its laws. Everything else follows with a little bit of added information here and there!

While the idea of the laws of nature is a powerful one invoked to understand the workings of nature, it nevertheless comes with its own baggage. Galileo's observation that nature is an open book whose laws are written in the language of mathematics, at one stroke relates the two essential components of modern science: mathematics and laws. The influential view that laws govern natural objects seems to add an agency to nature and gives nature authority over its objects.[3] Laws of nature are diktats on objects; they have to necessarily obey them. Laws themselves encode ideas of necessity in different ways. One of the influential ways of philosophically understanding laws is that laws are necessary relations between universals, which thus imposes on nature the metaphysics of necessity.

So nature governs the behaviour of objects and this explains why objects behave the way they do. But how does nature govern? Is it through these laws or are these laws only an instrument of a higher agency of nature? If we do not want to ascribe any notion of agency to nature, then we have to equate the governance of natural objects as being identical to the expression of the laws of nature. Laws then perhaps describe the uniformity and universality of natural actions and motions. However, given the primacy of laws in science, and their role in explanation and predictivity, such a 'secular' view of laws might be difficult to hold.

As Beebee (2000) points out, the fundamental difference between the necessity view of laws and the Humean view is that for the former, laws are seen as governing and for the latter they are merely descriptive.[4] For the former, there is a metaphysical consequence of laws, in that facts, and future facts, are grounded in laws: 'laws are the ontological *ground* of the future facts' (2000: 578). A law is required to make sense of a variety of phenomena like uniformity, repeatability, distinction between the accidental and the essential, explaining counterfactuals, and even predicting. These properties can be grounded within a real property of nature, something called laws, or they can be accepted as something that 'just happens'. Given that most scientists, as well as the claims within the discourse of science, seem to be committed to the governance view, it is necessary to consider the presuppositions of this belief. The realist theory of laws entails some notion of governance.

---

[3] See Feynman (2017), for example.

[4] There are different ways to understand the metaphysics of laws. One is to understand laws as necessary relations between universals (Armstrong and others). In contrast is the Humean view, the Ramsey-Lewis description of laws is that which understands laws as those 'generalizations which figure in the most economical true axiomatization of all the particular matters of fact that obtain' (Beebee 2000: 571). There is also a realist view of laws related to essential properties.

According to this view, laws of nature are real and present in the universe. The governance argument is that laws not only describe universal regularities but also *'govern* what will happen' (2000: 579). This also has an important consequence on the influential idea of determinism of natural phenomena.

Nature functions as an authority for science by being the ultimate justification for its knowledge claims. Scientific knowledge is always tested for its correspondence with nature, with the way the world is. The rejection of religious authority about the world is based on this incompatibility between the claims of a religion or a philosophy like the Aristotelian one, and the sensory experiences of the world. Every utterance of science is ideally to be compared with the world as is given. Thus, the authority of nature is based merely on its presence; by being what it is, it constrains what science can say about it. It is important to realize what has been done to both science and nature in this project: they are both reduced, idealized, and essentialized to laws. What is essential to nature are the laws of nature—the objects of nature are accidental and do not really matter to the workings of nature. Similarly, what is essential to humans are the laws that govern humans—particular individuals are accidental and do not really matter to the working of a society or of a human community. This is the strength and the price we pay for investing authority within nature.

Daston (2014: 579) points out that the authority of nature has been used right from early times and was used to support positions ranging from oppression to liberation: 'Nature's authority has been enlisted by reactionaries and by revolutionaries, by the devout and secular alike.' However, the domain of values which seemed to have characterized nature lost its hold in the nineteenth century when a distinction was made between the 'is' and the 'ought': The domain of facts and the domain of values, with nature being in the former. This is the well-known argument of 'naturalistic fallacy', first used by G.E. Moore in 1903, and has played a leading role in keeping ethics away from the domain of science, since science is seen to be about facts and not about values, which ethics is about.[5] Daston makes the important point that this presumed fallacy is really one that is based on a particular view of nature that develops during the eighteenth century.

[5] See Sarukkai (2009).

The useful lesson to learn from Daston's analysis is the influence of the construction of nature in modernity as the ultimate authority. If earlier in the European tradition, moral values could be grounded in nature, in the Enlightenment period across various domains including aesthetics and politics, nature comes to have 'sweeping normative authority' (Daston 2002: 409). This was possible in two steps: First, nature takes over the divine attributes and then 'de-divinize nature altogether' (2002: 409), which as a consequence leads to the naturalistic fallacy. But the de-divinization did not remove the problem of authority and only succeeded in replacing the divine agency with the problematic agency of the laws of nature. Daston also argues that authority, whether in the moral or the political domain, is always 'stratigraphic', namely that authority is always derived from a bedrock foundation. But, finally, what really links the imagination of the natural and the moral order together is the notion of order: Whatever the dissimilarities be, 'the moral and the natural are both intrinsically ordered' (Daston 2002: 411) and the consequence of this modern refiguration of nature meant that the moral order became more 'mutable' and nature became inaccessible as ground for it.

Naturalization itself is a process that essentially makes nature the ground for a phenomenon, that is, makes nature the authority for that phenomenon to be possible. Daston (1992), in showing how the female intellect was naturalized in different ways at different times and places, succeeds in showing how a history of naturalization is itself tied to different conceptualizations of nature. In its essential form, naturalization 'refers to ways of fortifying various social, cultural, economic, or political conventions by presenting them as part of natural order' (1992: 209). This is a move in which philosophers and scientists have participated in order to legitimize social conventions by taking them into a natural order. The articulation of the capacities of women has perhaps paid the highest price in this process of naturalization, which Daston refers to as 'ideology at full strength' (1992: 210). The processes of naturalization are so deep and not necessarily obvious—Galileo, she notes, '"naturalizes" the shaky political order of the Medicis by christening the newly discovered moons of Jupiter in their honour' and similarly Darwin naturalizes 'British political economy in the theory of natural selection' (1992: 210). Hobbes calls the great commonwealth, the Leviathan, 'but an artificiall Man' (Judd 2009: 52), and this model of man for society like in the model of caste is another pointer to the naturalization of a concept through an analogy with the body and the workings of the body.

Thus, we can understand how the very idea of nature is socially formed in order to highlight and frame some of its capabilities which makes it amenable for its use in the sciences. Some might point out that the ideas of the laws of nature are essential for physics but not for other disciplines such as biology. But the argument here is that at the time of the origin of the social sciences, and even in the times of Durkheim and others, the physics view of nature was dominant. Moreover, some of the philosophical assumptions about nature and its relationship to science have continued even in other disciplines like biology. The main motivation in offering this argument is merely to show how nature functions as an authority, what we refer to as 'non-agential' authority. This construction of nature is how modernity answers the question: How is authority without agency, without an author, possible? It is striking that the way the social comes to exert authority has many interesting parallels with this process.

Vedas and Non-agential Authority

There is a curious parallel that should capture our attention. This possibility of non-agential authority occurs in another context, which is the argument of the Mīmāmsa tradition about the author of the Vedas. What is of interest here is not the potential similarities between Mīmāmsa and modernist narratives of nature but more about what is philosophically needed to sustain a rational argument for authorless authority. For this is what the Mīmāmsakas aim to do—give a rational argument for the ultimate authority of the Vedas without invoking God as the author of these texts. As much as the recognition that what gives authority to nature is not the mere existence of something called nature but its laws and its language, so also is the recognition by the Mīmāmsakas that what gives authority to the Vedas is what Arnold (2014) refers to as the 'mind-independent reality of language'.

We can begin with a curious historical phenomenon of the lack of authorship in classical Sanskrit texts. In encountering Indian philosophy, for example, we are often struck by the absolute lack of the personal within the intellectual domain. Sometimes authors are not named and where they are named, they have no historicity about them. Pollock (1989) points to the astonishing fact that 'Sanskrit texts are anonymous' and the absence of a referential author is widespread across genres. Literary criticism till the tenth century makes no reference to individual authors, nor do philosophical texts who invoke nameless non-individuated debate with the opponents. Pollock points out that 'we can read thousands of pages of Sanskrit on any imaginable subject and not encounter a single passing reference to a historical person, place or event—or at least to any that, historically speaking, matters' (1989: 606). He then relates this lack of explicit historical reference to the influence of Mīmāmsa since they considered history to be irrelevant and antithetical to 'real knowledge'. For the Mīmāmsakas, the Vedas are transcendent texts and the aim of their philosophy is to show how this is so. One way to do this is to claim that language itself is transcendent in some sense.

Pollock discusses two arguments for the authorless and transcendent nature of the Vedas. The transcendent character is proved by the facts of there being no author and no beginning to the Vedas, which is furthermore supported by the ahistoricity of their contents. Pollock suggests that this argument of the Mīmāmsakas influenced the other classical texts in the Indian tradition and thus ends up erasing any form of historical referentiality or historical consciousness. Furthermore, he points out that since almost all classical texts traced themselves to the Vedas, they transferred the non-referentiality of the Vedas to themselves. As Pollock notes, 'Discursive texts that came to be composed under the sign of the Veda eliminated historical referentiality and with it all possibility of historiography' (1989: 610).

Similar arguments abound in the traditional understanding of the Mīmāmsa tradition.[6] There are some important implications of the Mīmāmsa argument about authorless authority, especially because of their stated aim of rationally proving this character of the Vedas. First of all, it gives a model of how something can be authorless and yet remain an authority. In the case of the Vedas, it is the very fact of being author-less that gives it authority—an interesting variation of the foundation argument. But the authority is also possible through the eternality of language and not just the lack of historical referentiality which Pollock

---

[6] See the volume by Pandurangi (2006).

refers to. While Pollock is interested in giving an explanation for the lack of historical referentiality in Sanskrit texts, we want to look at this as a paradigmatic model for agentless authority.

The non-agential mode of understanding Vedas needs some metaphysical support, which is really the task for the Mīmāmsa tradition. Kumārila Bhatta (seventh century CE), a prominent pūrvamīmāmsa philosopher, offers important epistemological arguments to rationally argue for the authority of the Vedas without an agential author. The Vedas are like nature in that both are the final authorities but there is no author, no foundation to that authority. Just as authorless nature grounds scientific knowledge (which itself is knowledge of nature) so also do the Vedas ground moral knowledge or dharma through the same mechanism. What is of relevance to us from this discussion are the parallels between the authority of the social (not to be confused with all social institutions or the political) and these non-agential authorities of nature and the Vedas. In the everyday social, our claim is that the different socials exert authority through these anonymous and non-agential ways.

The Relationship between the Natural and Social

An exercise such as this is useful to reemphasize the point that the structure of authority draws upon various forms of legitimization, and reconfiguring nature is one very important element. Therefore, to understand the changing nature of authority in our times it is worth paying attention to the subtle ways in which nature is being constantly recast in contemporary science, philosophy, politics, and so on. As we mentioned earlier, authority many times functions as a synonym of the everyday social. When people refer to the social in expressions like 'social pressure' or when they say that they have to do something because it is expected of them, they are basically referring to a notion of authority. In most cases, this authority is not embodied in any way: so, there is no specific individual or institution which has this authority. There is a large invisible space that exerts this pressure.

Many times in the context of the social, nature is used as an authority just as it happens in science. Natural is an alternate expression for authority, used when people refer to natural traits of women, caste-based qualities, sexuality, and so on. Through this, the question of authority rests on an ambiguous idea of nature. In the case of another important use of the social in the everyday world, the action of the social is often used synonymously for the 'action' of tradition. In both these cases of nature and tradition, in their relation to the social, there is a common element. They are both examples of non-agential authority in the sense that there is no specific agent who functions as the figure of authority. The fact that there is no specific figure of authority is really the essential marker of this form of authority. There is no agent who can take responsibility for wielding authority and thus this authority has no obvious notion of responsibility that is available. Tradition functions as a non-agential, diffused, ambiguous authority of the social, one that is legitimized in the everyday social repeatedly. These actions of the non-agential authority are many times far more powerful than those where the authority can be identified. Marriages in India are unaffordable for many families of the bride and yet they are forced to organize marriages which they cannot afford, leading to debt in many cases. In the many incidents of farmer's suicide, much in the news over the last few years, it was found that part of the debt trap they got into was because of marriage and other 'socially expected' expenditure. The power of the authority of the social is so strong that against all the power of individual autonomy it is able to make people perform actions which create great problems for them. Our aim in this analysis of authority in this chapter is to show how the most powerful of authorities is this non-agential one since it is the most difficult to resist or hold accountable. This is all the more reason why it is essential to understand the nature of the social that can influence such actions in a society.

The social acts through the invocation of the notion of tradition and that of the natural. One can distinguish this form of non-agential action from authority which is agential, and which arises as political authority. Political authority arises through agents of authority in a way that is different from the function of tradition as authority. In the case of the social, the primary task of authority is not order whereas in the case of political authority it is order. If social authority is diffused and pervasive, political authority is agented, situated, focussed, and spatially and temporally located.

The everyday social also speaks as if there is an ontology of the natural. Very often, the natural is described as if they are specific kinds of experiences. It is important to take seriously the ways by which nature appear to us as experiences in statements like 'smell nature', 'feel nature', 'breathe in nature', and so on. One might say that these are expressions whose denotations are not really nature, or something called the natural, but this argument may be nothing more than saying that material embodiment is the only sense of reality that we can have. If social science really has to learn something from the natural sciences, it is not merely some idealized methodology or emphasis on quantification. Rather, it is the engagement with the extremely rich ontologies that populate natural science, complex ontologies which are all not reducible to one kind of material entities. The social is also one such creature which becomes absolutely necessary for a meaningful understanding of the social in all its manifestations.

We will end with a final note on authority. Agentless or authorless authority is not a special phenomenon restricted only to the examples given above. There are many social phenomena which try to legitimize themselves on such authority. Rumour and gossip are very good examples of this. The way in which rumour and gossip act as authority—act as a source for some news, for example—is done in the same way as non-agential authority. Rumour and gossip really have no authors, nobody who can be held accountable. It is dispersive and generates power in its retellings. But it is also extremely influential, and many times can dictate social action, including drastic ones like communal riots. Rumours and gossip can have material impact on society. (There is always an intermediary role that language plays; this too is a characteristic common to the agentless authority of science and the Vedas.) Today, social media functions as the dominant source of gossip and rumour. This medium, like Twitter and Facebook, attempts to legitimize itself and begins to function as a form of social authority through a similar mechanism.

Unless we understand the nature of authority that operates in diverse ways in the everyday social, it would not be possible to really make meaningful social changes. Many important social movements, we would argue, have explicitly or implicitly understood the nature of this diffusive, non-agential authority of the social and acted on that basis. The response of Gandhi and Ambedkar to authority is illustrative of this claim. As mentioned earlier, politics is concerned with agential authority and thus looking at the social through this form of authority is to convert the social into the political. We can thus understand Ambedkar's claim about *Manusmriti* as an attempt to relocate authority into a specific agent since that allows politics to be possible.

7 Metaphysical and Lived Time of the Social

One response to our argument at the end of the last chapter could be that what we are talking about is nothing but the socialization of individuals which makes them act as if they are under the force of the social. While this is a reasonable way to look at this phenomenon, nevertheless it raises the question as to why humans get socialized so easily. How and why they are so effortlessly socialized into doing and believing so many things which they may actually find inconvenient or even harmful? Moreover, why after knowing that they are under the influence of socialization they are still unable to get out of it? The empirical model described here explains socialization because there is a concrete access to the social. Socialization is a response to the social and not independent of it.

In this chapter, we add another layer to the various qualities of the social, a quality which, in our view, is the most important element of the social—the ethical. Or more aptly, the experience of the ethical. A social is cognized through an affectual, ethical relationship along with its other perceptual modes. The special character of this experience is what marks out the uniqueness of the human social. Thus, our fundamental experience of the social is ethical. There are two aspects to this claim. One is that there is an experiential domain of the ethical in relation to the social, and the second is that the essential relation between different socials, the relation which marks them out as socials, is also an ethical one. At this juncture, we will not base these relationships on particular theories of ethics but use this experiential sense of ethics to describe these two forms of relationships. This chapter and the next will explore both these aspects in some detail.

Belongingness that characterizes the everyday social is primarily an ethical experience. It is the encounter with ordinariness that creates a minimum moral. Inequality is socially produced, starting with the experiences in a family, but so are 'higher' ethical principles. Belongingness of the everyday social is not a coming together due to utilitarian concerns or because it maximizes something for the individuals in that social. The sense of belonging arises as a spontaneous, embodied action, an embodied response to other humans with whom there is an experience of belonging. The ethics of belongingness is like the Levinasian ethics of face-to-face and Varela's embodied ethics. The everyday ethics is not developed through certain types of 'rational' thought but is one that is experienced as one of the experiences of the social. One of the primary components of this ethical response related to belongingness is moral equality, which is the expression of the symmetric nature of the experience of belongingness. Understanding the social has to be foregrounded in such a comprehensive field of moral equality. The experience of the social offers at least a moral minimum aimed at the elimination of hierarchy even in its perceptual form.

The experience of the social leads to the first awareness of a broader notion of equality—equality as it arises in being together. This equality is not the equality of material resources or positional good. Belongingness has been extensively written about by psychologists and although they accept the importance of belongingness to sociality, they still tend to view it as a decision made by the individual. So, for example, they talk about the 'need to belong' which involves various kinds of justifications for wanting to belong with others such as seeking 'positive social interaction with others' (Over 2016: 2). Thus, their understanding of belonging puts the onus of wanting to belong on the individual. But the belonging we are talking about is an experience of sociality and not a decision-making process. This is what happens in the processes of social belonging and this is primarily an ethical experience. This type of belonging is related to equality in terms of ethical resources such as decent treatment and affectionate attention.

Moral equality gets processed through such interactions that in turn are conditioned by the degree of affectionate attention that is inter-subjectively practiced by the members of the society as well as the degree of ethical commitment to decent treatment that is reflectively endorsed by the members of a social. Since equal attention, as an ethical need of a sentient being, is communicated through feeling, seeing (attention), and touching (treatment), it is internally attached to a normative social. In other words, the social is constitutive of moral equality which in turn is based on ethics of attention and human treatment that is essential to human flourishing. One cannot access moral equality even if it were to directly descend from the top of the normative scale of moral values. Similarly, it does not flow from an abstract universal. It cannot be accessed from the spiritual standpoint as well.

On following this line of argument, one may find it problematic to access moral equality through the perspective of Advaita Vedanta of Narayana Guru or the metaphysics of Gandhi, two influential crusaders against caste inequality and untouchability, since it is accessed through the experience of inequality which occurs in a particular context. Inequality is the experience of non-belonging or the rejection of belongingness. Hence, context-specific inequality acts as a barricade in terms of accessing such moral equality associated with the experience of sociality. It is in this sense that we need to appreciate the contemporary relevance of Ambedkar who explains how caste has been the insurmountable/irremovable barricade that has made it difficult for many to access moral equality. In fact, it has stalled our efforts even to comprehend a moral value such as moral equality which, for its realization, needs a continuous interrogation of what he calls 'graded inequality', emanating from and shaped by the caste system. Thus, it becomes necessary for us to foreground Ambedkar's position in the available context of Narayana Guru and Gandhi.

It is important to realize that moral equality in the form of the social arises not as an intellectual position but as one that is grounded in the experiences of the social. The implication is that the presence of the experienced social is the necessary precondition for moral experiences of equality, dignity, respect, and so on. This does not mean that every experienced social will be morally grounded. All we can say is that this is a necessary condition for human morality. The excessive shift to certain forms of non-embodied reason in ethics misses a most important point about human sociality and its relation to morality. This does not mean that every social is an ethical domain. We know otherwise. But the impersonal socials of institutions have been more brutal, violent, and destructive as the history of Europe in the last century shows.

Narayan Guru and the Question of Equality

It is instructive to consider two profoundly important thinkers, Narayana Guru (NG) and his foremost disciple, Nataraja Guru (NaG), and their response to the question of the inequality in caste. Narayana Guru consistently rejects any notion of caste distinctions and hierarchies. The theme of oneness is very important for NG's philosophical and spiritual vision. At one level, the claim to oneness is quite simple: it is merely an assertion that all humanity is one and that the differences one sees are only in the world of appearances. The answer to why Advaita becomes very important to this project lies precisely in this simple claim that the appearance of the world is illusory and that the true reality of the world is a form of unity. Can this claim, which repeatedly occurs in NG's and his disciples' writings, do enough work for the eradication of caste distinctions?

Jāti Mīmāmsā is a poem written by Narayana Guru. NaG gives a commentary of this poem in his book *The Word of the Guru*. NaG suggests that NG's use of *manuṣyatvam* (humanity) is primarily about the recognition of all humans as belonging to one common species. However, this would not really be true of the larger Indian philosophical understanding of being human. NaG argues that all human beings are equal, and the caste hierarchy is a product of social forces. As he notes, 'While historical, sociological, economic, or even dialectical circumstances may have caused the complex configurations of caste this does not mean that it has a raison d'être of its own' (Guru 2008: 280). Placing the origin of caste within specific historical and sociological influences misses the central idea of caste that it indeed has a raison d'être of its own, one which is philosophical in nature. In fact, this philosophical origin of caste—and it has two faces—makes the phenomenon of caste consistently escape the sociological and the historical. An implication of this is that if caste was merely a socio-historical-economic phenomenon then one could in principle eradicate caste by removing those conditions which enabled it in the first instance. However, the difficulty in eradicating the imagination of caste and its current consolidation in India points not just to the difficulty in eradicating the social conditions that sustain caste but also the difficulty in eradicating the metaphysical presuppositions supporting it.

NaG was aware of the philosophical foundations of caste and he seems to have overlooked this, at least in his commentary on the *Jāti Mīmāmsā*. Nothing explains why one needs a deep engagement with philosophical systems to eradicate caste unless there was a philosophical problem at the heart of caste. To make the statement that all humans are equal does not need philosophical argumentation. It does not need a serious reading of the Advaitic tradition. At first glance, it might seem that NG does not directly deploy Advaita in any serious manner to critique caste. While there is an obvious extrapolation of non-dualism to the claim that there is really no difference between human beings since there is one single unity, it is nevertheless an unclear claim. To use non-dualism to argue that all humans are 'equal' needs a lot more work, and NaG does not do that in his commentary on the *Jāti Mīmāmsā*. By not doing that, he misses the fundamental insight in NG's approach to the question of caste. NG's invocation of the long philosophical tradition of Vedānta, and Advaita in particular, is a recognition that social action needs to tackle—along with the social factors—its metaphysical presuppositions. The two fundamental metaphysical notions that philosophically uphold caste are the notions of untouchability and karma, both of which should be seen in their metaphysical garb and not only as the forms of their instantiation in our world.[1]

While there is some unease about metaphysical approaches to caste emancipation in current social politics, there is no such ambiguity in NG's own invocation of Advaita and his understanding of its link to emancipatory politics. So, one can see his work as consistently enlarging and interpreting Advaita for his context. Whether it is his *Darśana-Māla* or *The Vedānta Sutras*, he is engaging in recording and interpreting Advaita for a common understanding. This itself is the first political step of recovering non-dualism for potential social emancipation. In NG, oneness in human beings forms the essential part of the ideal social. Even in Gandhi this oneness also forms the part of the ideal social. But Gandhi, unlike NG, uses the concept of

---

[1] For a discussion on the metaphysical presuppositions surrounding untouchability, see Guru and Sarukkai (2012).

metaphysical time (self-in-incarnation) and the theological spaces like temple as the context within which he seeks to establish his notion of the social. Moreover, the concept of rebirth or incarnation in Gandhi is complex and deep and is not at all simple as it is made out to be by his critics. He says, 'I do not want to be reborn. But if I have to be reborn, I should be born an untouchable, so that I may share their sorrows, sufferings, and the affronts levelled at them, in order that I may endeavour to free myself and them from that miserable condition' (Gandhi 1921: 144).

This idea of incarnation in Gandhi has been endorsed by Mahadev Bhai Desai who produces the following quote from Gandhi: 'He who does not believe in it [incarnation] cannot have any real faith in the regeneration of fallen souls' (Chatterjee 1983: 25). Who, according to Gandhi, is a fallen soul? We could say that it is a person who fails to serve society or, to put it differently, a person who is interested only in self-service (service of the self). It is needless to emphasize here that Gandhi would suggest that such regeneration (moral equality) of Indian society has to be achieved in lived time only. For this regeneration, he chose different spaces, the ashram being the dominant one, but also the temple, which forms one of the important spaces for such an articulation. Arguably, for NG, the question of social equality mediated through temple spaces seems to acquire an abstract character in that it becomes symbolic. He does not want to put an idol in the *garbha gruha*, the inner shrine of the temple, and instead suggests putting up a lamp in the inner sacred core of the temple. This is quite fascinating and a step forward.

But Gandhi's effort to redeem the value of justice and equality in lived time is also evident from his unfailing support for the Temple Entry movement. Gandhi does say that foreign invasions that destroyed the temples in India in historical time are wrong, but he also said the denial of temple entry to Harijan was a much more serious social devastation; a crime committed by the high caste Hindus. Gandhi seeks equality in the karmic spiritual time. He seems to use karma theory quite innovatively in favour of equality. He achieves this goal through the demobilization of the high caste Hindus from their deep-seated prejudices that militate against the value of equality. Let us put Gandhi in proper perspective through paraphrasing his overall take on the role of sacred spaces in constructively mediating between inequality and equality. Thus, in the spirit of Gandhi, we may say, if you think that temples are the sacred sites of ritual purification where you can wash your sins of the past and if you think that untouchables have become untouchable as a consequences of their sins that they committed in previous birth, then it becomes your sacred duty and responsibility to allow them to enter the temple so that they could wash their sins.

In this regard, it is also important to note here that Gandhi, like Ambedkar, suggests the locus of action to be the same temple and not a parallel temple or a separate temple. He is not asking the untouchables to create their own temple. Gandhi was forcing limits on orthodox forces by not approving the construction of a separate temple. He was using the notion of rebirth with a cosmic desire to become a bhangi (untouchable scavenger) in the next birth, only to reassert the importance of individual scavenging.

Rebirth, when viewed from the Gandhian position, is aimed at establishing equality in spiritual time and not in lived time. The notion of rebirth also suggests the impossibility of individuating the obnoxious practice of scavenging in lived time. Taking our cue from Gandhi, we can make a hermeneutic move to try and establish the link between the temple as sacred spaces and the creative process of moral regeneration through the idea of incarnation. As mentioned above, Gandhi is not suggesting the creation of a separate temple for the untouchables but wants the same temple to be opened out to them. This insistence on the same temple has two significant aspects. First, it forces limits on the orthodox section of the high caste Hindus, and second, it has the moral force to convert the space from being empty, even in its sacred sense, into a space filled with the normative substance of justice and moral equality. The ideal social engulfs into its normative grip even a sacred site such as a temple. Perhaps other conglomerations such as the *Kumbha Mela* or *Varkari Dindi* (in Maharashtra) can also be thought of as forming a part of this social. Thus, we may argue that the temple itself undergoes a transformation through this process. By allowing the social to enter its shrines, the temple achieves its 'mokasha', or becomes the active site for mokasha, that is *Manuski* in Marathi and 'dignity' in English in Ambedkar's normative vocabulary. The temple-entry movements by Ambedkar, and less by Gandhi, are aimed at giving life to spaces that are socially lifeless (in the sense of the social discussed above) such as a temple with proscriptions on entry. The calibre of justice leading to equality has to be understood in terms of the social meaning being present in the structure with its normative calibre. Both Gandhi and Ambedkar are in agreement in as much as both of them are using the temple to underscore the point that the high caste Hindus need to acknowledge Dalit rights to justice and equality that could be realized in lived time.

The Social in Karmic Time and Lived Time

What is ethical or unethical about caste practices? As we mentioned in the beginning of this chapter, the different socials are characterized by ethical relations. Thus, an interactive relationship regulated by caste has a definite bearing on the ethical relations between two socials. We begin with caste because caste practices illustrate well this relationship between socials. We can look at one much-discussed problem within caste, namely the inherent inequality between the different castes. What is the nature of this inequality? The nature of inequality becomes discernible through its conceptual capacity to contrast with equality. The idea of equality is central to the understanding of modern conceptions of justice; however, one of the most difficult tasks is to clarify exactly what this concept means. This is especially true when we talk of the equality of all human beings. We begin with the observation that inequality is itself a relation between socials which often gets expressed as if it is a relation only between individuals. When inequality is proposed as a point of comparison between two individuals, it is often a comparison of the social representations of these two individuals. Much of the misunderstanding about inequality is because of its individual-centric meaning, instead of its foundational meaning that arises as a relation first between different socials. It is these different socials which are related to each other through a sense of inequality, and it is this inequality that permeates the individuals within a group. In the case of the inequality in caste, we will see how these inequalities are sustained primarily because of the ontology of karma, hereditary birth/rebirth, and so on. All these are 'social terms' and it is impossible to reduce them to individual characteristics alone.

What kind of inequality characterizes inequality in caste? In the case of caste, the assertion that all humans belong to one species is not enough to guarantee equality to all human beings. This is primarily because the biological and species notion of the human does not exhaust the space of being human. This incompleteness has been at the core of all theories of the human since there is always something to distinguish one biological human from another. There is always a level at which humans can be distinguished and then hierarchized. The notion of rationality is one good example by which humans were distinguished not just from animals, but from one another, as well as from one civilization to another. Thus, there are limits to our understanding of ontological equality, although this conception can be used against those who discriminate on the basis of colour or race.

Caste inequality is sustained by a process of naturalization which marks out the speciality of caste experience. By its very definition, it does not make sense to say that inequality can be naturalized since inequality is a social judgement and not a personal characteristic. This is the reason why difference is not the same as being unequal. We accept differences, such as the difference between any two individuals, but we do not accept that they are unequal. However, there have been many attempts to naturalize inequality. The invocation of race, brain size, colour, and caste are potent examples of the attempt to justify inequality between individuals and groups by taking recourse to some natural characteristic. The inequality in society faced by women, Dalits, and others are but a reflection of the success of this naturalizing tendency. As discussed in Guru and Sarukkai (2012), even untouchability gets naturalized and comes to be seen as the property of an individual. As we saw earlier, such a constant articulation of the natural is but a consequence of the formation of the social.

One way by which caste gets naturalized is through its association with karma. Weber's argument that karma legitimized the caste system is part of the everyday understanding of caste. Echoing popular variations on the theme that the present status one has is a consequence of past actions in earlier births, Weber went on to argue that rejecting one's caste belongingness would be punished in future reincarnations (Milner 1993). Many writers have rejected Weber's claims on various grounds and the many complex and local narratives of karma point to the limitation of Weber's view. However, the idea that one pays in the present what one has sowed not just in this life but in earlier ones is a theme that is replayed over and over again from vedāntic texts to folk tales. What is most surprising is that we see this in popular narratives of caste in today's society, particularly from the growing strident voice of upper castes who are against the caste mobilization of the other castes. We also see this equally stridently in the narratives of genetics and their relation to caste. In fact, both these arguments (karma and genetics) are a form of the naturalization of caste.

The relation between caste and Hindu eschatology is possible because both of them are 'systems of structured inequality' (Milner 1993: 302). Milner goes on to list three central features of caste: (*a*) The lack of mobility across (relatively many) caste boundaries, (*b*) caste membership based solely on 'inheritance and ascription', and (*c*) significant energy devoted to maintaining caste distinctions (1993: 303). He then argues that the three major elements of Hinduism, namely samsara, karma, and mokṣa, are the structural inversions of these three characteristics of caste. Samsara is mobility across births. As Milner correctly notes, religious texts have continuously stressed how a sinful life will lead to birth in a lower caste; the key point here is that in Hinduism, there is continuous mobility across births but no mobility in this world (1993: 304). The recognition that this worldly existence is incomplete—at least for final judgements of any kind—is fundamental to how we conceptualize ethics and inequality in Hinduism. This will also lead us to reconsider the question of inequality among castes.

Karma as merit, according to Milner, is the structural reversal corresponding to the second characteristic of caste: that caste is based on inheritance and ascription. As Kane points out (quoted in 1993: 305), the law of karma makes existence deterministic. By this token, the law of karma is a true law of justice which works across many births instead of just one. It also points out that a principle of justice and of inequality restricted to the lived world is always underdetermined and hence cannot be exhausted by enworlded situations.

So, to answer what exactly is unequal in a caste hierarchy it is necessary to broaden not the 'space' of equality, which Sen (2009) rightly criticizes, but the 'time' of equality. First of all, the very notion of equality has to be broadened to take into account this intergenerational karmic process. Within this process, there are at least two distinct domains of inequality: one is the local or embodied inequality (inequality in the present world) and the other is a generational equality (equality across rebirths). In other words, the domain over which we aggregate measures of equality or inequality is not just of the experiences of this world but experiences across rebirths. In the overall sum of generations, equality is not only sustained but is enshrined as a fundamental principle. But in the localized mode of one existence, equality is not guaranteed. It is easy to see how themes in justice map out in this theory, such as the relation between retributive justice and generational equality.

The principle of 'intergenerational equality' is that all human beings are completely equal when counted across generations. One is always in a transient caste in this life because you do not know which caste you will belong to in your next life, if you are reborn as a human in the first place. The twice-born nature of Brahminhood is only an allegory of the repeated birth one takes through rebirths and an indication of the possibility that one is not guaranteed birth in the same caste in each rebirth. The problem of caste inequality at an experiential individual level is negated through this argument that the state of being in a caste is only temporary—even for the untouchables. That is, in the narrative of karma, an untouchable can go out of that state and be reborn in a caste or even attain liberation and not be reborn as a human at all. And equally, a Brahmin who does not practice what he is supposed to can be reborn into any other caste or as an untouchable or even as an animal.

Thus, one might understand this to say that across generations, across the span of rebirths, there is a fundamental principle of equality. This is not the equality of human individuals but the equality of individual souls. In other words, the most fundamental principle of equality is given to the essence of the embodied humans, their souls. Souls have no caste, no class. They do not carry these 'temporal' markings but only 'value' markings. In their very embodiment they lose their equality and it is these embodied humans who now carry the possibility of inequalities.

This fundamental principle of equality of all beings, not in their temporal embodied manifestation but across the span of rebirths, can justly be called the principle of justice in any philosophy that upholds the doctrine of karma. We could call this 'intergenerational equality' as equality guaranteed across generations. The inequality which characterizes caste hierarchy should be seen as inequalities which arise by the very act of embodiment of these souls and thus are representations of an 'embodied inequality'. This is the reason why caste hierarchies cannot be reduced only to sociological, political, or economic conditions.

The metaphysical grounding of these hierarchies arises at the first instance of embodiment and birth. Thus, it should be no surprise that the moment of birth is so fundamental to the dialectic opposition which sustains caste, namely the hereditary inherence of caste in both the Brahmins and the Untouchables.

One might respond to the above argument by arguing that modern ethical principles have no place for notions such as rebirth, karma, and so on. However, if a significant number of people use this narrative to make sense of their lives and if these notions are part of everyday cultural practices of a society, then how do we construct a meaningful ethical discourse other than by claiming that they are all mistaken or superstitious? The everyday social is suffused with these narratives. By asking this question, we are not suggesting that the karmic theory should be accepted within modern ethical theories; rather, what we need to understand is that to counteract the pervasiveness of the caste discourse, we need to target many such conceptual structures which invisibly act as the foundation of the caste social. Also, the argument around rebirth is quite independent of the act of rebirth in that the formal structures around this argument are reproduced even in theories of justice which do not have terms like rebirth in them.

The crucial point about this argument is that the metaphysical baggage of caste creates an obstruction to the possibility of a desirable relation between the different socials (more on this in the next chapter). This is because the caste social can never be fulfilled as a social in our world, meaning that the caste social always exceeds the experiential space of caste through its relation to karma and intergenerationality. The destabilization of caste as a social process is reinforced through its connection to the domain of the natural and borrows its authority from it (see the earlier chapter).

Most interestingly, these principles that support caste contribute to the task of creating 'social time'. The idea of caste through its association with heredity and rebirth is actually a creation of 'social time', ways in which time is experienced and narrativized in social experiences. In general, these are the complex ways by which time is experienced and spoken about in the everyday social which is pervaded by culture, caste, and religion. To understand the significance of this relationship between the everyday social and time, we will take a brief look at the way time is configured socially.

Social Time

If there is one axis around which modern societies function it is the idea of time. But there is no one single conception of time and hence part of being or becoming a social is also to reconfigure time along with the social which leads to a particular notion of time. Equivalently, the ontology of the social is like the ontology of time. A parallel discussion, made famous by Henri Lefebvre, was about the relationship between space and the social. From the aforementioned discussion on caste, it is possible to claim that the caste social is a social modelled on particular conceptualizations of time. The parallel between the ontology of the social and the ontology of time is also captured in the way we invoke these ideas so effortlessly, as well as experience them or at least talk as if we experience them. In our everyday world, we do not reject an ontology of time, the 'reality' of it in some sense nor try to reduce it to physical elements. But social scientists, by and large, have tended to do this with the social and to assume that the social as an entity is not imaginable, except as an aggregation of physical entities. So, there is nothing really odd about the way the social can exist as a 'real' entity, even though it is not physical like individuals are. The relation between the social and time is not new and one can argue that every epoch of new socials corresponds to new visions of time.

Cultural beliefs about time have had a great impact on the way we live and on the way we think. Early Indian theories viewed time in a variety of ways including the following: Time as the controller, time as the cause of the origin and the destruction of the universe, and time as Absolute (Balslev 1983: 12). In the Mahabharata, time is described as *sūtradhāra* (story-teller like a compere) 'of the universe, permitting events and preventing them from taking place' (1983: 12). The word for time in Sanskrit is '*kāla*' and the root of this word means 'to count'. The root also means 'to devour' and so kāla also means death. These 'physical' accounts of time have played an important role in the creation of the notion of social time.[2] The social is first formed as a temporal process. The very act of aggregation is also an act extended over time and is part of the dynamics of temporality. But social time

[2] For an interesting account of a cultural anthropological view of time, see Munn (1992).

is much more than the mere counting of time for aggregation to take place. It is that notion of time which orders the aggregates and creates the specific socials. This is common to all social formations, including that of modern industrial society which too begins with a particular notion of controlling time. The invention of the clock changed the world order and gave the European cultures a position of primacy in comparison to the colonized people (Adas 1989). Colonial discourses on India often refer to the incapacity of Indians to understand and follow clock time. Much of this cultural characteristic of time can be traced to the creation of mathematical time. This view of time makes time a quantity and not a quality, makes it measurable and allows the identification of the number line with the timeline. Progression of time is like the progression of numbers; it should not surprise us, therefore, that time was seen to be somehow related to arithmetic (just as space was related to geometry). Just like an interval between numbers can be broken into smaller intervals, so too could an interval of time be reduced to much smaller units. Today, we very easily talk of time at the nano scale—an extremely small duration. It is in this view of time that it becomes linear and irreversible.

Judith Walker (2009: 483) points out that after the invention of the Pendulum Clock in 1657, 'everyday activities have been ... governed by quantifiable units of time'. Following Marx, one could say that the capitalist modernist tried to 'control time' (the worker was also controlled by clock time) but in the globalized economy, there is an attempt to 'outsmart', 'commodify', 'obliterate' time. Walker addresses the question of how these changing ideas of time in the globalized world impacts education, particularly in what she calls as 'academic capitalism'.

Pre-modern societies had a different relationship with time—when almanacs are used instead of a clock, there are obviously different ways of ordering our experience and our expectations. Time was literally 'slow' before the advent of the clock since changes were slow. Capitalism, as many scholars have pointed out, shifted the meaning of time into one of efficiency (Adam Smith) and value (Weberian 'time is money'). When time becomes money, then, as Walker points out, it can 'be wasted, saved or spent' (2009: 486). It should not be a surprise to note that Weber considered the wastage of time as the 'deadliest sin', a view which is in consonance with his attempt to create moral values around time. Hard work and denial of 'idle talk and leisure' become moral virtues and not just utilitarian ones. Walker points out how different writers concur that in a globalized world, time is compressed and not well compartmentalized as earlier, such as the carryover of work into homes now leading to a piquant situation where we seem to have lost control over time.

Industrial time is related to labour and production. It even simulated a belief that somehow time was under our control, since work was under our control. The relation between work and time had serious consequences for what followed in capitalistic economies. The claim that 'time is money' created a value for time that soon transformed from an economic one into a moral value. The Weberian principle of the morality of time meant that wasting time was immoral. The guilt associated with leisure is a remnant of a long acculturation of this view which, among other things, leads to the anxiety to make time productive in every sphere of life. All this seems to suggest that an important form of relationship between the individual and the social is through the idea of time. Time is social in the sense that the very nature of the social is defined by the time that characterizes that social. Different socials often will have different notions of time that influence the experience of that social. For example, in a study of Canadian scholars, it was discovered that the 'cult of speed, compression of time and intensification of work' has greatly impacted academic practice and has changed the nature of the academic world today (Menzies and Newson 2007: 496). That is, the sociality defining today's academic world, for example, is different from that of earlier times commensurate with the changing conceptions of time in these socials.

There is a special character to this social time which goes to constitute social phenomena, and this is related to time's capacity to unify. The unity of social processes like caste across time is related to this capacity of time. These ideas of time are also exemplified in processes that are sensorially accessible, like the social. This is the idea of time that is encoded in music, which is also one of the primary agents of creating the sense of the social as discussed in the earlier chapter on sensing the social. Music is a very good example of time consciousness, a point from which Husserl draws fundamental insights into the phenomenology of time. Phenomenologists point to one special experience of time: time-consciousness unifies different instants into one whole. Listening to music is not merely listening to instants, to disjoint pieces, to the last note alone but to a synthesis that happens over time, over a duration and not at one instant. This synthesis must 'preserve' each tone and keep the full melody, as well as relate each tone. All our experiences need a 'temporal horizon', as exemplified by melody. To give an account of this experience, Husserl suggests three levels of time: world/objective time, personal/subjective time, and consciousness of internal time.

But what is special to the idea of the social is that it is not reducible either to world/objective time or the personal/subjective time. The social time of caste is deeply related to the sociality of caste and defines the kind of social experiences that are shared by members belonging to a given jati. One of the defining dynamics of the caste experience is that of a unique notion of time that is related to rebirth, heredity, and intergenerationality. We can now understand the meaning of inter-caste marriages which are not just about the marriage of two individuals belonging to different castes but is the creation of a sociality based on a new sense of social time. Inter-caste marriages bring the question of justice from an intergeneration equality to equality in the lived domain.

We can see reflections of this complexity in the way social reformers looked towards inter-caste marriages as a way of diluting the hold of caste. For Tagore, inter-caste marriages were a form of social martyrdom. For Ambedkar, too, this was an important issue. In spiritual time, marriages are arranged in heaven whereas *satya shodhak* (truth-seekers) marriage, as propounded by Jotirao Phule, self-respect marriage suggested by E.V.R. Naickar, and Buddhist marriage advised by Ambedkar are all 'arranged' in lived time. Within some religious traditions, it is commonly said that marriages are arranged in heaven.

Given this complexity, perhaps the only way to destabilize the caste social is by recasting some fundamental principles of ethical reasoning. The social serves as an important reference point to normatively evaluate certain rituals and actions that are otherwise considered to be individual or private. The social which is given a priori will remind us of this question: Are marriage unions social? This question can be handled by a singular reference to the social which is already universally available. For example, the universal values of dignity, equality, freedom, and friendship are primary moral goods which should attract everybody, irrespective of his or her own particular location. One's ultimate universal interests lie in creating this social and that is possible if one follows this given social before one's union with another individual either through friendship or marriage. Phule, Periyar, and Ambedkar, who were seminal thinkers of modern India, codified the a priori social into oaths of marriage. But the oaths uttered during the marriage do not become articulable on their own; their validity can be established only through the everyday practices of these oaths. That is, truth given in oaths is not a sufficient condition for creating the vibrant social. So, the a priori social remains hypothetical and to prove this hypothetical truth one has to involve oneself in righteous and morally consistent action. Hence, the given truth in oaths produces a social through the practice of these codified values and the values which come from the historically tested experience of the social.

One such reworking of ethics in the social context is through reformulating ideas of the ethical as an interaction between socials which is not reducible only to individual ethical action. In the next chapter, we argue that *maitri* is a concept which captures this unique relationship between the socials. It is a term that we borrow from Ambedkar. Although this term has been understood in various ways including that of friendship, these meanings do not capture the essential importance of maitri as a relation between different socials and not between different individuals. The analysis of inequality is illustrative of how maitri functions as a relation between socials. The resistance to meaningful maitri as a relation between socials in the case of caste socials arises from the relation of inequality between these socials and not from the inequality between individuals.

8 *Maitri*: Ethical Rationality between Different Socials

We have so far described the ways by which we can conceptualize the many socials that are part of everyday experiences. We have tried to make sense of the everyday forms of social communication that make an ethical commitment to the experiential domain of the socials. We have also explored notions of self, agency, and authority, as well as inequality and time in relation to the social. In the beginning of this book, we had started with an observation that the idea of the social as a mere collection of human beings is incomplete on the count that it is not able to demarcate the nature of human collections in contrast to non-human collections. In the preceding chapter, we suggested how the question of ethics is central to the experience of the social. In this final chapter, we are interested in understanding what the cultivation of this ethical amounts to and in so doing, try and explicate what the quality of being human contributes to the ontology of the social.

The two important qualities of the sociality of humans are that of rationality (seen broadly to include forms of thinking and communication) and morality. Both these qualities, unfortunately, have been individualized to such an extent that one tends to see the capacities of rationality and morality as individual characteristics. But we make a different claim. As discussed in the previous chapter, the everyday social is built on a foundation of a primal response which we identify as ethical—for example, the experience of belongingness. The feeling of belongingness, when in the company of a group with whom there is a feeling of sociality, can range from a feeling of affection to complete dissolution of the self in the group. These experiences are ethical in the Levinasian sense as described earlier since they are ethical responses to our recognition of other humans around us. Hatred towards particular groups of people are acts which are 'socialized'. Thus, our starting point is that the ethical experience of the social is intrinsically character-ized by equality and hate is a learnt behaviour. The moment of the formation of an experience of the social is also one that is primarily marked with the cognition of the ethical. People live together, enjoy being together, even in the midst of suffering and deprivation. It is the interactions within the everyday socials of their lives that sustain them. It might even be possible to say that the origin of ethics lies in this experiential space of the everyday socials.

In this chapter, we will extend this approach by arguing that two socials have a relation of belongingness to each other analogous to the individual having a relation of belongingness to a social. Just as individuals come together through the experience of being-with, two socials, comprising of individuals who are independently part of them, can also be in a similar relation of being-with each other. Any mean-ingful model of society which has many socials has to accommodate this possibility of different socials being in a relation of belongingness and being-with each other. In this chapter, we argue that the only way to make sense of spontaneous human goodness is by identify-ing a specific character of the everyday socials—the special relation between the different everyday socials. This special ethical relation between socials is not reducible to ethical relations between individu-als belonging to these socials. The idea of a relation between the dif-ferent socials is not uncommon and this claim can be substantiated by quite a few everyday examples. For instance, consider the relation between institutions. Very often, institutions sign a Memorandum of Understanding (MoU) between themselves and, as such, are a par-ticular form of relation between two group entities. The individuals belonging to the institutions are the ones who will collaborate accord-ing to the MoU. However, the governing force of their action which is based on the MoU will regulate the relation between institutions to different degrees. Nations sign agreements and enter into a relation-ship with each other as collective entities. Corporates sign agreements that can be enforced legally. In all these cases, these are relations that are primarily between 'social' entities, even though many times it is the individuals belonging to these entities who act in accordance with these agreements. Our primary argument in this chapter is that the social too functions in a similar manner; the dominant form of the interaction between the socials is like the relations which two entities enter into. These relations are not written or legal nor governed by formal agreements. The most important of these relations is the ethical one and we suggest that meaningful ethical social action—as well as any ethical action of an individual—arises first as a special form of relation between the socials. The question of inequality which we discussed in the last chapter is an example of this phenomenon. We borrow a term from Babasaheb Ambedkar—maitri—and will propose that maitri is the term which stands for the ethical relation between the different socials that constitute the everyday social.[1] Maitri is the social MoU which influences ethical social actions. Unlike influential claims that human societies are primarily and fundamentally hateful, selfish, and have to be controlled, we argue that fundamentally the socials that are an essential part of any human society are characterized by an innate sense of compassion and goodness that are related to the experience of belongingness and being-with. Recapturing the social is to recapture this essential ethical core that is present in the formation of the everyday socials.

Ethics of the Social

The experiential space of the everyday social challenges naive presuppositions about the notion of the individual, especially in relation to the social. The individual seems to be an integral part of the construction of the social while at the same time the everyday response to the social is as if the social is hypostatized as an individual. That is, individuals act as if they are mediated by social selves and act under agentless authorities, while the socials act as if they function as individuated

---

[1] Ambedkar's views on maitri are extremely important and needs much more work. His definition of maitri through the *apoha* process—defining through negation what friendship is not—is another important connection between his views and Buddhism, since apoha theory is an extremely influential Buddhist theory of meaning. For more on this, see Ambedkar (1987: 283). Here, we are keeping the 'spirit' of his idea of maitri but placing it in a different framework.

autonomous entities. The experiential domain of the social reinforces these ideas. Although this is particularly true of the Indian socials, these phenomena are endemic to many social formations in other parts of the world.

Why take this picture of the social seriously? Perhaps, the most important reason in this context is that focussing on an autonomous individual as the unit of action leads to a confused picture of social action. This is best manifested in a common Indian phenomenon, one which we believe is being manifested globally. In India, it is now quite impossible to isolate individual action since it always tends to be seen as part of a collective social identity. For example, many claim that there are no historians in India but only Left and Right historians, thereby subsuming individual action under a social identity. The social presence of the author dominates texts and ideas to such an extent that books are read or not read based on the caste, class, and gender of the author. Written material takes on the characteristics of caste, class, and gender to such an extent that they begin to function as social beings. While we believe that it is extremely important to recognize that the author's socialities are an integral part of her writing, the impossibility of stepping out of those socialities is one powerful illustration of how the individual (author) is always presented as a social entity with little agency and autonomy of her own. This is true of almost any domain of action in India—from academics to sports, from activism to academics. Even when the notion of the individual can be extracted, it is often through recognition of another social formation.

This tension between the social and the individual is not new in the history of India. The early Hindu practice demanded renunciation as the last stage of a person's life. In contrast, the ascetic traditions which were so essential to the Buddhist and Jaina practices, were essentially about the possibility of liberating oneself from the social. To achieve this liberation, one had to abandon the social in all its manifested forms right from the beginning. Thus, one of the most common tropes of recovering a 'true individual' out of a 'socialized individual' is by training the self. Ironically, liberation of this kind also leads to the dissolution of the individual self into a much larger notion of the self, most often a transcendent self. It is almost as if it is only by giving up self-identities that we reach the true state of an individual.

This difficulty in separating the individual from the social has important implications, particularly for understanding social action in the everyday social. For example, we could consider the difficulty in dealing with the question of caste in India. As is well known, the practices around caste are spread across all religious communities, and even today exert great influence on an individual, right from the choice of education and profession to the choice of a marriage partner. There have also been many attempts to promote dissolution of caste identities through promotion of activities such as inter-caste marriages. As discussed in the last chapter, Ambedkar's call to annihilate caste is one important example of an attempt to remove an entrenched social practice. But today we could say that caste practices are still well-entrenched. Matrimonials based on caste preferences continue to flourish even as there are interesting mutations of caste affiliations that allow for a more fluid marriage agreement between different jatis. The lack of prospective brides among particular caste groups has been one of the most influential catalysts for inter-caste marriages since some jatis get absorbed into a particular varna to allow arranged marriages of individuals belonging to different 'castes'.

A major part of the problem in understanding, as well as evaluating, social action lies in the presumed inability of the individual to come out of social practices in order to take up a position that is individuated and not representative of a social group or social ideology. However, we also tend to expect that social action should be reduced to individual action in that it is the individual who has to act—to annihilate caste, for example. Actions can be agential at the level of individuals or larger aggregates like organizations. Thus, to remove certain caste practices, a society can act as a social group ideally acquiring ontological form to transformative social institutions. Caste and patriarchy, particularly in the Indian context, put up stiff resistance to such a meaningful social ontology. In general, it becomes easier to give agency to embodied entities such as an individual or an organization operating through rules and laws. This also implies that any notion of ethical action in the context of a society gets reduced to that of individual or institutional action. So, the ethics of resisting certain caste practices are seen to belong to the domain of the individual or the institution of law. However, since the individual in the everyday social is seen as a socialized unit, her ethical decision is often seen as a default decision of the socialities that she operates under. Thus, where exactly do we situate certain kinds of ethical action—is it between individuals or between different socials? What really is the nature of ethical social action?

We will begin with a particular model of ethical social action. A society is not just made up of many individuals; it is also made up of many socials. Individuals belong to these socials and they relate to each other even though they may belong to different socials. These socials are not fixed but fluid and dynamic. Thus, the belongingness to these socials is also fluid and dynamic. However, what is important is to understand how the socials as autonomous entities themselves interact. Ethical action in the context of the social is first defined through a relationship between different socials and not between different individuals belonging to these socials. Reduction of all social action to the individual leads to a major misunderstanding of these actions.

Individuals are also extremely important, and we are not negating this importance. However, when can we say that an action by an individual is entirely located within the individual's individuality or when it is only an expression of the different socials 'inhabiting' the individual? In fact, we can go to the extent of saying that an individual really functions in the fullness of her individuality only when her actions have the capacity to create a new social. That is, truly individual actions are those which actually create new socials and it is in this possibility alone that we recognize true individuality.

It might seem that today the world has moved more and more into possessive and disembodied individualism leading to more isolation through personalized technologies. But this is only partially true because this individualism is being supported and protected by a powerful presence of the social. This social which often takes the form of desire and hedonism gets reproduced through consumer capitalism. The invisible social has finally taken over individualism. It has truly become a carapace like caste is in India. In this hyper-individual world, there are more Facebook friends than those we would have had if we had only been individualistic. There are more social interactions through the web which makes us deal with many more individuals, views, and opinions than ever before. Very sparsely populated countries have become like India and China in that the virtual population that the individuals in those countries deal with have become very high. But, as we discussed in an earlier chapter, this is not a 'true' social but a virtual one. The sensory, experiential mode of perceiving the social as well as the experience of being-with is absent in these virtual socials.

Being versus Knowing: Ethical Rationality of the Social

What kind of ethics describes the ethics of the social as we have described it here? Modern ethical theories have invested too much in particular notions of rationality as a core element of ethics. But what does this mean for relationships based on the sensory experience of the social? Arguably, the conception of rationality is a slippery one in that it can as easily be applicable to social systems that are regressive in nature. The rationality of wars, of the Holocaust, of racism, and of all types of discrimination must force us to rethink the relation between ethics and rationality in a way which allows us to retain both but in a more 'humane' sense. The caste system is one such system which is a self-enclosed totality based on a unique criterion of rationality. Caste-based rationality is instrumental as it tends to ensure the stability of the caste system. Thus, transgressing social norms that regulate the caste system could be seen by authoritative members, who exist in every caste group across the board, as an irrational act. For a high-caste Hindu, following the caste dharma is a rational social action. Similarly, crossing boundaries of lower castes is also considered as adharma by the members of such castes. The question that we need to raise here is this: Is there a possibility of the ethics *of the social* in such structures of caste-based rationality?

First, we will begin by trying to understand a broader conception of the social that is relevant to social action or actions of the social. How does ethics operate at the level of the social? We are not talking about the ethical questions that arise from the action of social institutions such as corporates. We are trying to make sense of the social origin of the ethical based on which the ethical actions of the individual can be understood. One way is to begin with the idea of vulnerability—both of individuals and societies. Individuals are vulnerable in a biological sense (related to death) and in a social sense (related to insecurity). As mentioned above, they are similarly related to desire (biological sense) as well as desire-as-power (social sense). When we commonly talk of desire-as-power, especially in the context of rapes and the Me Too campaign, we have to recognize that this relation is a social relation or a relation between socials and not an individual action alone. Simplistically, these social relations might be seen to express the social conditions that allow desire to be converted into power—for example, the social conditions that make powerful men use their position to sexually harass women working under them. The movement from the language of desire to power is an illustration of the presence of the social, and a meaningful ethics of human action in such a case has to find ways of talking about relationship between socials and not just individuals. Here is why the social ethics of maitri become extremely significant as an ethical term operating between different socials.

Unlike generic collections, there are unique marks of the human social, when humans congregate into various socials: two such marks are those of death and desire. Just like rationality and morality, these two terms have become almost completely absorbed into the individual and thus it becomes difficult to view them as qualities of the social. But death and desire are indeed 'social' qualities in their richest sense. Death is always more than the mere cessation of bodily activities and, in fact, is one of the most powerful social concepts that have been instrumental in the creation of societies. So too is desire. Both these together create a rationality of vulnerability which centrally marks the degree of the social. There are societal manifestations of this as in the following: Where the vulnerability is greater, where death intrudes in uncontrolled ways, the greater is the sense of the social of those who live under its actions. Where desire is boundless and goes beyond the domains of the vulnerable, the social collapses into the individuals. Both death and desire have a core sense of vulnerability around them and it is this that makes them essential to the formation of any social. The vulnerability of desire, even for the consummation of the most unbridled desire, is the loss of the social that goes with it. If there is a special kind of rationality associated with the social, it is the rationality of dealing with death and desire. Even utilitarian accounts of rational action are relatable to this larger space of rationality. It is also these characteristics that distinguish mere scientific rationality from the rationality of the social. This rationality which is the foundation for any possibility of the social is not one that is only about calculative action but one in which notions such as death and desire figure deeply, even if not prominently on the surface. The Ambedkarite notion of maitri offers one possible way of understanding such an ethical rationality between the different socials.

We could begin with the pair of terms 'being' and 'knowing', and isolating an important difference between them. As social beings, we interact with one another with some amount of knowledge—knowledge about the other, about the world which we share, and so on. But 'being with' another is a very different form of existence which is not reducible to 'knowing that' individual. You can be with somebody without really knowing much about them or even wanting to know everything about them. Friendship and familial relationships arise dominantly through the relation of 'being with' rather than 'knowing that'. (One could, perhaps, see some relation between this formulation and the well-known distinction between the two kinds of knowing, know-how and know-that.)

This distinction is important in the context of the formation of the social for many reasons. One of these is that hierarchies are catalysed through categories of knowing, and articulated and legitimized through these epistemological categories. Knowing something influences behaviour; being-with can only be silent about this aspect. Sometimes we may not want to know anything about a person but prefer just to be with her or him. This leads us to consider the possibility of a rationality of being and not the rationality of knowing. Rationality and justification are most dominantly associated with the idea of knowing. Rationality itself is closely linked to the concept of justification. For Habermas, an influential writer on this topic, rationality is fundamentally linked to knowledge; not to the content but about how we *acquire* and *utilize* it (Dallmayr 1988). Batens (1978: 25), for example, argues that rationality is primarily about justification and what he means by justification is not application to beliefs and so forth, but to processes that lead to justified beliefs.

Justification is an important idea in the formulation of what could constitute valid knowledge, but justification can as well be invoked in explicating the valid ways of being with others. The rationality of being with others, a central form of the ethical rationality of the social, lies in coping with the irrationalities of the other. It also offers a way of engaging with the transcendent—which is the non-reduction of the transcendent to oneself. We must note that this notion of the transcendent is a profound human condition and is not restricted to notions of god alone. It is the relation with a transcendental notion that influences the social in deep ways. The rationality of being also includes a meaningful framework to act within structures of the irrationality of desire.

The possibility of being-with is challenged most strongly by the presence of social death caused by caste or race and the desire for privileged insularity. In this sense, these are great obstacles to the possibility of creating a stable social. One of the major challenges to theories of the rationality of social action is the 'irrationality' associated with both these notions. What we suggest here is that it is ethical rationality which can engage meaningfully with these natural/social 'facts' of being-with, death, and desire. The justification which has to be found at the foundation of ethical rationality has to be based on the idea of being human.

The first ideas of a historical social actually are concomitant with articulations of the rationality of social and biological death and desire. Some of the most important texts in the world are ways of coping with the challenges posed by death and desire, when they move from their 'natural' state to the social one. That is, the creation of the social lies as much in the socializing of the concepts of death and desire. Since they are wrongly seen as something to do with individuals and not the social, the response to death—making meaning of that event—is often expressed in terms of the irrationality of the cosmos. There is almost no death which is not viewed with a sense of betrayal, a sense of a special loss, a yearning for some more years, and so on. Biology and medical science are primarily about this attempt to understand the nature of life so that death does not become a natural part of life. The constant attempt to postpone death also carries with it an acknowledgement of death's power to escape any simple notions of control and prediction.

It is a similar case with desire. If desire is seen as a fundamental human condition and not just as a psychological one, then we have to consider the possibility that desire and our response to our own deaths have to be at the basis of any understanding of many everyday social actions. The everyday social is pervaded by responses to, as well as articulations of, death and desire. This poses a challenge to the study of the everyday social as well as to the formation of the socials. Even the modes of analysis have to be different, for some of the most profound ways of dealing with death and desire in the everyday world have come from literature and art. In the everyday social performances, these have become ways of coping with the challenges arising from them. This rationality of coping through telling, and telling through a variety of forms is an important element of the rationality of human action. These stories, narratives, and metaphors generate an ethics which is based on the primacy of being and not necessarily on the primacy of knowing. It is these rationalities—understood not as control and prediction but as ethical and reasonable at the same time—that are needed. In the language of the everyday, saying 'I am there for you' is often enough; it is an ethical response because it is about being-there for somebody. Family and friends are those whom you would like to be 'there' for you; you may not even need them to do this or the other, but to be just there. The sense of absence is the void of non-being, not being there when you want somebody to be there. We rationalize this non-being through stories, metaphors, and narratives. These are the structures of justification of being and not of knowing. In the everyday social, stories, music, and dance function as fundamental social actions which are intrinsically related to the ethics of being-with.

There is yet another deep relation between these states of vulnerability and the social. It is the social which functions as the bulwark against the vulnerability of individuals and groups. Individual vulnerability often translates into the vulnerability of the social. Indian cities, towns, and villages have many pockets where the poor reside. The social world in which they live is one that challenges ideas of privacy, comfort, leisure, hygiene, and so forth. The social is one that is as vulnerable as their individual lives; their society is one that is often in danger of being the site of conflicts, riots, disease, and power and water cuts. Death and desire live side by side in these localities—both are celebrated and mourned in equal measure. There is really little difference between notions of vulnerability and death in the individual and the social domains. The coming together into the social is the protection—ironically, these 'little' socials are a protection against the dominant society which has discarded them. The social gets strengthened through this capacity of being-with as a primal mode of sociality.

Maitri functions as the rationality of being-with rather than knowing-that. It is the relation between socials that first communicates this possibility of being-with and it is from this experience of the social (manifested all the time in the everyday social) that we learn friendship (and its related cognates) as individual ethical action.

Social Decomposition

Do the socials in India fit into this model? They may not if there is a resistance to the stability of the socials leading to social decomposition arising through inequality, oppression, and so on. The normative aspect of a social is to create spaces for the victims to fight the structural forms of alienation, de-socialization, and self-imposed alienation. As events in contemporary India are unfolding, it seems as if the normative social seems to be rushing rather fast to its moral decomposition. The acknowledgement of such decomposition is evident in the expression of people who say that they can use morally offensive language without personally knowing the victims of social terror. This is moral decomposition of the social. The Twitter attack on the journalist Gauri Lankesh after she was killed is one such recent and tragic incident. Such a socially disastrous tendency operates on the market principle of exchange of moral value which would thus make Gauri's life ironically valuable to those who are interested in creating terror among the possible dissenters or the critics of Hindutva. So dissenters, in a utilitarian sense, have the exchange value that makes the crusader dispensable for what is considered as the superior value of a particular religion. This decomposition has a corresponding link with the social decomposition of the untouchable self. Inversely, this process of alienation leads to the decomposition of the untouchable into a social death. Social decomposition of a Dalit necessarily involves the feeling of being neglected, being seen as a source of nuisance, repulsion and disgust or moral menace, not worthy of attention, and being an object of constant suspicion. The dissolution of the self into moral insignificance is constituted of unseeability, untouchability, and unapproachability. Civilizational violence is another name for self-decomposition. Unseeability destroys that optical process that is so necessary to bring the active face into play and a face which is expected to offer not the 'tight' smile but a genuine smile. Intersubjectivity gives rise to a notion of friendship in which a person is a concrete, unrepresentable being. The feeling of compassion has to further graduate into the social relationship of friendship, which then becomes one single moral frame in which all different attitudes can be united.

Social decomposition is not a natural process; in fact, it leads to the production of insularity which for Dalits could be quite persecuting.

It could be persecuting in terms of self-imposition of debasement, servility, inferiority, demeaning mentality, or the feeling of insignificance and subordination. Accepting inadequacy in communication that happens at different levels could also constitute decomposition. Hence, the social has a deep existential dimension. It would mean that the struggle to overcome this self-decomposition becomes personal, which, as a consequence, would keep the larger structures outside the purview of such struggles.

The existential logic tends to suspend, if not completely eliminate, the possibility of strengthening a social good such as intersubjectivity or being-with together. There are many non-Dalit castes in India and white racists in America who continue to maintain pathological distance from the untouchables and the Blacks respectively. However, one need not generalize as there are some from among the upper castes in India or Whites in the US who do not exhibit this pathology. In fact, there are several ethically sensitive persons in both these groups who show their firm commitment to produce normatively desirable conditions of intersubjectivity. They know that the truth of intersubjectivity is embedded in the suffering of others that is narrativized through the reading of autobiographies, for example, of the Dalits. They, in fact, find the act of knowing the suffering of others by adopting the mode of reading which is not symbolically violent. In such cases, reading acquires a mediating role in bridging the social gap between two persons or two groups, mediated through reading symbolically violent social relations. For example, consider the sympathetic feelings that are expressed by one of the leading Marathi literary commentators, Bhalchandra Phadake, who after having read *Akkar Mashi*, (an autobiography by one of the Dalit writers from Maharashtra) said, 'When I read the autobiography I felt that I was being bitten by a thousand scorpions' (personal communication). This ethics of confession suggests the possibility of converting a neutral or indifferent self into a passionate self who would then find universal purpose in communicating the moral significance of human suffering as portrayed in the Dalit autobiography. Such ethics of communication is processed through certain moral concepts such as empathy, human concern, and mutual recognition of equal dignity. This kind of ethics of confession is not interested in just downplaying the mutual reification or alienation or humiliation but it actively disapproves of such an attitude that is socially a moral disaster. Thus, the ethics of confession is one of the crucial conditions that is fundamental to the realization of maitri. The ethics of confession becomes a matter of learning to be-with and is different from reading merely in order to know.

Alienation, on the other hand, is counter to such confession or knowing. This is particularly true in the Indian context which in effect points to a kind of depletion of moral resources. This depletion takes place at two ends of Indian society: the *Varchi ali* (in Marathi) or *agrahara* (in Kannada), the upper layer, and *Khalchi ali* (Marathi) or *cheri* (in Kannada), the lower layer. Alienation at the lower layer is morally significant as it has the potential for its transcendence. An untouchable in a historical sense finds an emancipatory purpose in fighting against alienation that becomes the fate of his/her community. Ironically, the privileged alienation of an upper caste does not arise by itself and is based on the contribution that the untouchables make in producing their own alienation. Alienation at the lower order results from the untouchable's failure to meet the social norms decided by the upper castes who produce them to strengthen and perpetuate the pathology of distance. These upper castes take this pathology of distance so seriously that they deny themselves the ethical advantage of producing even the tight, if not soft, smile on their faces. Some persons, particularly from the upper castes, even today, do not feel an ethical need to see the face of the untouchable. This is evident in the act of erecting the wall of separation that is aimed at reproducing ethically offensive conditions of unseeability. However, walls of separation have become a common resource even for the untouchables who would use it for material purposes, and not social or civilizational purposes. This hastens the process of social decomposition which is based on either social insulation in the case of the upper castes or material appropriation in the case of the Dalits.

Untouchables could be held guilty in as much as they also contribute to the process of a slow decomposition of the social in India. The social in India produces not the consciousness of the body but the consciousness of the mind. Dalits, instead of becoming the spectre of the mind for the Brahmins, end up becoming the victims of their own spectre. This self-alienation deepens because there is a lack of third-party intervention that is necessary to first dilute and then finally destroy the untouchable's capacity for social decomposition. The third party should have the virtue of humility that is necessary to enhance the credibility of intervention on the part of a non-Dalit as a third party. Many such people fail to use the moral quality of humility that is internal to the act of knowing and acknowledging, rather than the arrogant act of dictating to the Dalits. There is good reason to claim that we in India lack the notion of a third party that has a sincere commitment to public reason. A third party could be defined in terms of those members of society who have the necessary moral stamina to test their given social position against the universal agreed upon values such as humility, which stands for mutual dignity for all. This moral lack has to be understood in terms of the preponderance of caste imagination over the thinking faculty of the members of Indian society.

In contemporary India, particularly in the political space, people have not been interested in making the transition from emotions such as hatred and repulsion to more harmonious feeling such as compassion. Emotions such as hate and repulsion, which are morally disgusting feelings, find their roots in the malignant social that is constitutive of offensive prejudices. Caste and patriarchy are among the worst examples of a malignant social. Such a social runs counter to the natural goodness that is inherently present in every human being who has the moral capacity to reflectively summon it into his or her active consciousness and social practice. Prejudice which gets fossilized through the malignant caste social necessarily disrupts the transition from basic emotions to redemptive compassion. This disruption happens because the basic emotions are not only unpleasant, but they are morally offensive. Through Twitter they express hatred against a dissenter such as Gauri Lankesh and repulsion against the untouchables. Reason obviously fails to facilitate this transition from basic emotions to compassion. Caste, as social, converts natural feelings of empathy into unnatural basic emotions such as repulsion, contempt, disgust, and even hatred. Caste thus serves as the mechanism that produces such conversion. The social has to create such empathy as an initial condition that is necessary for the emergence of a reflective endorsement of what is 'naturally' good in every human being. This reason has to be cultivated through everyday practice in order to reflectively endorse this goodness.

Maitri

The social serves as an important reference point to normatively evaluate certain rituals and actions that are otherwise considered to be
individual or private. Are marriage unions social? This question can
be handled by a singular reference to an already available social with
values of dignity, equality, freedom, and friendship, which are primary moral goods and should attract everybody irrespective of their
particular location. If one follows this given social before one's union
with another individual, either through friendship or marriage, questions about marriage as discussed earlier will not occur at all. Periyar,
Ambedkar, and Phule codified the a priori social into oaths of marriage
such as in self-respect marriages, *satya shodhak* (truth-seeking) marriages and Buddhist marriages. But the oaths do not become articulable on their own; their validity can be established only through the
everyday practices of these oaths. That is, truths encoded in the oath
are not a sufficient condition for creating the vibrant social. So, the
available social remains hypothetical and to prove this hypothetical
truth one has to involve oneself in righteous and morally consistent
action. Hence, the given truths in oaths produce a social through the
practice of these codified values and the values which come from the
historically tested experience of the social.

Based on the experience of the everyday social, we could say that
the organizing principles of this social will include humanity, mutual
respect, peace, friendship, and commonwealth. If injustice thrives on
the indifference of the people, can we really put this organizing principle into actual practice? This question becomes important in the present context where certain social classes have treated it as a given that
some others exist only due to the 'courtesy' of the former. For example,
minorities have been given to imagine that for their self-expression in
the public they have to depend on the permission of the privileged.
The arrogant self with its oversized ego is subordinating the autonomy
of the other for its own social ambitions to remain on the top. People
who exist in the social space need to interrogate this courtesy-mode
by intervening whenever the members of the minorities are put to this
violence. But the social space is shrinking even in terms of its moral
capacity to accommodate the difference principle that existed through
cultural practices such as food. Thus, in a liberal sense, one could find

some value in social groups practicing their culture differently today. In recent times, the everyday sense of hate against the Muslims has exposed the limits of this multicultural thinking. The social spaces that existed between the two communities or between two individuals are being filled with an element of indifference and as a consequence this is creating a deep sense of passive injustice in India.

The social is an embodiment and experience of virtues, like friendship and emotional generosity. These go beyond emotions particularized within individuals and thus are not to be seen as mere psychological states. They are substantial in an important sense and form into meaningful social and historical conditions. In the Indian context, it is fair to ask the 'Ambedkar Question': Were these moral virtues, such as the ones mentioned above, ever part of the Indian social, seen as an amalgamation of different socials? The Ambedkar answer is undoubtedly Yes, to the extent that it has a bearing on the Buddhist concept of maitri. Maitri in the ethical sense has to be understood as an anchoring concept or bridge concept connecting different social groups to each other with the sense of deep compassion and love for the members of such groups. But this project that is internal to Buddhism gets interrupted by the onslaught of the caste ideology of mutual isolation. The history of the Indian caste system is the history of holism that entails the organizing principle according to which different fragments of caste defined their essence across time and space. This is perhaps the single principle of caste that regulated the operation of 3000 and more caste groups from Kashmir to Kanyakumari. The different socials in the Indian context get contaminated by the hierarchical logic of caste. Caste is constituted by certain social conditions such as isolation and dissociation. These conditions are produced and reproduced historically.

However, the upper caste does not seek a dignified isolation from the Dalits or untouchables. In fact, they can, and do, deploy emotions which are quite basic to human nature. One might argue that the basic emotions of caste are primarily those of repulsion and contempt. The idea of caste brings along with it a 'natural/social' propensity to belong. It is belongingness that really marks the most essential aspect of caste even though it may be exemplified in various social and political ways. All these different ways can be seen as different expressions of belongingness. In the Indian context, caste has become a 'natural' social condition to which people belong and hence they also share the basic emotions that are the very essence of the caste system. In the articulation of such basic emotions, the concept of discretion has only a small role in terms of moderating the emotions in favour of a benign social: a social with a strong interactive presence of empathy, love, care, and affection. The social ridden with caste on account of its rigid rule eliminates the possibility of such discretion.

Like nationalism, the caste-ridden social does not invoke the exercise of discretion. Members of caste society do not use their discretion to remove the blocked-in social interaction. In stark terms, they need to progressively defy the social rule in order to render the social exchange free from rigid rules. Arguably, nationalism is a blocked exchange since the secrets of the nation cannot be sold to the enemy. However, the social cannot be a blocked exchange and has to be based on the reciprocal recognition of complementary favour and not individual talent. The social that is driven by caste and ethnicity also results in a blocked exchange in the sense that it is a non-negotiable moral good. It is a moral mandate and hence non-exchangeable and non-changeable. It is in this sense that the notions of the national and caste enjoy the same moral status. The caste system blocks the exchange of ethical resources such as friendship.

On a radically humanitarian note, the social becomes imminent in the political. The social is the reciprocal return of the ethical such as maitri. It should not be seen as social generosity shown to a destitute or a needy person. The mutual interaction between two persons has to be unconditional. For example, a Dalit does not expect the upper caste to treat him as a mere object that is in need of maitri. Maitri does not result from the advantage of holding the source of moral patronage. It does not involve a top-down ethical flow. This would bring an egalitarian content to the ethical relationship, liberating the physical space through an invitation into the house, sharing of food, and so forth. In such a situation, caste pride as the essence of the social gets replaced by the ethical expressed through maitri.

The argument that should sound quite exciting is the foregrounding of the idea of a social into the moral conditions that are constitutive of maitri. Before we discuss maitri as the moral condition that assigns definite coherence to the collection of many socials, a point of clarification is in order. We are not discussing maitri in the sense of friendship as discussed in Aristotle or Derrida. In Neo-Buddhism, Ambedkar finds the highest human value in maitri. As Joshi (1977: 14) points out, Buddha considered maitri as the core of his teaching. Obviously, maitri is not a moral value that is a given. In fact, it has to be created through the constant reflective endorsement of compassion that is present among human beings. The human need is to annihilate mutual hatred and fill the social with an adequate degree of *manuski* (dignity), to use Ambedkar's expression in Marathi—in other words, to recapture the original moments of sociality. What was the nature of the social and the natural moral that provided the constituting conditions for the idea of social that encapsulated maitri during Buddha's time as well as Ambedkar's time? It could be argued that the Buddhist moral emotions such as compassion could not be imagined without the existence of emotions such as rage and repulsion, hatred and humiliation, anger and arrogance. During the Buddhist period, it has been argued that it was the ideology of Brahminism that was the source of these emotions. Buddhism suggested compassion as the moral route to transcend them.

Survival as a mere existential need becomes a burdensome state of being that tends to exist at the cost of the others' survival. Surviving at the cost of others gives rise to certain emotions such as rage, anger, hatred, contempt, repulsion, and violence. As the history of the social suggests, such emotions, under the leverage of casteism, seem to have taken over the ethical affinity or goodness which is arguably natural to human beings. In Buddhism, the notion of maitri was the moral device to overcome these emotions. Compassion is the mutual ethical ground that makes this overcoming possible. Humanity is the condition of all value and maitri is the social condition of humanity and vice versa. Maitri is not a kind of social relationship that could be realized between two people or a family but it normatively encapsulates the entire society through the reconfiguration of relationship between the different socials.

In the relationship of maitri, emotions are active and not receptive. Emotions that are received by the mind or the heart acquire a passive character and seek to have a redemptive impact on a person. For example, an upper caste feels emotionally pained after having read a morally tormenting autobiography of a Dalit as mentioned earlier. S/he would not ask the following question: Why should I sympathize with you? Maitri in its active sense rather than in a receptive or passive sense has the conceptual capacity to produce a moral reconfiguration of the various mutual socials. It is this relation of maitri between socials that influences how they are ultimately experienced.

Maitri: A New Configuration of Ethical Relations between Different Socials

Maitri, as we have argued here, promises a new configuration of social relationship that would involve the realization of moral equality. Put differently, it will undermine and ultimately eliminate the possibility of hierarchical ordering of moral values. It will flatten the maxim of ascending and descending sense of reverence which is the hallmark of any socially graded society.

Maitri in the Buddhist sense is not a virtue that is self-evident. In fact, for its own realization it requires some morally necessary conditions. Communicating through human interaction at different levels (social and conversational levels) constitutes one such crucial condition. In maitri, no state of human silence or muteness is permissible. Communicating both pain as well as pleasure with one another is a human need. Those who are placed and operate in the narrow confines of their particular social of caste and gender or race are invited to make their maitri coextensive with the other socials, but on a more abstract level of interaction and communication. A second condition, which results from the first, is the participation of not an argumentative Indian but, much more importantly, of a passionate subject who would rather unconditionally participate in relations of human suffering and not just on the occasion of happiness. Maitri is neither a sphere of cognitive credibility that therefore may assume the argumentative Indian nor is it a sphere which will base human relations on the logic of calculation. Maitri has a much larger promise to offer. The language of suffering that is at the core of maitri in Buddhism corresponds to the language of understanding between two passionate subjects.

Maitri as an enlarged social relation gets instantiated in the passionate subjects through everyday forms of conversation and modalities of communication. Maitri becomes discernible primarily through the process of unfolding oneself into larger spheres of unconditional human interaction. This flowing self does not wait for the help or direction of others but takes the initiative in facilitating such an interaction. This is the ethical core of Buddhism. Maitri thus is the opposite of a socially regressive phenomenon such as mutual reification or mutual cancellation of each other. Such phenomena find their malignant as well as violent expression that is inherent in mutually exclusive, if not embattled, socials. Maitri is the context within which one could seek the replacement of such phenomena by generating what could be called moral generosity. Moral generosity is an important dimension of maitri in which passionate subjects accept normative values without bothering to know who the originator of such values is. A passionate subject should count as a source or creator of normative values irrespective of his/her being a Dalit or a woman or a tribal.[2] These values acquire their universal validity without reference to the social background of the proponents of this value. Maitri finds its basis in such universalizable value. Maitri is not a sphere where there are only a particular set of people who grant the rest of the people values such as the recognition of worth. It is also not the sphere in which one could grant recognition to others without requiring it for oneself in turn. Thus, if Ambedkar is proposing the value of manuski in the seamless sphere of maitri, it has to be acknowledged without any reference to his caste. Individuals need to be morally generous to others as well as to themselves. The articulation and expression of maitri thus does not depend on the either direct or subtle use of power. In fact, maitri acquires its moral significance on account of its eschewing the power element.

Maitri as the new ideal social that could be realized on an everyday basis emerges from the decomposed forms of the social which are sociologically constituted, historically arrived at, and politically articulated. Caste and gender are two socials that are processed through history, politics, and sociology. As mentioned above, the decomposition in the Indian context is constitutive of inequality and mutual reification which underlies a deep sense of humiliation (Guru 2009). Our argument is that the ideal social has to come from the process of the reconfiguration of the decomposed social on the lines of maitri and that it cannot be brought from outside. It necessarily emerges from a radical dismantling of the regressive socials such as caste, patriarchy, and race.

---

[2] See Mulgan (1977: 7) for a related discussion.

What kind of a model of the social can best capture these characteristics? We emphasize the fact that the everyday social is also the origin of social moralities and maitri is a relation between the different socials and not between different individuals who might belong to these socials. There are different socials that operate, and they are not reducible to terms like 'community' since community is only one instantiation of a particular social. The sociality of a group which considers itself as Hindu is different from the sociality of its caste experience or of its religious sect. The social corresponding to being Indian may bring a different sense of sociality to the group but within it there may also be other socials operating. The advantage of using the space of the social to describe what might have been described as communities or identities is that with the latter the character of aggregation is again distributed into individual action. So, identity politics becomes certain kinds of action performed on the basis of identity and described through forms of individual actions. But replacing this perspective with that of many socials is to find ways that capture how the socials interact with each other. The nature of such interactions is very different from the interactions of individual agents.

The socials do not interact like individuals do. When two socials are related to each other in 'friendship', for example, it does not mean that everyone 'belonging' to these socials have a relationship of friendship. It may seem like relations are only embodied through human individual agents, but it is the relation between these experienced socials that really matter in the formation of meaningful ideas of the social. What this implies is that belonging to a social does not arise through counting or being told that one belongs to a group. Belonging to a social is also an expression of being influenced by the social, of actions being dictated by the particular social one belongs to based on their experience of the social. This description captures the ambiguity of individual agency within the social since individuals do not seem to have complete autonomy of action while being part of a social. Even simple examples of autonomy such as choosing one's clothes are influenced quite deeply by various social forces. In some societies including India, individual autonomy can often be subservient to a family's interests, including in the choice of education or of a spouse. The point is actually not about individual autonomy at all but about the types of autonomies that can coexist with the social. In this sense, belonging to a social is like belonging to the ubiquitous economic market—we do not belong to a market, nor are we members of a market or decide to have an identity with the market. We belong to the market in the way that our actions are dictated by it in known and unknown ways. This embodiment of the social is not a physical embodiment but an embodiment through action and this is an important meaning of the social.

The model of maitri is that of a particular form of relationship between the different ontologies of the social. This relation may well get exemplified within individuals but that is not necessary. Two socials that are related through maitri may have examples of individuals belonging to the two socials who also have a relation of the instantiated maitri between each other. This relation between two individuals is not only emotional. For example, 'caring friendship', which might be one characterization of maitri, may be present between two individuals of the two socials. But this caring friendship need not only be at the level of emotional relation between the two of them. It is also to be seen in its embodiments in forms of practice and action between the two individuals. As mentioned earlier, a more useful way to understand belongingness to a particular social is not through identity or assertions of belonging but through acting according to the needs and demands of that social. How we act decides to which social we actually belong to. When this relationship of maitri between the socials reduces to a relationship of maitri between individuals then we move more towards Gandhi. So, one might discover this crucial distinction between Ambedkar and Gandhi in the location of the agency of maitri—for the former, between socials and for the latter between individuals influenced by these socials.

The moral configuration of the social would involve ethical rationality and moral discretion. The universal principle of impartiality induced through Weberian rationality is inadequate to produce the normative social. One needs to aid such impartiality with discretion as a moral force behind it. Discretionary moral power acquires validity when it is driven to impress upon those who are less likely to follow the universal principles. Those who are mired in caste or gender are less likely to follow either Kantian autonomous subjectivity or Weberian objectivity, not because of their innate incapacity but because of the way the rational and ethical are acted upon by the social. The tendency to locate the ethical within some problematic notion of individual autonomy (individual in opposition to the social) leads Kant and many others of his kind to deny the rationality of the ethical to women and those of colour.

The social is not the ideal that lies outside the everyday life or in the distant future but has to be realized on an everyday basis where it is already present. Its essence, which is dignity, has to be experienced in the everyday form of human experience. An alternative conception of the social has to emerge from the available conception of the social. If the available social forgets the experiences of the belongingness of the everyday socials, then the alternative conception has to be normative in character. It should include even-handed attention, mutual respect, and freedom from the negative feeling of being abandoned by the members of the social. The collection of many socials, which constitutes 'society', has to be both universalizable and realizable. It should not be an absolute platonic ideal which cannot be realized. The normative project within which society has to be realized has to contain the perpetual professing of common good.

What is, therefore, important is to treat maitri as a normative good that has to be perpetually possessed by every member/collective of the new social. The other socials, such as the institutional socials not related to the everyday socials, have to be not only imagined but more importantly realized as a higher moral ordering of society. What are the grounds that can organize this higher order of the social? Can these be theoretical, testimonial, or experiential? As we have discussed in detail earlier, we can experience the social through the various senses. Are there equivalent experiences of the social through the political or legal? The most formidable obstacle in achieving this higher moral ordering particularly in the Indian case is caste and gender. Human beings have to be wrenched off from the social infirmities associated with these two. In order to do this, we need to press in service the ethics of friendship, and the larger notion of maitri, which are available in both Gandhi and Ambedkar.

References

Adas, Michael. *Machines as the Measure of Men*. Ithaca: Cornell University Press, 1989.

Ambedkar, B.R. *Ambedkar, Writing and Speeches of Babasaheb Ambedkar, Riddles of Hinduism*, Vol. 3. Mumbai: Government of Maharashtra, Education Department, 1987.

Arendt, Hannah. *The Human Condition*. Chicago: University of Chicago Press, 1958.

Arnold, Daniel. 'Kumārila', *The Stanford Encyclopedia of Philosophy* (Winter 2014 Edition), Edward N. Zalta (ed.), https://plato.stanford.edu/archives/win2014/entries/kumaarila/.

Aspers, Patrick. 'The Second Road to Phenomenological Sociology'. *Society* 47, no. 3 (2010): 214–19.

Baindur, Meera. *Nature in Indian Philosophy and Cultural Traditions*. New Delhi: Springer, 2015.

Balslev, Anindita. *A Study of Time in Indian Philosophy*. Wiesbaden: Otto Harrassoitz, 1983.

Batens, Diderik. 'Rationality and Ethical Rationality'. *Philosophica* 22, no. 2 (1978): 23–46.

Beebee, Helen. 'The Non-Governing Conception of Laws of Nature'. *Philosophy and Phenomenological Research* 61, no. 3 (2000): 571–94.

Benton, Ted and Ian Craib. *Philosophy of Social Science*. Basingstoke: Palgrave, 2010.

Bhatt, Govardhan P. *The Basic Ways of Knowing*. Delhi: Motilal Banarsidass, 1962.

Brockmeier, Jens and Donal Carbaugh, eds. *Narrative and Identity*. Amsterdam: John Benjamins Publishing Company, 2001.

Bruner, Jerome. 'Self-Making and World-Making'. In *Narrative and Identity*, edited by J. Brockmeier and D. Carbaugh. Amsterdam: Johns Benjamins Publishing Company, 2001. pp. 25–37.

Castree, Noel and Bruce Braun, eds. *Social Nature: Theory, Practice, and Politics*. Oxford: Blackwell, 2001.

Chakrabarti, Arindam. 'I Touch What I See'. *Philosophy and Phenomenological Research* 52, no. 1 (1992): 103–16.

Chatterjee, Margaret. *Gandhi's Religious Thought*. London: The Macmillan Press, 1983.

Dallmayr, Fred. 'Habermas and Rationality'. *Political Theory* 16, no. 4 (1988): 553–79.

Daston, Lorraine. 'The Naturalized Female Intellect'. *Science in Context* 5, no. 2 (1992): 209–35.

―――. *The Tanner Lectures of Human Values*, 2002. Utah: The University of Utah.

―――. 'The Naturalistic Fallacy Is Modern'. *Isis* 105, no. 3 (2014): 579–87.

Demeulenaere, Pierre. 'Comment: Where Is the Social?' In *Philosophy of the Social Sciences*, edited by C. Mantzavinos. Cambridge: Cambridge University Press, 2009. pp. 60–6.

Durkheim, Emile. *Suicide: A Study in Sociology*. Edited by George Simpson, translated by John A. Spaulding and George Simpson. London: Routledge, 2005.

―――. *The Division of Labor in Society*. Translated by W.D. Halls. New York: The Free Press, 1984.

Feynman, Richard. *The Character of Physical Law*. Cambridge, Mass: MIT Press, 2017.

Furedi, Frank. *Authority: A Sociological History*. Cambridge: Cambridge University Press, 2013.

Gandhi, Mohandas. *Young India*, 4 May 1921.

Giddens, Anthony. *The Constitution of Society*. Berkeley: University of California Press, 1986.

Guru, Gopal, ed. *Humiliation: Claims and Context*. Delhi: Oxford University Press, 2009.

Guru, Gopal and Sundar Sarukkai. *The Cracked Mirror: An Indian Debate on Experience and Theory*. Delhi: Oxford University Press, 2012.

Guru, Nataraja. *The Word of the Guru*. Delhi: D.K. Printworld, 2008.

Halewood, Michael. *Rethinking the Social through Durkheim, Marx, Weber and Whitehead*. London: Anthem Press, 2014.

Harre, Rom. 'Metaphysics and Narrative: Singularities and Multiplicities of Self'. In *Narrative and Identity*, edited by J. Brockmeier and D. Carbaugh. Amsterdam: Johns Benjamins Publishing Company, 2001. pp. 59–73.

Heap, James and Philip Roth. 'Phenomenological Sociology'. *American Sociological Review* 38, no. 3 (1973): 354–67.

Heatherton, Todd F. and C. Neil Macrae, and William M. Kelley. 'What the Social Brain Science Can Tell Us About the Self'. *Current Directions in Psychological Science* 13, no. 5 (2004): 190–3.

Henry, John. 'Metaphysics and the Origins of Modern Science: Descartes and the Importance of Laws of Nature'. *Early Science and Medicine* 9, no. 2 (2004): 73–114.

Jammer, Max. *Concepts of Space*. Cambridge, Mass.: Harvard University Press, 1954.

Jawaare, Aniket. *Practicing Caste*. New York: Fordham University Press, 2018.

Jenner, Mark S.R. 'Follow Your Nose? Smell, Smelling, and Their Histories'. *The American Historical Review* 116, no. 2 (2011): 335–51.

Joshi, Laxman Shastri, 'Introduction'. In *Buddha Leela*, edited by D.D. Kosambi. Maharashtra: Government Press, 1977 (first published in 1914). pp. 9–16.

Judd, Diana. *Questioning Authority: Political Resistance and the Ethic of Natural Science*. New Brunswick: Transaction Publishers, 2009.

Kalberg, Stephen. 'Max Weber's Types of Rationality: Cornerstones for the Analysis of Rationalization Processes in History'. *The American Journal of Sociology* 85, no. 5 (1980): 1145–79.

Latour, Bruno. *Reassembling the Social: An Introduction to Actor-Network-Theory*. Oxford: Oxford University Press, 2005.

Little, Daniel. 'The Heterogeneous Social: New Thinking About the Foundations of the Social Sciences'. In *Philosophy of the Social Sciences*, edited by C. Mantzavinos. Cambridge: Cambridge University Press, 2009. pp. 154–78.

Mantzavinos, C. 'Explanations of *Meaningful* Actions'. *Philosophy of the Social Sciences* XX, no. X (2010): 1–15.

Matilal, Bimal K. *The Character of Logic in India*. Albany: SUNY Press, 1998.

McHugh, James. *Sandalwood and Carrion: Smell in Indian Religion and Culture*. New York: Oxford University Press, 2012.

Menzies, Heather and Janice Newson. 'No Time to Think: Academics' Life in the Globally Wired University'. *Time & Society* 16, no. 1 (2007): 83–98.

Milner, Murray. 'Hindu Eschatology and the Indian Caste System: An Example of Structural Reversal'. *The Journal of Asian Studies* 52, no. 2 (1993): 298–319.

Mulgan, R.G. *Aristotle's Political Theory*. Oxford: Clarendon Press, 1977.

Munn, Nancy. 'The Cultural Anthropology of Time: A Critical Essay'. *Annual Review of Anthropology* 21 (1992): 93–123.

Muranjan, Sumant. *Purohit Wargache Varchsva ani Bharatacha Samajik Itihas*. Wai: Pradnya Pathshala, 1973.

Nerlich, Graham. *The Shape of Space*. Cambridge: Cambridge University Press, 1994.

Omvedt, Gail. 'Caste, Race and Sociologists I'. *The Hindu*, 18 October 2001.

Over, H. 'The Origins of Belonging: Social Motivation in Infants and Young Children'. 2016. *Philosophical Transactions of the Royal Society* B 371 (1686): 20150072.

Overgaard, Saren and Dan Zahavi. 'Phenomenological Sociology: The Subjectivity of Everyday Life'. In *Encountering the Everyday: An Introduction to the Sociologies of the Unnoticed*, edited by M.H. Jacobsen, 93–115. Basingstoke: Palgrave Macmillan, 2009.

Pandurangi, K., ed. *Purvamimamsa from an Interdisciplinary Point of View*. New Delhi: PHISPC, 2006.

Pawar, Jaisinghrao, ed. *Rajarshi Shahu Maharaj*. Kolhapur: Maharashtra Itihas Prathistan, 2001.

Perrett, Roy. 'A Note on the Navya-Nyāya Account of Number'. *Journal of Indian Philosophy* 13, no. 3 (1985): 227–34.

Pettit, Philip. 'The Reality of Group Agents'. In *Philosophy of the Social Sciences*, edited by C. Mantzavinos. Cambridge: Cambridge University Press, 2009. pp. 67–91.

Pollock, Sheldon. 'Mīmāṃsā and the Problem of History in Traditional India'. *Journal of the American Oriental Society* 109, no. 4 (1989). pp. 603–10.

Ruby, Jane E. 'The Origins of Scientific "Law"'. *Journal of the History of Ideas* 47, no. 3 (1986): 341–59.

Sarukkai, Sundar. *Translating the World: Science and Language*. Lanham: University Press of America, 2002.

———. *Indian Philosophy and Philosophy of Science*. New Delhi: Motilal Banarsidass, 2005.

———. 'Science and the Ethics of Curiosity'. *Current Science* 97, no. 6 (2009): 756–67.

———. 'Possible Ideas of Necessity in Indian Logic'. *Journal of Philosophical Logic* 40, no. 5 (2011): 563–82.

Searle, John. 'Language and Social Ontology'. In *Philosophy of the Social Sciences*, edited by C. Mantzavinos. Cambridge: Cambridge University Press, 2009. pp. 9–27.

Sedikides, C. and M.B. Brewer. *Individual Self, Relational Self, Collective Self*. New York: Psychology Press, 2001.

Sen, Amartya. *The Idea of Justice*. Cambridge, Mass.: Harvard University Press, 2009.

Spirn, Anne W. 'The Authority of Nature: Conflict and Confusion in Landscape Architecture'. In *Nature and Ideology: Natural Garden Design in the Twentieth Century*, edited by J. Wolschke-Bulmahn. Washington: Dumbarton Oaks Research Library and Collection, 1997. pp. 249–61.

Taylor, Charles. *Sources of the Self: The Making of the Modern Identity*. Cambridge, Mass.: Harvard University Press, 1989.

Thomasson, Amie. 'Foundations for a Social Ontology'. *Protosociology* 18–19 (2003): 269–90.

———. 'The Ontology of Social Groups'. *Synthese*. 2016. https://doi.org/10.1007/s11229-016-1185-y.

Vallee, R. 'Who Are We?' *Canadian Journal of Philosophy* 26, no. 2 (1996): 211–30.

Walker, Judith. 'Time as the Fourth Dimension in the Globalization of Higher Education'. *The Journal of Higher Education* 80, no. 5 (2009): 483–509.

Wilson, R.A. 'Group-level Cognition'. *Philosophy of Science* 68, Proceedings (2001): S262–S273.

Index

scientific knowledge 147, 151

secular voice 65

Sedikides, C. 114

seeing (attention) 156

segregation 52; foul smell and 59

self 115, 171; argument of 110–13;
    existence of 110–11, 117, 121;
    vs group 121; idea of 110–11,
    114–15; idea of Taylor on 118; as
    private 116; as reflection of onself
    116; understanding of 114; sense
    13, 79, 177

self-alienation 184

self-decomposition 182–3

self-imposed alienation 182

self-representations 114

self-respect marriages 169, 186

Sen, Amartya 163

sensation, individual 52

senses 46; non-visual 50; social 13,
    79, 177

Sevagram ashram 57

Shahu Maharaj 82

Shaking hands 68–9

shared-touching 70

Shiv Sena 49, 112, 125

smell 5, 7, 10, 12–15, 46–61, 63, 72,
    80, 84–5, 113, 197; aestheticized
    54; Brahminical food in 54;
    categories of 56; common 48;
    in cultural asymmetries 49; and
    Dalits 52; and death 55; foul 3,
    54, 57–9; ghettoization of 50;
    global 57; gross 57; as indicator
    or marker 52; individual 52;
    karmic past and 53; medical
    traditions and 55; metaphysical
    level 58; metaphysical position

about 57–8; moral sense and 55;
    nature of 53; ontological beliefs
    about 49; 'outside' agency for
    57; particular 49, 58; permanent
    55; repulsive 58; role of 52;
    sensation of 50–3, 113; sense of
    15, 47–8, 51–3, 55, 57–8; sewage
    49, 54; social 9, 47–8, 58; social
    function of 55; social in 48; as
    social stigma 57; tactile source
    of 59; through categories 56;
    understanding of 51

'smell world' 54

sociability 61, 130

social 6, 10, 22, 56, 98; as abstract
    entity 5, 19; aggregates 25, 57;
    ambiguous nature of 17; analogy
    with space 20; anonymous 31;
    assaults 77; authority of 16, 132,
    135–6, 152–3; belongingness
    to 7; body image of 8; brain
    science 114; competence 115;
    conceptualization of 12–14;
    conditions 21, 83, 158, 178,
    187, 189; as consciousness of
    society 22; corresponding 75,
    192; decomposition 182–94;
    definition of 9–10, 29, 55; diverse
    manifestations of 5; domination
    21, 78; drinking 74; ethics of
    173–94; experience of 1, 5, 8–10,
    12, 14, 22; as experiential entity
    5–6; as form of persuasion 135;
    formation as conscious action
    112; formation of 3, 6, 14, 40, 71,
    75, 110, 112, 125, 162, 167, 174,
    179; fundamental experience
    as ethical 154; generosity 84,
    188; idea of 4, 6–8, 10–13,
    15–16, 18, 21, 23, 26–7, 29, 34,
    109–10, 114, 116, 132, 169; of

About the Authors

Gopal Guru retired as professor, Centre for Political Studies, Jawaharlal Nehru University, New Delhi, in 2018. He is currently editor of *Economic and Political Weekly*. His research work spans a variety of themes and has most recently centred on 'experience' as well as the political phenomenology of 'touch'. His books include *Humiliation: Claims and Context* (2009) and *The Cracked Mirror* (2012) (co-authored with Sarukkai). He has published numerous research articles in edited volumes and research journals. He wrote the entry on 'Caste' for the *Encyclopedia of Anthropology* (2018). He was awarded the Malcolm Adiseshiah Award in 2013 for research in social science.

Sundar Sarukkai is a philosopher based in Bengaluru. He was, till recently, professor in philosophy at the National Institute of Advanced Studies, Bengaluru. His work is primarily in the philosophy of the natural and social sciences. He is the author of the following books: *Translating the World: Science and Language* (2002); *Philosophy of Symmetry* (2004); *Indian Philosophy and Philosophy of Science* (2005); *What Is Science?* (2012); and *The Cracked Mirror: An Indian Debate on Experience and Theory* (2012) (co-authored with Gopal Guru). He is the series editor for *Science and Technology Studies* and the co-chief editor of the *Handbook of Logical Thought in India*. He has also been very active in outreach programmes to take philosophy to different communities and places as well as bringing philosophy to the public through his writing in *The Hindu*.